PRAISE FOR TRANSPARENT

"Deeply felt and well-informed, *Transparent* tells its story from a sharp and fresh perspective."
—*Time Out New York*

"*Transparent* is a remarkable book—captivating, powerful, funny, and wise. Without ever upstaging her subjects, Beam explains how she fell in love with them, and so allows us to do the same. This is literature of the first order."
—Andrew Solomon, author of *The Noonday Demon*

"*Transparent* is a testament to the resilience of young adults trying to find themselves in a world that would prefer them lost. I couldn't put it down."
—Rachel Simmons, author of *Odd Girl Out: The Hidden Culture of Aggression in Girls*

"Putting aside the gob-smacking strength, humanity, and hard-won wisdom in both the writer and her subjects, *Transparent* is just an astonishing book and Cris Beam, an extraordinary talent. This is everything that writing should be: gripping, desperate, heart-breaking and joyous."
—David Rakoff, author of *Don't G        rtable*

"Beam knows how to tell a story. . . . Whe                       g statistics from a study conducted by the                       trol and Prevention on homeless youth                       sgender people in prison violates the Eigl                       eps it stimulating. . . . But it's also a love story                       woman reaching out and helping another one claim       in the world."
*San Francisco Chronicle*

"Beam vividly conveys the alienation that shapes their lives as she peeks into the bleak underworlds of prostitution and black-market hormones." —*Entertainment Weekly*

"Gripping, illuminating and deeply moving portrait of transgender teens. . . . [Beam] seamlessly blends memoir, reportage and advocacy. The result is a vivid and fiercely empathetic narrative that juxtaposes dead-on portraits of these young women with clearly articulated fury at a culture that's not only fearful of anyone who deviates from traditional gender roles but treats minorities and the poor with contempt." —*Publishers Weekly* (starred review)

"Every once in a while you come across a book that feels necessary, a book so engrossing that you want to put a copy of it into everyone's hands. *Transparent* is one of those books."
—Alison Smith, author of *Name All the Animals*

"Keenly observed and deeply felt, *Transparent* is essential reading—as illuminating as *Random Family*, with hard-won personal insight."
—Janice Erlbaum, author of
*Girlbomb: A Halfway Homeless Memoir*

"Cris Beam has written a terrific book, both tender and tough, about brave sexual travelers who violate borders in search of new worlds."
—Richard Rodriguez, author of *Brown*

"These kids are most usually known *about* rather than known. But Cris Beam knows them. Bless her for so eloquently and respectfully sharing their stories with the rest of us."
—Kate Bornstein, author of
*Hello, Cruel World: 101 Alternatives to
Suicide for Teens, Freaks and Other Outlaws*

*transparent*

# transparent

## LOVE, FAMILY, AND LIVING THE T WITH TRANSGENDER TEENAGERS

### CRIS BEAM

A Harvest Book
Harcourt, Inc.

*Orlando   Austin   New York   San Diego   London*

www.HarcourtBooks.com

"Wild Geese" by Mary Oliver, copyright 1986,
used by permission of Grove/Atlantic Inc.
Lyrics to Dolly Parton's "Little Sparrow" © Velvet Apple Music.
Used by permission.

The Library of Congress has cataloged the hardcover edition as follows:
Beam, Cris.
Transparent: love, family, and living the T with transgender teenagers/
Cris Beam.—1st ed.
p.   cm.
Includes bibliographical references.
1. Transsexual youth—California—Los Angeles—Social conditions.
2. Transsexual youth—California—Los Angeles—Biography.
3. Transsexual youth—Education—California—Los Angeles.
4. Transsexualism—California—Los Angeles.   I. Title.
HQ77.95.U6B43   2007
306.76'808350979494—dc22     2006011373
ISBN 978-0-15-101196-4
ISBN 978-0-15-603377-0 (pbk.)

Text set in Adobe Caslon
Designed by April Ward
Printed in the United States of America
First Harvest edition 2008

A   C   E   G   I   K   J   H   F   D   B

FOR ROBIN

# contents

# PART ONE

You do not have to be good . . .
You only have to let the soft animal of your body
love what it loves.

—Mary Oliver, "Wild Geese"

# I

# SCHOOL

*H*ERE'S WHAT YOU SEE when you drive down Los Angeles's Santa Monica Boulevard just east of La Brea: a 7-Eleven, a Shakey's Pizza, a low concrete building with fish painted on the side, and a taco stand. There's a Chinese takeout place and a triple-X video rental shop, a filling station, and four lanes of traffic, two in each direction. Old people waiting for the bus. Young mothers dragging children in flip-flops. A discount dollar store, a Laundromat, and a bunch of teenagers standing around and smoking. If you stare for more than a minute, you may note that most of these teenagers are girls, and that they're more ethnically varied than other cliques in this segregated town. But that's it. Santa Monica Boulevard's got the sun-bleached, chain-store feeling of most of L.A.

If you're a transgender girl (meaning you were born male but live as a female), you might notice something extra along this stretch of Santa Monica. It's here that you'll find girls trading secrets about how to shoot up the black-market hormones purchased from the swap meets in East L.A. If the hormones don't work fast enough to manifest your inner vision of wider hips and C cups, you can find out about "pumping parties" out in the Valley, where a former veterinarian or a "surgeon's wife" from Florida will shoot free-floating industrial-grade silicone into hips, butts, breasts, knees—even cheeks and foreheads. Of course, this is dangerous when the oils shift and form hard lumps in the armpits and thighs, but you'll look good for a while.

On Santa Monica, you can learn which dance clubs, like Arena (with its crudely painted ocean mural on the outside), let in underage kids and have go-go boxes for dancing. You can learn which motels, one block up on Sunset, are safe and clean and have weekly rates. You can find out about the telemarketing company that hires transgender youth, no matter what they look like, to sell garbage bags and first-aid kits over the telephone. Of course, for the job you'll have to memorize a script saying that you're handicapped and that these household items are offered at higher prices because they provide employment to mentally handicapped people like yourself. And though it makes you sick to say it, this technically won't be a lie; transgender people are still dubbed "mentally ill" by the medical community, the way gay people were in the seventies. This is how the telemarketing firm gets away with cheap labor.

On Santa Monica, you can walk with a friend to the Jeff Griffith Youth Center—one of the few outreach agencies that knows about, and feeds, struggling transgender kids under twenty-four. It's right on the corner of Sycamore; you'll recognize it by the thick bars on the windows and the hand-drawn sign that says NO FIGHTING. Here you can sign up for a shower or get free bus tokens or a subsidized meal on a tray that looks just like the kind served in the high school cafeteria you ran from. There's also a big TV and a pool table with no billiard balls, and you can hang out until the place closes at six o'clock, without cars stopping you on the street and asking, "How much?"

And when the center closes, you can traipse over to Benito's, the twenty-four-hour clapboard outdoor food stand and "Home of the Rolled Taco," for yet another dinner. Teenagers can always eat.

At Benito's, over the sizzle and pop of day-old grease, kids preen and throw insults and drink oversize sodas from waxy paper cups and look into cars for cute boys who might roll by. As the girls wait for night, when the dance clubs open, the Benito's parking lot fills with them, laughing and squealing and running up to one another with halfway air-kissy hugs, like they haven't seen each other in ages and yet don't want to muss their clothes. Most look nothing like the drag queens or cross dressers that stereotypes dictate or outsiders expect. They're young and soft faced and wear jeans and T-shirts or, if it's a Saturday night, clingy dresses and big hoop earrings.

"Tracy, girl, I haven't seen you since like *last month*! You look good! Where you staying at?" This is the kind of banter one might hear as girls bump into each other buying post-taco Slurpees at the 7-Eleven.

"Angel! I know, it's been a long time—that's 'cause I'm not staying in Hollywood no more, *chica*. I got me a husband and we moved over to Culver City."

A husband is a stretch, but it's a term kids commonly fling around in an attempt at permanence or stability. When Tracy asks Angel more questions about her man, Angel will likely demur unless the two are legitimately good friends. Teenagers are known for stealing one another's boyfriends, especially when there's a perceived scarcity, like there is in this community.

Standing on the corner of Highland and Santa Monica, you can feel positively cultured, as canned classical music is piped out of a loudspeaker and into the parking lot all night long. I heard that it was the Chinese restaurant that put this in, in an oddly misguided attempt to curb loitering. But teenagers like Vivaldi as much as anyone else, and they gather there, shouting over its trills, bobbing their heads in four-four time. Gossip speeds along the sidewalk, as kids swap secrets about crushes and losses, and dish about what no-good ho stole another girl's man. Some kids, though certainly not all, climb in and out of cars—hustling for cash. In this crowd there's competition for men and money and good clothes and popularity just like at any high school in America, and on the Boulevard you can find out who's winning. The Boulevard is also where you can hear about who just got her breasts pumped and looks damn good, and who went back home to live with her mother, becoming a boy again. It's where you can learn from the older girls that not everyone has surgery and not everyone wants it, because a woman can have a penis and—girl!—no one can tell her she can't. It's where you can listen to the new Pink CD on your friend's Walkman and play video games at the all-night Donut Time. It's where you can feel normal, connected, hip. It's where you can be a teenager.

Around the corner from Santa Monica and up the street, on Highland, is an unremarkable brown office building. It's the kind of place that houses dozens of low-rent and high-turnaround businesses: limo services, temp agencies, computer repair places, accounting firms. Every weekday morning a handful of transgender kids stumble in with the rumpled brown suits and briefcased folks, because in the basement of this building is a high school, of sorts. Or was, when I became a teacher there.

I don't even remember how I first heard about Eagles, the small, scrappy high school for gay and transgender teenagers. Probably just from a new acquaintance in a passing conversation. But it had piqued my interest; I was curious who would go there, since when I was a kid, there was no such thing as a gay school, and hardly any such thing as a gay *student*. Would these kids be harassed, troubled, in need? I wondered if I could help in any way. By then I had been living in Los Angeles for six months, and an itchy boredom with the town had begun to creep up my spine. Having moved from New York so my partner, Robin, could get a Ph.D., I was missing an urban edge and lonesome for community beyond my dining-room table. I worked at home as a freelance magazine writer, and I had extra time to volunteer, maybe once a week, maybe twice. So that winter (which didn't really feel like a winter at all), I rang up the school.

"Eagles!" a gruff voice answered my call. And then, "Fiona! Put down that straighten iron! The outlet is for the coffee pot!" I heard a muffled crash. "I'm sorry. Eagles Academy. Can I help you?"

"Yes," I said. "My name is Cris Beam. I'm a writer who just moved into town, and I'm calling to find out about your school: what it's about and whether you need—"

"Fiona!!" the person shouted, without covering the phone. The voice was masculine sounding, but without the deep tones of a man—like an adolescent boy whose voice hadn't changed, except this person was clearly an adult. I detected a slight German accent. "I'm sorry. I'm going to have to call you back."

I found out later that this person, whose name was also Chris, was a transman, meaning a male who was born female. Chris hadn't started taking hormones at that time, but when he did a few years later, his voice dropped into the full male register, his face became more angular, and he grew facial hair, like all men on testosterone do. When he called the next day, he was apologetic, and when I told him I was interested in possibly volunteering, he got excited and launched into the hard sell, his accent thickening. He called himself the "volunteering office manager." His phrasing was clearly non-English.

"Eagles, it's a school for GLBT children. Well, not children always—some students, they are like twenty years old. This is because, you understand, our students have very hard lives. They do not always have parents, and they do not always come to school. Our books, it says we have one hundred students, but today we have only five. We used to be in a church, but now we are on Highland Avenue. You know Highland? You are gay too?"

I was startled by Chris's rambling bluntness but only for a moment. I told him yes, but that I never would have made that public in high school. Growing up in San Francisco where I did sounds like a soft launch for a gay kid, but actually, the other students were so worried about being stained by their location that they mocked or tortured anyone remotely suspicious. Including me. I remember girls in the bathroom turning and leaving in disgust when they spotted me at the mirror. They intoned, darkly, so that I could hear, "Dyke!" And then, to each other, "Get out of here fast!" as they pushed each other, laughing, through the swinging door. "I'm amazed there is a high school for such kids," I said. "How did it start?"

In his charming clip-clop English, Chris explained that Eagles was founded by a former high school teacher six years back. Despite its fancy name (which was an acronym for Emphasizing Adolescent Gay Lesbian Education Services), Eagles Academy wasn't a full-fledged school, exactly, but more of a continuation program for kids who had been—or would be—beaten up at regular schools. They were the boys who looked too girlie or the girls who looked too butch; they were the homeless kids living in temporary group homes or on the street; and they were, as Chris said, transgender. I said I didn't know transsexuals could be so young.

"Transgender can be anybody," Chris said, firmly. "You will see. Come tomorrow at twelve? Or earlier? Okay, good-bye." And he hung up.

The next morning, after squabbling with a security guard who claimed to have never heard of the school, I made my way to the basement, where I found a sheet of paper taped to a wall with the word "EAGLES" scrawled in a Sharpie. I followed the arrow on the sign, and at the first open door, I saw a person squatting, rifling through a cardboard box on the floor in a tiny room that was musty and too warm. Folding chairs leaned against piles of battered textbooks in every corner. A stack of cardboard boxes served as a table for a cracked coffeepot.

"Hello!" the person said warmly, standing to shake my hand. He looked like a man, but I could tell he had bound his breasts. This must be Chris. He was wearing faded blue jeans, black boots, a tight white T-shirt, and a black leather bomber jacket, ten years out-of-date. His hair was short and dark black, slicked like a skull cap to his head. He pointed to a chubby, ruddy-faced white man with a button-up collar that was far too tight, talking on the phone. This man sat at the kind of teacher's desk that I remembered from my public school days: a green metal base with a faux-wood top, heavy as a tank. It took up most of the room. "That's Jerry."

"Hello, hello!" Jerry gushed, interrupting and banging down the phone. His strawberry toupee shifted back and forth as he pumped my hand. He didn't make eye contact but instead looked at a clock on the wall, next to an enormous framed photograph of himself lying on the grass with two tiny fluffy white dogs with bows in their hair. "Oh! Chris—look at the time! We have to go get the lunch!!"

Jerry turned back to me and said, "You wouldn't mind watching the kids, would you? I can't remember what it is you teach, but I'm confident you're an excellent teacher." He pointed to a door. "They're all in that room right now. No one's teaching them."

Jerry grabbed Chris by the shoulder and hustled him out. I stood for a moment, stunned. The clock ticked; I knew I could walk away if I wanted to. Instead, I crept toward the door. Loud dance music was blaring on the other side, and I heard someone shout "Girl!" like a command. I turned the handle.

Inside was what looked to be an oversize storage room. It was windowless, furnished with a ripped orange couch, an oblong card table, and metal folding chairs scattered about. There were no books, but there were about eight teenagers, mostly hanging out in pairs in different corners of the room. One was braiding another's hair; two were sharing headphones and doing some kind of synchronized dance. One was asleep, and another was drawing patterns on her forearms like tattoos. Some kids looked like women while others looked like adolescent boys with breasts; they all were African American or Latino. One girl with dark skin and a high forehead was wearing a flowy white blouse with tight red jeans. Her makeup was flawless, but her feet, in rubber flip-flops, were dirty. Another kid of indeterminate gender wore jumbo khaki jeans, cut off just below the knee with tube socks pulled up high. She, or he, wore a Dodgers baseball cap backward and was cracking up at something a short girl with black lip liner and a white tank top was whispering in her, or his, ear.

When the door opened, they glanced up at me and then blandly looked away. For reasons I still don't understand, I dropped my book bag on the table to get their attention.

"Gather around!" I said. I was buoyed by the sound of my own voice, which had, weirdly, taken on the tone of a two-bit magician. "A class like you've never seen is about to begin."

The kids were curious, and bored, so six of them gathered. I had no idea what I was going to do.

"We," I said boldly, gesturing to everyone, "are going to make a Magazine."

It was the first thing that came to me; I had worked on magazine staffs for years—it was the only thing I knew how to do. Surprisingly, the kids cocked their heads and quieted down. They liked magazines; they had some in their bags. They liked hair magazines, they said, drifting closer toward the table, the kind of thing that could teach you something useful, something practical. One girl with tight cornrows said she hated magazines that just "talked a lot of BS," like politics or news, and another—the one in the cap—retorted, "Except for *Vibe*. That's got news, but, girl, it's the kind of news you need."

I knew after the first few minutes that I liked the kids. They carried fake Prada bags and wore scuff-free sneakers and chomped on bags of Doritos dramatically and wouldn't share. Some looked exhausted, but they were boisterous and opinionated, and seemed content to tell stories to a perfect stranger who had never been properly introduced.

"In, in, in!" I grew accustomed to shouting at 10:30 each Thursday morning, acting as a human school bell and pushing teenagers down the hall into my classroom. After lunch that first day, Jerry had crowned me the lone writing teacher, without so much as a head toss toward the résumé I had laid on his cluttered desk. Had he looked, he would have noticed I was utterly unqualified for the job (I had babysat; I had tutored; I spoke English), but he bartered with me nonetheless. He wanted me to teach two or three days a week, help him craft the bylaws and mission statement for his school, and run a weekly newspaper. I told him I could only donate a few classroom hours a week, and he shook his head desolately.

In my first few months, I learned to disregard the school district rule that teachers weren't ever to touch their students. Any touching could be misconstrued, administrators reasoned, but for me, shoving was often the only way to get kids into my room. When I arrived each day, I never knew what I would see: kids could be loitering in the hallway, bothering Chris or Jerry to make more coffee in the dilapidated coffeepot, or staggering out of the bathrooms, high out of their minds. Kids came to school late or not at all, and they brought weapons and boom boxes and wigs and drugs and sometimes even their own children to school.

My experience, I found out, matched Eagles' reputation. When I told people where I was working, they'd often wince, citing stories they'd heard of drug dealing or violence, or they'd shake their heads slowly, saying what a pity it was that such a good idea was handled so poorly, that, of course, the "gay school" was wild and administratively ignored. I discovered that GLASS (Gay and Lesbian Adolescent Social Services), the one foster agency that specifically places gay and transgender kids in group homes and with families, wouldn't send their teenagers to Eagles. This was because, a top GLASS employee told me later, "we haven't had a kid yet that succeeded at that school."

But I didn't care, really. I simply grew to love the kids—their attitude, their will, and their immense creativity in the face of such adversity compelled me. And I thought if anybody needed writing skills, these kids did, so I stayed. I initially marveled that they came to school at all, but I came to understand that Eagles was a nest, a social safety zone, where they could reimagine themselves and test out new identities. Lots of kids migrated weekly between "boy" and "girl," changing their names, donning wigs or falls, and pinning together skirts made of T-shirts, breasts made of socks. It was part of the game when I took roll each morning, identifying these new characters when they wouldn't respond to their old names.

Of course, they could just be acting insolent too. Eduardo, for example, was a student with a shock of platinum blond curls who didn't like his boy name, so he preferred to be called nothing at all. He marched into class with one eyebrow arrogantly lifted, and with his chin cocked at an angle high above the other students' heads. His eyes were slightly closed as he clutched his binder, covered with cutouts of the Spice Girls, against his chest. His headphones buzzed audibly, and he ignored me when I said his name.

"Okay, sit down, sit down," I ordered. Sitting, too, was an exercise in politics. There was the whole issue of *where* to sit, as the wrong association could dent a reputation, and then there was the issue of *how* to sit: did you drop and cross your legs to show off your high boots, or did you sit with a head toss to signal a new weave?

This parade was more than a fashion show; it was a hunt for approval and for reflection. Most of the students had little to no contact with their families of origin, and while they shuttled between shelters and group homes and court-appointed placements, they desperately needed friends to appreciate their clothing choices as they stumbled to adulthood. A very small minority of Eagles students lived with their biological parents—most of whom were too tired or overwhelmed to care that their kids were attending a dangerous and sad gay school. One of these students was a transgender girl named Shavonne (originally spelled Chavon, then CaVone, then Shawvawn). Shavonne's mom was a legend at Eagles because she took this daughter who was born a son to get manicures (acrylics airbrushed with sunsets!) and wasn't ashamed. The kids were jealous of this parental acceptance, but Shavonne's mother also had four children in a studio apartment in a bad part of town, and Shavonne often didn't have enough to eat. Shavonne's mom felt lucky when her children went to school—any school—at all.

There was, when I first started teaching, one exception to the ever-transient gay and trans student body: a straight boy named Cid. Cid was a short, green-eyed gangster who had, at seventeen, done prison time as a murder accomplice. The district thought a gay school might be the only place where Cid's gang loyalties wouldn't flare, so they assigned him to Eagles. Oddly, he fit in. He was tender with the boys in heels and the girls in tats; his serious life and even more serious crime gave him a worldliness that made him overlook people's appearances. And the kids respected Cid for his lockdown survival; most of them had served time only in juvie or in camps for infractions like hustling or ignoring curfew.

In fact, for all their adolescent taunting, Eagles kids were broadly tolerant of one another. They were, after all, misfits themselves. Aside from Cid and Eduardo and Shavonne, there was Nina—born in Mexico as Adelio—whose extended family had rejected her when they caught her in a dress at twelve. And Bella, a transsexual girl also from Mexico who had run away from her mother and siblings in Tijuana to end up in the foster care system of Los Angeles. And Domineque, also in foster care, who always wore a red or black bandanna folded into a triangle over her long braided hair. Domineque had sad eyes and never did any schoolwork. She also had some kind of hold over Eduardo, who rarely befriended anyone but was in love with the idea of tragic, doomed beauty, which Domineque seemed to embody. Together, Domineque and Eduardo discussed stars like Marilyn Monroe and the model Gia, women they deemed "just too beautiful to live."

And then there were the genetic boys who really wanted to be girls but still came to school dressed as boys. One of these was Luis, who wanted to be called Ariel during the school day—after the mermaid in the Disney movie. Ariel was a shy one. She dwarfed herself in baggy T-shirts and khaki pants and then sat in corners giggling or staring off into space. Jadon, a student who didn't admit his girl name, was terrified he was too fat to pass as a girl. His father caught him in the bathroom once wearing his sister's high heels—which he promptly beat him with, after pinning Jadon to the wall. Then there were plain old gay boys, like Deshane, who wore jogging suits and iced-out chains and sat, with arched eyebrows and pursed lips, haughtily surveying all who passed. Deshane and Nina were hustlers who lived on the streets.

There were a few genetic girls too—toughies like KC and Carmen, who bound their breasts and hid their bodies in slouchy jeans. Or Shemeka and Angel, who had both delivered babies before they realized they were lesbians, and then, because they were such young and ill-equipped mothers, had their children taken away. Pain came in waves at Eagles; you could see it shimmering and hovering at the periphery of all we did, like the horizon's visible heat, rising up from the street.

At first, I thought my students would actually write in a writing class. Then, I learned that about half didn't know how to turn words into sentences—and those who did, simply wouldn't. I ended up teaching writing via acting, which was one thing my students would do as a cohesive group, occasionally. Many of my lessons looked like this:

"Okay, in stories, there's something called a point of view. Does anyone know what that might be?" I asked one morning.

"An opinion?" Bella ventured, her Mexican accent both thick and sharp. Bella was smart.

"Something like a tower?" another student asked, spacily, twirling a pen. There was always a student like this—someone I had never seen before and would never see again, wandering into my classroom and muttering non sequiturs.

"Uh, sort of. The point of view is the perspective from which a story is told," I said. "You can think about it as the person telling the story, even if the person doesn't say his name or announce he's the one doing the telling. It's his perspective—or, as Bella says, his opinion—coming through. So the story will change depending on who's telling it, depending on the point of view."

The kids were starting to glaze over. I had to work faster. "So let's try it," I said. "Someone name a fairy tale."

One girl said in slow motion with dripping condescension, "'The . . . Three . . . Little . . . Pigs.'" I ignored her tone and asked Eduardo to act out what the wolf's perspective might be.

"Well, being a wolf, I get hungry," Eduardo immediately started, standing up and getting into character. I don't remember Eduardo's outfit on that particular day, but he was probably wearing snug, tomboyish clothes—like tight jeans and platform white sneakers with a faded red or baby blue T-shirt that offset his platinum blond curls. The shirt would have been cut feminine, with two-inch cap sleeves that disguised only the top of his homemade tattoo, which was the fancy scripted letters of *A., T.,* and *C.* "And when I get hungry, I want *carnitas*. Well, yesterday I got arrested by some pig cop for just being myself and going out looking for pork. Damn!"

Eduardo continued, cocking a hip: "I had found a little pig, done up in a straw house, thinking she was all beat with her hay furniture and shit. I yelled, 'Miss Thing! What is your T? You know it's time to go to the tea party!'" Eduardo pursed his lips and looked another student up and down, slowly, disdainfully, like he was the pig. "I was trying to get her to come outside, but she wasn't having it. That pig thought she was too pooch for me. So I told her, 'Bitch! I am gonna blow y'all's house down if you don't show me your business. Don't you make me huff.'"

Here Eduardo sat down, for impact, and let his face grow mournful. "You know what that pig did? She got her big-assed transsexual sister who was rich and shit, living in a big ole brick house, to try to boil my ass in a pot. In. A. Pot. And I was just hungry. Damn!"

Eduardo was fifteen and transgender, on the verge of being a self-proclaimed transsexual. As my days at Eagles piled up, I learned what this meant. Transgender is an umbrella term—used to catch anybody who looks or acts outside the bounds of traditional gender norms. Transgender, for example, can be the femmy boy (gay or straight) who likes to wear makeup and sometimes even skirts. Transgender can be the genetically female girl who goes by the name

BJ and binds her breasts into a flattened mass beneath her T-shirt. And transgender can be the person who looks singularly male or female on the outside but internally feels like an amalgam of both, a person who falters in front of public restroom doors, momentarily not sure which to choose.

Transsexual is more specific, though it's a primary category under the umbrella. A transsexual is someone who feels entirely like the opposite sex. This person doesn't have to *do* anything about this feeling; she just has to *feel* it. Sooner or later, though, most transsexuals will start to "transition." This can mean dressing in the clothes of the opposite sex, taking hormones, having surgeries, or any combination therein.

The transsexual community of men and women is as diverse and varied as the world of genetic men and women. There are rich transsexuals and poor transsexuals, brain surgeon transsexuals and garbage collector transsexuals, transsexuals from the country, the suburbs, and the city, from religious families and secular. People who say they've never met a transsexual just didn't know what they were seeing; most transsexuals blend and fit and pass.

Many of my students at Eagles were transgender in some way. Some male-to-females (MTFs) had breast implants, some took legal or illegal estrogen hormones, and some did neither, living part-time as a boy, part-time as a girl. Contrary to popular name-calling, there were no transvestites—defined as straight men who like to wear women's clothes for fetish. And while most of the transgender kids were genetic boys who lived as girls (transgirls), there were a few genetic girls who did the reverse (transboys). All of these kids were called the pronoun of their choice.

Los Angeles, it's been said, is a place where people start over. If Vegas is a city you go to, to escape, and New York is where you go to establish yourself, then L.A. is where you go to emerge. You see it in the signage. "I'M NEW!" proclaim the giant retail ads, fighting for air space with the palm trees. "I'M HOT!" declare the billboards hawking fashion on Sunset Boulevard or restaurants on San Vicente. You'll never see signs as big and sexy as you will in L.A., advertising things as regular and puny as copy shops or *taquerías*. With ten million residents, you can be anonymous in L.A., but you don't want to go unnoticed. Which makes it the perfect place to slip in—a small-town kid from nowhere—and emerge a rock star, a celebrity, a big-city player. In Los Angeles, you can be anything you want to be.

Or so goes the promise. Of course, it's not always true, but it's part of the prevailing mythology that makes Los Angeles a particularly potent magnet for transgender youth. While there have always been transsexuals in all pockets of the globe, never before have there been so many young ones—twelve, fourteen, seventeen years old—collecting in the big cities, determined to live out their lives as a sex they were not born. I met over fifty transsexual kids during the five years I lived and worked in Los Angeles, and they came from as far away as Alabama and Mexico and even Hawaii. Some hailed from smaller California towns in the Central Valley or up north, and some grew up in L.A. proper. Most had tattered, strained family relations, and many had been kicked out when their parents caught them (their sons!) trying on a dress in the bathroom or stashing stilettos in a schoolbag. These male-to-female transgender kids, who even a generation ago may have suffered silently in their bedrooms not knowing what to call their strange feelings, were now seeing images of transsexuality on daytime talk shows or in music videos. Oprah was talking about it and so, regrettably, was Jerry Springer, with his "Your girlfriend's a man!" exposés. RuPaul was a drag queen, but he was popular and beautiful. While these representations weren't always positive or perfect, at least they helped the kids to know they weren't alone. They allowed them to try out new identities—to dress up and even, sometimes, tell a few friends. Parents, however, weren't catching up, so the kids ran away to Los Angeles in search of a new community, and some help.

For all its troubles, Eagles really did try to be this help. After my first few months teaching in a storage basement, we moved to a larger space in an equally drab office building on Hollywood Boulevard. Thanks to a grant, we were able to move into offices, with windows this time, and roll-around chalkboards and more donated chair-desks. The hallway was decorated with a few rainbow flags stapled to the walls and the kind of generic inspirational messages printed on thin cardboard ("GO FOR IT!" or "OUR SCHOOL RULES!") that adorn every public classroom. In the rooms, gray industrial carpet met pale yellow and peeling walls, which led to flimsy ceiling panels and fluorescent lights. One of the classrooms was for Laura, a full-time teacher hired to teach history and math and social studies, another for whatever volunteer (like me) was teaching that day, and the other, the corner office, was for Jerry. Unfortunately, because the rent was cheap, the school was positioned on a major drug block where kids in puffy black jackets whistled like birds to indicate what exactly they were selling, or to warn one another about the vice around the corner. Eagles was also situated just a few blocks away from the two major prostitution thruways, which affected the student body's after-school activities.

When the kids got on the elevator with their multiple piercings and tight clothes, they elicited mutterings and dark glances from the building's other tenants. These people—employees of the nondescript, numbered offices that filled the other floors—were likely dismayed by rumors of underage sex in the fire-escape stairwells and drug dealing in the trash alley. Though I don't know this to be true, I'm sure Eagles prompted several complaint calls to the managers and landlords. I do know we stayed in that building for only a year.

Most of the Eagles volunteers lasted a few weeks or months, but I taught journalism there for two and a half years. I stayed because— despite their voguing in the hallways or dropping out for weeks at a time, despite their standing up in the middle of a lesson to shout and snap, "Miss Thing's got her work on. Down!" for no apparent reason—I liked it. I was endlessly amazed by a kid's ability to be so desperate, sleeping in cars and tricks' hotel rooms, and then show up at school wearing knockoff Chanel and Versace, notebook in hand. I bonded with the teenagers who kept coming back and, less valiantly, I attached myself to the thin satisfaction that came from believing I was impacting their lives in some way.

After I had taught at Eagles for a good six months, more than a few students confessed to me that, more than anything, they really wanted to graduate from high school. That this was a matter of pride. They had romantic visions of their delinquent families suddenly showing up, remorseful, at their graduation ceremonies, with carnations in hand, begging to be a part of their now-successful child's life. This student usually would imagine accepting his diploma and then giving his teary parents the middle finger while shouting, "Ha! I did it despite you, and now you'll never get me back!" It was a version of the "they'll all miss me at my funeral" fantasy so many of us nurse as kids, and I longed to help them make their victory march.

Still, wanting to graduate and wanting to do the work to get there are entirely different things. I kept the promise I had made the first day to make a magazine, but it was harder than I thought.

"This is boring!"

"I don't want to be a writer."

"I hate you."

As soon as we stopped planning the magazine and started working on it, these became my students' Thursday-morning battle cries. I had to play teacher-cum–circus juggler, constantly ditching my lesson plans to ignite their attention. When the kids were either particularly insolent or especially deflated, I would turn my back on them and shriek like an opera singer. Then I would whip around and make them jump up and touch their toes ten times. If I could surprise them enough with my antics, they'd often go along with me. Or I'd tell them to tilt in their seats and pretend that they were on a luge sled zipping down a mountain. Anything to get them engaged.

Whenever they could, my students, like all students, would talk about sex. It was one of the topics that kept us communicating as a cohesive group, so I usually let it slide. I think specifically of the time Shavonne came back from juvenile hall and choreographed a dance about prison flirting, with a short poem attached to give it classroom potential. Shavonne was the transgender girl with the sunset-painted acrylic nails, the one with a mother who actually accepted her. Shavonne had been arrested for prostitution, but since it was a first offense, she was sentenced to several days in a juvenile detention center. Because she was genetically male, Shavonne was sent to the male ward and had to revert back to her boy identity, Darnell. This, for most transgirls (especially those who take hormones and have breasts), can be a major problem, as "chicks with dicks" tend to inspire sexual assaults and beatings. Sometimes the more sensitive facilities will try to protect the transgender inmates by putting them in solitary confinement, but this, too, can wreak psychological havoc. But Shavonne was so saucy and spirited and adaptable that she redonned her boy mode as though it were an outfit, and then snapped and swished her way through the ranks of the tougher boys. By the end of her time, she said, "every man in there wanted a taste of this booty. Down!"

I remember when Shavonne actually was Darnell, back at the start of my Eagles tenure. She would probably hate this now, but at the time, Darnell reminded me a bit of Michael Jackson. Not the freaky, nose-crumbling, mask-wearing Michael Jackson, but the prior white-gloved creature with the spangled socks. I'm thinking of the Michael Jackson who seemed both cherished and somehow broken, a live spark who mitigated these inconsistencies with genuine creation—using style to rise above a complicated past. Darnell did this too.

Unlike most students, Darnell came to school every day. He was only about five foot six, but his white platform sneakers or his high-heeled zip-up black boots gave him extra inches. His black hair was braided and sometimes gluey from the latest weave, the ends frayed like old paintbrushes. Often Darnell would tie this back with a rubber band, and other times he would borrow a wig from one of the transgirls and march into class, arrogant, like a runway star. Just before he reached his seat, he would twist back around, flipping the blond wig, and grin, welcoming us into the charade. Then he'd stick his bum out and shake it like a rattle. A victory dance.

Darnell's body was amazing—all taut, sinewy muscle layered over a perfectly aligned bone structure that could fold, like a toy, in any direction. Darnell was usually dancing, even when he was sitting still: a toe pointed forward when he sat at his desk, or a shoulder jutted back like a ballerina about to pirouette. During breaks he would dance for everyone in the hallways—a unique combination of elegance and rhythm, like break dancing merged with a model's catwalk.

His shift to womanhood, when it came, looked from the outside like incremental variations on a theme: The wig he'd don for class would suddenly stay on all day; the strategically ripped T-shirt would one morning reveal a sports bra beneath and on another day a bra with hooks and lace. Soon the short-shorts became a skirt (just a quick snip at the seam), and Darnell started asking us to call him Shavonne, with all those crazy spellings.

Darnell/Shavonne was good in class, eagerly answering questions and listening, head tipped, to the other students talk. When I passed out reading assignments, Shavonne would finish first and then quietly watch herself, making tiny dance moves reflected in the window. When I asked the kids to interview someone they respected, Shavonne chose her mother, and we published a story about a woman who had four children and no phone, but could scrounge together coins to buy Shavonne the clothes appropriate to her new gender. Shavonne actually worked on the rewrites I assigned her, as she was a perfectionist, and proud.

So we were all surprised when Shavonne got arrested. She said she had to "ho it" because she needed the money for more clothes and that she'd only hustled a few times when she got picked up. "And look!" she said, presenting me with her "Prison Passion," she'd even worked on her writing while she was in the hall. Glad to see Shavonne back in class and seemingly unscathed, I rode along with her enthusiasm and let her perform it.

I've scoured my files for a copy of this poem, and while I've found Shavonne's essays about her mother getting pregnant and her cousin getting shot and some lighter ditties on fashion, I can't find it anywhere. I vividly remember, though, that the dance depicted an exercise scene in the juvie workout room where Shavonne kept dropping her dumbbell, forcing her to crawl around on the floor to pick it up again. The dance was delivered from this vantage point, where Shavonne gazed up at her fellow captives and imitated them bench pressing. Every boy in the song, it seemed, was particularly sweaty that day, and needed Shavonne to rag them off. There was a lot of grunting from the lifting, and Shavonne danced her way through the weight room, "accidentally" touching her toes to stretch her hamstrings as a fellow inmate passed her backside. The "poem" was a few well-timed rhymes and groans, and rhymes that rhymed with groans, and Shavonne was so outrageous and so theatrical that the whole class laughed and made her do it again. Laughter, even when it's rooted in the raw mulch of pain, is obviously healing, so I let the X-rated delivery slide. I'm sure this is questionable pedagogy.

On lucky days one or two students would actually write something, a paragraph or two, on binder paper framed in doodles. The rest would pick up pens when prompted only by a hard stare, and then drop them when I looked away. Still, we inched along. Every week I collected what I could, after teaching basic writing skills, like when to capitalize letters and what a comma means. Some of the best writing was slipped to me after class, when other students weren't around. One kid would hang back when the others trailed out, picking at his backpack zipper, retying his shoe. Then he'd hand me a piece of paper, folded into a tiny square, and say, "Here. Tell me if it sucks or not."

Ultimately, miraculously, we managed to pull together enough pieces to make a magazine. *Out & About* was alternately sad and hilarious, with fashion reviews of the stores next door, obituaries of friends the kids had lost, and all sorts of advice, like transgender "Hints from Heloise." We ran Bella's medical story, called "Hormones: Are They What *YOU* Want?"—which basically warned girls that they wouldn't get the body of a goddess as fast as they probably wished no matter how many pills they popped. There were also large doses of angsty teenage poetry. A young lesbian named Arcelia, who was homeless after her parents caught her with another girl, wrote a fantasy poem about an imaginary aunt who "loved and accepted me the way I am." And sometimes their earnestness was comical— especially in their advice columns. In our first issue, we published two columns side by side: "Getting out of a Gang" and "When Your Grandma Finds Your Drag Clothes." (I've actually used advice from both.)

The final version of *Out & About* was a twenty-page glossy zine, courtesy of a printer who donated his services, and designed by a small graphic design firm I'd convinced to contribute their skills. We printed hundreds, and the kids were proud. They carried stacks of them back to their old neighborhoods, leaving them in cafés and bodegas, and sneaking into the schools where they'd been beaten up or expelled, to leave piles in the cafeterias when no one was looking.

## 2

# EDUARDO/GERI/CHRISTINA

$B$Y THE TIME I had been at Eagles for more than two years, I was burned out and ready to quit. I loved many of the kids, but their attitudes, and the occasional danger and regular tragedies, were exhausting.

I knew I'd see the kids again, though. Robin and I regularly went to any transgender youth event that the Gay and Lesbian Center held, and we lived off of Santa Monica Boulevard where some of the kids hustled, so I often stopped to talk or buy some former student a meal. The kids were usually hungry for something nutritious or nurturing or hot. They laughed at me for my interest and still called me "the teacher," but they always wanted to talk nonetheless. As with any subject I care about, I started writing about it, and I soon began taping conversations with kids, and getting introduced around. Everyone wanted a book about transsexual young people to exist (well, they really wanted a TV show) because they'd never seen themselves reflected anywhere and, besides, they liked to listen to themselves on tape and critique their voice quality. But my interest, at base, was personal. So few adults were watching after these kids. I cared about their welfare, so I kept coming back.

A few months after I quit, I ran into my student who played the wolf, Eduardo, who was now calling herself Christina. She was per-

forming at a benefit for Bienestar, a major bilingual AIDS education
and social service agency in Los Angeles. The Bienestar offices in
East L.A. and Hollywood were nonprofit shabby, with worn couches
and a scattering of heavy desks in large windowless rooms, flanked
by folding chairs and ancient coffeepots seared with permanent burn
marks. On nearly every messy surface, there was a fishbowl full of
condoms, and the walls were bright with AIDS posters and flyers
announcing rap sessions for gay men and their HIV-positive partners, for older Latina lesbians facing menopause, and for transsexual
teenagers just coming out. Bienestar was one of the few agencies that
the kids at Eagles really loved; they would hang out there in the afternoons and fill giveaway bags with condoms and folded-up instructions for bleaching needles. (These would later be doled out to
kids exactly like themselves on the heavily prostituted corners.)

Every month, Bienestar hosted a talent show called Sabor a Mí,
to raise money for the center and to provide a stage for their drama-
drenched and audience-starved community. Many of my students
would concoct an act, with full costumes sewn from scraps and thrift
store giveaways, and they would vogue or lip-synch, dance or rap,
with a startling focus and precision that I never saw in the classroom.

When a student first invited me to the show, however, I was dismayed by what I saw as cliché: here were all these transsexual kids
behaving like drag queens and singing in falsetto. Drag queens, I
knew, were not transsexual; they were gay men who dressed like
women just for performance, and I thought it was counterproductive
for transgender kids to act high camp, when they were desperately
trying to be seen as "real." But then I realized this show was their
chance to go over the top, to be called beautiful or talented by a
roomful of people, or their chance to be outrageous, to try a style
they'd never risk on a city bus. Plus, I recognized, lip-synching and
drag shows are cultural; they're like lesbian bars.

My father always says he can't understand why people would want
to hang out in bars and, if I weren't gay, I might feel the same. But
like it or not, bars are where the lesbians are, so I go there sometimes

to relax and to blend, and to let down that burdensome watchfulness experienced by any minority. Drag shows are the same way. For decades piano bars and cabarets have been the safe zones for gender experimentation. It's tradition.

And, certainly, not all the transkids did music acts. Any Sabor a Mí had its share of mediocre poets, leather daddies giving talks on safe sex, activists selling the next big rally. The night I saw Christina, a bunch of young lesbians had already sexily crooned Spanish rap, and a drag king with a paste-on beard had done a puppet show with vibrators shaped like bunnies and ears of corn. Christina's act followed a man in a too-large sombrero slowly and drearily lip-synching to a ranchero ballad.

In a pair of black bell-bottoms, black platform boots, and a black fishnet half-tee, Christina walked to the spotlight, dramatically gazed down and to the left, and raised her hand to cover her face, fingers spread wide. I laughed when I heard the first notes of "Oops! I Did It Again"; I remembered Christina loving the Spice Girls when they were huge stars—apparently she had transitioned smoothly on to Britney Spears.

After the show, I walked up to Christina and asked if she remembered me. She did, of course: I was her teacher "a long time ago." She was breathless and eager to run off, but she scribbled her phone number on the back of a fast-food receipt. I noted that she wrote "Geri/Eduardo" above her number, even though her friends were calling her Christina as they ran by and congratulated her on her performance. This was surprising because it looked like Christina had developed actual cleavage in the nine months since I had seen her and was probably on hormones; most transsexuals utterly avoid using their boy names at all once they've started to transition. (I found out later that the cleavage was only due to a particularly tight binding with extra-adhesive duct tape, which actually left permanent comma-shaped scars on her skin.) Maybe she thought that Eduardo was the only way I'd remember her.

Eduardo had been my favorite student at Eagles. I watched her more closely than the other kids, noticed the way she started straightening her hair to make it look longer, and how, over the months, her tight pants grew tighter or how her T-shirts suddenly had a bra line beneath them without so much as a bump in the chest. One day, when she was supposed to be writing an essay on freedom of speech, I caught her writing "Eduardo is dead" again and again across some loose-leaf paper with a purple gel pen. Shortly after that day, all the kids started calling her Geri, as though through some collective subconscious programming. "Geri 4-ever" was suddenly scrawled along the base of Eduardo's white sneakers, and thin black lines appeared at the edges of her formerly naked eyelids.

After class I asked her why she chose the name Geri. She reached around to the backpack with a glitter adhesive of a devilish cat's face and pulled out a copy of Geri (Ginger Spice) Halliwell's biography. Despite its being checked out from the Los Angeles Public Library, she had underlined the huge book throughout. Geri told me that Ginger Spice was her biggest inspiration—that she had been through such hard times in England with all those eating disorders and suicide stuff, but—girl! (and here Geri got louder)—Ginger Spice made it through. Plus, she said, all sparkly and moony, Ginger Spice's voice was soooo pretty.

"You know, and I been through such hard shit with my mom and being homeless, and, you know, I can make it too," she said. "And Geri Halliwell made a band. Just by being herself. Girl, you know I gotta be down with being myself too."

I asked if that was the only reason she picked Geri, and she admitted that she also liked it because it sounded gender-neutral. She imagined it could be the kind of name her family might one day accept; it didn't sound too far off from a pet name she could have been given, as a boy or a girl.

Besides, she didn't like girlie-girls, and she didn't want her name to sound too femmy. She had always been a tomboy, climbing trees and fences as a young kid, loving her Tuffskin knockoffs from the swap meet—though she never once felt like a little boy in these clothes. At high school, she slicked her platinum curls back into a tiny knot at the base of her neck, and outlined her lips in beige or brown. (Even today she hates bright lipstick, as it clashes with her no-frills style.) She walked like a *chola,* as she liked to say—with a slow, badass street swagger and a sultry, even gaze. Even before she started stuffing her bra or doing up her face, some men on the streets saw her as a woman and catcalled her into their cars—because her aura was undeniably female. They didn't read "boy" in her five-foot-five frame; they just noticed her thin arms and hazel eyes and thought "sex." Of course, other men called her "faggot" in those days and threw eggs at her or chased her down the street. She'd been beaten up plenty of times.

Geri's best friend was Domineque, the sad-eyed transgender girl from my class. Domineque had begun transitioning when she was fifteen, and she was living with a foster mom who was required by law to lock up all the knives and sharp objects in the house, for fear Domineque would hurt herself. She had before.

Domineque had been born to a mom heavily into crack cocaine, and she was the oldest of four children. Her mother was addicted throughout Domineque's childhood and moved the kids from motel room to boyfriend's house to motel room again monthly, and sometimes even weekly or daily, depending on her mood or poverty or connection to a dealer. It was often up to Domineque to forage for her siblings, which she did by hitting up bodegas and begging for chips.

Together, Geri and Domineque looked like any Latina tough girls from South Central or East L.A., with tight shirts and big earrings and handbags with appliquéd Playboy Bunnies. Domineque was several inches taller than Geri, and her skin was a richer shade of mocha. Her breasts were naturally large, and her belly, though trim, was soft, so there was something wilted and maternal about her, even as she practiced looking sexy and tossing her head back, laughing too hard from whatever drug she'd recently taken. Geri tried to keep Domineque off the substances and yelled obscenities at men who catcalled from cars. Domineque passed as a woman impeccably and was rarely if ever "clocked"—the term all the kids use to mean discovered, or called out as a genetic male. (On the East Coast, the term for this is sometimes "spooked.") The men lined up for Domineque, possibly sensing a succulent victimhood, which clung to her like a scent.

So the two filled each other's needs perfectly. Domineque needed a protector, and Geri needed a mentor who wouldn't try to mother her. Domineque's own drag mother—the person who helped her transition into womanhood—had been a wispy, blond little teenager named Juliana who lived on the streets with Domineque during a bout of homelessness. I knew Juliana as a sometime student at Eagles. Domineque tattooed Juliana's name around her upper arm in homage, where a sailor would tattoo "MOM." For many transgirls who have had to raise themselves in some fundamental way, their drag mothers are totemic; they become part of their own personal creation myth. Even though, for example, Juliana had her own problems and couldn't really address all of Domineque's, Domineque still thought of her as a strong mother figure and wore her tattoo proudly. Juliana ultimately grew exhausted by the street and decided to move back to her biological mother's house in Texas—under her mother's condition that she live as a boy. Juliana wasn't strong enough for herself, let alone Domineque, so Geri sidled up as best friend/protector/confidante.

Geri didn't want a formal drag mother, but Domineque knew she could quietly help turn Geri out by playing to Geri's theatrics. Geri, the ham, loved having her photograph taken, so after school she'd head to Domineque's foster mother's house and dress up. She hung Domineque's crosses around her neck and cast her eyes upward, as if she were receiving salvation, while Domineque took her picture. Or Geri clung to the banister on the porch stairs, one of Domineque's wigs messily strewn across her eyes and makeup streaking tear marks down her face. With Domineque, Geri felt safe acting the girl; she could try on Domineque's lingerie and boots, and Domineque would snap her photograph from behind, Geri tossing her head back and laughing like a model.

A few weeks after I saw Geri/Christina perform the Britney song, I called her up. I asked her where she wanted to meet, told her we could go anywhere, and she chose a Jack in the Box off Hollywood Boulevard.

Over large fries and a double bacon cheeseburger, Christina explained the reason she called herself Christina but wrote Geri on important papers. "I've said many times that Christina is for now, but Geri is forever," she said, talking with her mouth full and leaning forward, eyes glinting. She explained that she was now dressing as a girl full-time and still told people her name was Geri. But this moniker didn't stick, largely because Christina, now sixteen, was modeling her movements, her clothes, and her makeup on the pop star Christina Aguilera and people noticed the likeness. "I mean, I'm Christina now, but there's gonna be a time I'll go back to Geri."

She meant she would go back to being a boy, a boy named Geri, as she never felt like an Eduardo inside. "This will be in the next two years or something," Christina asserted. She looked down, kicked at a ketchup packet on the floor.

"But why?" I asked. "You're passing well right now."

"'Cause it's going to be even harder in two years—you know, your body changes. And I'm not going to take hormones, that's one thing for sure."

Christina explained that she wanted to have a baby one day, something that would make her mom proud. She would donate her sperm to some girl and then she'd take care of the kid (the practical details here were murky), and she was worried that hormones could damage her sperm count or its potency. I knew the kids' street knowledge of anatomy was beset with wishes and plagued by mythologies, so I told her that if she stopped taking the hormones, her sperm count would go back up. Christina raised her eyebrows, plucked into such high arches that she looked like she was in a permanent state of surprise, and said she didn't believe the doctors I had talked to.

"Besides, I just want to leave my mark and say, 'Okay, I was able to be who I wanted to be born as, and I was able to trick everyone.'" She paused. "And I'll have pictures to prove I was passable."

Christina was obsessed with pictures. In her backpack she had dozens of them—mostly snapped at strip-mall photo studios where she could pose with a giant champagne glass or teddy bear, or drape herself sexily against a fake Greek column. She would give these out to men on the bus, or men passing in cars, or men hitting on her at the Pic 'N' Save. Whenever she liked the guy, she would sign the back "X-tina," and when she didn't, she would sign it "Gia." This way, if they phoned her, she could immediately tell their ranking by the person they asked for. If a man misread her tricky signature and simply called for "Tina," she would know he hadn't been listening when she told him her name on the street, and she'd hang up on him.

Christina loved codes and symbols and anything that could foretell the future in some way. Whenever she found a key on the street, she'd keep it; it meant an opportunity would be opening for her soon. If she cried on a birthday, it meant she'd be crying for a whole year. And if the first thing a man noticed was her eyes, which are enormous and bright hazel, then he could see into her soul. She would end up hating him anyway, as she said she hated all men as a matter of course, but she'd still look back upon him with the kind of romantic sheen only a sixteen-year-old can muster. (Christina once told me about a boy who carved her initials into his arm when he was serving time in juvenile hall. This was, to her, the dreamy equivalent of getting a boy's class pin, even though when I asked her who he was, she said he was just some guy she gave a blow job to behind a 7-Eleven.)

Even when she was sitting at the window in the Jack in the Box, looking out onto four lanes of cars and a strip of auto-body shops across the street, men stopped and stared at Christina. Christina was beautiful, but it was some kind of taut control atop a fierceness, I think, that men reacted to. Her face was round and soft, with vaguely Mayan features and a tiny gold stud in her nose. Her hazel eyes were wide set and almond shaped, and her full lips were both pursed and pouty. She looked like she could be twelve or twenty in her tight jeans appliquéd with blue glitter stars. When she smiled, it was gentle but with a look in her eyes that said, "I could kill you and you'd like it."

At this point in her life, Christina enjoyed the power of making people afraid of her. She was street-smart and scrappy and carried a steak knife in her purse; she had been in a street gang as Eduardo. She was also a teenybopper, who would switch effortlessly between tales of chasing off crackheads to a soliloquy on the wonders of Angelina Jolie. It was this younger Christina that I connected to; I felt the violence was a bit of an act. She relaxed with me during our first three-hour stint in Jack in the Box, because I neither scolded nor feared her, and because I had lasted as a teacher in one of the toughest schools she knew. Still, I was often charmed by her clever subject changes, tricked off course into talking about a silly shirt designed by Selena, instead of Christina's harder days in the gang. I was the experienced reporter and I should have noticed the slippage, the way she could seamlessly wrest control of a conversation. But Christina was smart and funny and fun to be with, and I often just followed her thread, wherever it went.

That first day it went back to her earliest childhood. She was born in 1983—a year after her parents arrived in East L.A. Her mother, Gloria, and her father, Eduardo Sr., had fled Guatemala City and its terrible years of civil wars, failed coups, and death squads to rent a one-bedroom apartment in a rough part of town. Shortly after they arrived, Gloria's several sisters and their various husbands and boyfriends also paid to be shuttled across borders in the middle of the night. Beds filled every available space. When Christina turned four, Gloria became pregnant again, with a girl.

Some months later Christina showed me a videotape from this time period. It's a baby shower in the apartment, and all the beds are pushed up and tipped against walls. Gloria is hugely pregnant with Christina's sister, Victoria. She laughingly accepts presents from the neighbors and cousins streaming in the door and squeals when a man takes her by the waist and twirls her to the beat of the *cumbia* music. The sound quality on the tape is poor, but you can see clearly that Gloria's happy. Her husband, Eduardo, appears only once, sulking in through the front door, drinking a beer. He has a black mustache and a flat expression, and when he realizes the video camera is angled at him, he grabs a balloon and stuffs it up under his shirt like he has a baby too. Then he's gone.

Christina, who is Eduardo Jr. in the video, is wearing shorts and big white sneakers. Aside from his hair, which is cropped and cowlicked, he looks like a little girl—buoyant, somehow, as he bobs around the room, reaching up toward one of the many aunts to get her to dance with him. He skips and hops, watching a balloon he's clutching by the string float along behind him, and he leans into the sides of women, burying his face into their thick waists. There's another little boy at the party, with a toy gun he aims at table legs and balloons. Eduardo watches him shyly.

"My dad was probably screwing the neighbor lady, even during the party," Christina told me. Some weeks after Vicki's birth, Eduardo Sr. left Gloria, moving in with a woman who lived in another apartment in the building, a woman who had been Gloria's friend. The two quickly moved across town and Christina didn't see her dad again until she was thirteen years old.

When her father left, Christina said, her mom got bitter. She remembered her mom flying into violent rages when she felt one of the kids crossed her. These battles sometimes ended with an exasperated neighbor calling the cops and the kids getting placed in protective custody for a few weeks or months, until another court date, when Gloria would promise to be better.

"My mom would hit us like you'd hit someone on the street," Christina explained, casually, licking salt off her fingers and peering into the french fry box, looking for scraps. She showed me little scars along her cheek, on her arms, from the times she said her mom hit her with extension cords, with the aluminum piping from a closet organizer, with an iron. I also saw fresh scratches on her arm. Thin razor lines, about eight of them, in the pale fleshy inside of her left forearm, in a kind of random crosshatch pattern—like long scattered pine needles. I raised my eyebrows and nodded toward the newer cuts. She paused for a second, avoiding my eyes. "Oh, that's from a cat. Anyway. I would have to tell the school that my sister and I had been playing, that she'd flicked me with a belt or whatever. Or that I fell on the stairs. You know, the typical stuff."

Once in a while an aunt would take the kids in for a bit, but predictably Eduardo and Vicki, once the storm passed, would want to go home again. Home felt comfortable to them. When Eduardo was seven years old, Gloria got a boyfriend named Esteban, who moved in, along with his own daughter. For the next several years, the five of them shared a small apartment with just one bathroom. Sometimes when Esteban and Gloria were fighting, Gloria would sleep in the room with Vicki and Eduardo, taking Eduardo's twin bed and bumping him to the floor. There wasn't much room, ever, for Eduardo to dress up like a girl, though he had started to try in first and second grade.

"The first time I did it for real, I was at Roxie's house and it was with socks," Christina said, explaining that Roxie was her best friend in seventh grade—a girl who already had a training bra to hand over to Eduardo to stuff. At this point, Eduardo was loosely modeling his style after the gangsters in his neighborhood: oversize baggy T-shirts, long shorts, and white tube socks. Eduardo never would have confessed his desire for tighter, more feminine clothes, so he was relieved when his friend sensed it. "Roxie knew I liked this guy named Dante, and we talked about girl things, and I don't know—one day we were in her room, and she just handed me a skirt and said, 'This would look good on you.'"

The skirt led to the bra and to makeup—first eyebrow pencil, then eyeliner, then nail polish—in the privacy of Roxie's bedroom.

Roxie's family owned their own business, so they were often out of the house, but one afternoon the girls were in the living room when Roxie's father came home. He wasn't surprised that his daughter's male friend was wearing a dress; Christina said he just told them they looked pretty and encouraged them to go shoe shopping at the mall. They did, and Roxie's father filmed them walking away with the family video camera. Christina thinks now maybe this was a little, as she said, perv, on his part, but right then she didn't care. "I was just like, 'Oh my god, I'm showing my legs.' It felt so good."

Before then, when Christina was Eduardo, he had tried on girl clothes, his mom's or his sister's, only in hiding—furtively during bath time and behind a locked door. He had a tube of Chap Stick he liked to smear on his eyelids when no one was looking because it made him feel like he was wearing eye shadow, except it was invisible. Once, when he was ten, an aunt nearly caught him at the mirror with a T-shirt wrapped around his waist like a skirt, but Eduardo dived under the bed and pretended to be looking for a toy, just in time. Eduardo's mother scolded him for "running like a girl" only once; still, he instinctively knew to hide his proclivities.

I asked if, when she was in primary school, Christina wished she were a girl, and she said, flatly, "I never thought I was a boy." But surely people treated her like one? Kind of, she said. Teachers called her Eduardo, but they didn't really expect her to play like the other boys. When Eduardo wore his slickest rain boots to school so he could intentionally slip on the playground and make another boy fall on top of him, the yard aides looked the other way. And his teachers tolerated his closeness with other girls when he whispered with them during nap time or played house during reading hour. As for strangers, Christina said, they were often confused about her gender.

"One time I was at the mall and I saw this lady with a really cute dog. I was probably like seven or eight," she recalled. Eduardo asked the woman if her dog was a boy or a girl, and instead of answering, the woman gazed down at him and responded, "Are *you* a boy or a girl?"

After the episodes with Roxie, Christina grew bolder. By eighth grade she had started wearing her own bra to school, putting it on after her mother left for work and slipping it off before she came home, unhooking it on the bus. Gloria was starting to notice her son's femmy touches, discovering mascara that wasn't hers at the back of a bathroom drawer or watching Christina march out the door with a change of clothes stashed in her schoolbag. Gloria wasn't having it. She thought her son was probably gay, which, for her, was a black mark upon the family, an indictment of her already-questionable parenting. She told Christina she wished she would just die of AIDS if she was going to act this way; she called her "whore," "*puta*," "slut" and, in their nastier fights, would throw her out, once even changing the locks. Later I would learn that Christina attended five junior high schools in the span of two years as she shuttled between foster care and homelessness and her mother's house, but that day at the Jack in the Box, Christina kept it simple. "My mom has a black heart. I couldn't stay with her very much."

It's not an external environment that "causes" someone to be transgender; Christina felt female before her dad left. Her sister, who grew up under the exact same conditions, is not transsexual at all. Plus, transsexuals hail from all kinds of backgrounds: no studies have found links between upbringing and gender identity, though transsexuals from urban areas or loving families might come out younger, for instance, simply because they believe they'll be supported.

So what, scientifically, does cause transsexuality? It's a hard question to answer, because we don't know what causes gender. Scientists haven't been asking that question; rather, they've been asking about the differences, neurologically, between men and women. And then, building on a base of research that presumes two distinct and stable sexes, people have been looking for a reason for, and sometimes proof of, the anomalous transsexual. Which means, basically, that they've often been looking to find a "female" brain in a "male" body or vice versa. In reality, as humans we may be a lot more complex than that binary model allows.

Still, they've had some success. In a famous Netherlands study, scientists found a region of the brain where transwomen look precisely like genetic women. It's a group of cells deep inside the brain, in the limbic system, and it's called the "bed nucleus of the stria terminalis" (BNST). Ten years ago scientists counted the number of regional neurons in nine postmortem heterosexual and nine homosexual males, along with ten heterosexual women and six male-to-female transsexuals of undetermined orientation. They found that the gay men and the straight men had about 70 percent more neurons in the BNST than the women—and the male-to-female transsexuals.

What that means isn't entirely clear, unfortunately. The BNST is often considered part of the extended amygdala, which is a part of the brain that plays a role in such things as fear, emotional memory and learning, attention, and possibly many other emotions. The BNST itself is believed to mediate the release of a pituitary-adrenal stress hormone. Beyond that, we don't really know what it does or what the difference in the number of neurons signifies.

When scientists go looking for the *causes* of any brain differences, they often start with hormones. Again, looking at the so-called "normals," the story goes like this: Fetuses are sexually undifferentiated until they're eight weeks of age. If, at that point, a fetus has XY chromosomes, he will begin to develop testes, which will generate testosterone, which enters his brain and starts creating male neuronal markers—and shutting down the female ones. A popular "what causes transsexuality" hypothesis is that babies got too much of one hormone or the other. Often called the "hormone wash theory," it says that for some reason (researchers often blame stress) a small percentage of pregnant women produce extra hormones that wash through the womb. Too much testosterone and a girl baby is born a transsexual male. If too much estrogen hits the male fetus, you get the reverse.

The hormone theories are largely born of animal studies and from watching early childhood behavior. For instance, there's a growing body of research on small female mammals like rats and guinea pigs that indicates that a shot of testosterone on the day they're born will make them live and act as males. Conversely, castrated rabbit fetuses will develop as females. Scientists can't perform the same experiments on humans, but a medical group in London sampled the testosterone levels in the blood of nearly seven hundred healthy mothers and then tracked the behavior of their children through three and a half years of age. They found that those moms with the highest levels produced girls who favored masculine toys and behavior in preschool. Their sons showed no such correlation.

Some of the newest research goes beyond the hormone wash theory entirely and indicates that there may be some gender to the brain before any hormones splash in and make it male or female. Birds, for instance, are default male rather than female. When a scientist in Amsterdam implanted female forebrains into the brains of Japanese quail embryos before their gonads developed, the male hormones kicked in but the birds still didn't act or sing like male birds, nor did they have fully developed testes. Their female brains prevented their development, indicating that a prehormonal brain, at least in some species, may determine gender.

Gender in this prehormonal brain may be found in the genes themselves. At the University of California, Los Angeles, the chief of medical genetics, Eric Vilain, has looked at the twelve thousand genes in mouse brains—and found that fifty-one of them are expressed differently in male and female mice *before* gonads have formed. He's beginning a series of experiments on what are called "knockout mice," wherein he'll inactivate certain of these fifty-one genes, one by one, to try and figure out how each one impacts male and female behavior.

So far Vilain has focused on the SRY (sex-determining region Y) gene, which is on the Y chromosome and "tells" previously undifferentiated gonads in utero to become testes. Vilain has found that turning certain genes on and off doesn't result solely in what's traditionally considered "gender expression," meaning it doesn't make subjects "act like a girl." Manipulating the genes can show us the different aptitudes that males and females have in areas like motor or language skills, vulnerabilities they have for disorders, and so on.

Vilain told me, "There's a whole new emerging field, which is gender-based medicine. We're finding males are more susceptible to schizophrenia and females are more susceptible to MS or whatever—so I imagine a lot of the differences we'll find will be related to motor function or susceptibility to a disorder. They won't be related to gender identity."

As for the people experiencing transsexuality, they usually don't need proof of their biological difference. All transpeople I know, and most in the literature, felt "different" from the moment they became conscious. Many knew by age two or three that they were supposed to have a different body or be called a different name. Many felt entirely secure in this early knowledge; it was the rest of the world that was confused.

Despite this common denominator, the varied environments in which transkids grow up make for different kinds of transgender experiences, which is why it's so difficult to talk about transsexuality in general sweeps. T-girls, or TSs, as they'll sometimes call one another, from the inner city are poles apart from t-girls from tony suburbs or farmlands. Granted, many will end up in the big cities where there's safety in numbers, but often what forms their later life choices and beliefs continues to be the backgrounds they hailed from—their nurture as well as their nature.

Christina was one kind of homeless transgender kid: homeless because of familial instability, which was going on long before Christina ever wore a dress. There are, however, plenty of kids in Los Angeles who are homeless precisely because their parents threw them out for being trans, and there are kids who ran away because their parents didn't approve. But these are variations on the "difficult home life" theme: if you're transgender in a more stable home environment (rich or poor), then your parents ideally help you and support you. You don't end up on the streets. A good example is the transkids who starred in the Sundance Channel documentary series *TransGeneration*. This show tracked four college students from different cultural and socioeconomic backgrounds for one year. Three out of four of the families had struggled, to varying degrees, with the news—but none would have abandoned their children entirely. (The fourth came out to his unaccepting mother after he was securely enrolled in graduate school.) At their respective schools, all found friends and lovers and campus support groups, and one girl's grandparents even paid for her surgery.

Of course, parents can struggle with the shock and the adjustment, and parents can try to change their kids, and parents can make mistakes. But it's probably safe to say that the bulk of homeless transgender kids in Los Angeles come from damaged family lives; their families didn't make them transgender, but their families could have made them homeless.

Which is why you'll see more homeless adolescent transgirls than transboys in L.A. While there's no precise breakdown, clinical estimates say that transwomen outnumber the men by three to one. (Some activists claim that the totals are more equal; transwomen are just more likely to alert the medical establishment and land on tallies with their surgeries.) My experience is that parents are more likely to throw out a "son" to fend for himself when he's embarrassed the family by dressing like a girl. They won't, however, throw out a daughter when she looks like a boy. Part of this is sexism—it's fine for daughters to want to be men, but for sons to be women? Unthinkable. Finally transgirls are more numerous on the street because of economics: there's a viable prostitution market for teenage male-to-female transsexuals, and there's a reason for them to be loitering on

corners. This is compounded by the fact that there aren't enough social services—like foster parents or schools or group homes—that
support transgender kids specifically. Take Domineque.

Domineque's mom was also poor, poorer than Christina's, and
her father was also missing. She told me she never met him and
heard that he was dead. Domineque, then called Javier, was the first
of what would be seven children and, she said, was a shy and withdrawn little kid. Domineque said her mom used crack nearly every
day and, like many addicts, became furious and violent during her
down times. Domineque remembered getting awakened in the
middle of the night, her mother screaming at her to get on the bathroom floor and search for the drugs she had dropped, because her
six-year-old eyes were better than her mother's.

"She was making me look for a piece of crack on a white tile
floor; that's like trying to find a needle in a haystack," Domineque
said to me once over lunch at a Mexican restaurant. Her hair was
tightly cornrowed into braids down her back and covered with a red
bandanna kerchief. She had ordered enchiladas but was mostly just
twirling the cheese around with her fork. "I couldn't find it and she
got mad. The thing I hated most was when she pulled my hair. Even
now when I get extensions, I get really aggravated because they have
to pull my hair. When they do that, I'm like, 'Fucking shit!!!' Then I
have to be like, 'I'm sorry, my head is really sensitive.'"

Domineque's mom and the kids and a sometime boyfriend lived
in various motel rooms, and Domineque walked to schools in bad
parts of town. When a neighbor called the Department of Children and Family Services (DCFS) because the kids were begging
for food, a social worker showed up with the police. Domineque/
Javier was seven, her younger brother Tadeo was five, and two sisters
were babies.

"My mom was crying and yelling, 'Why are you taking my kids
away?!' And the social worker just lifted up my shirt to show all the
bruises," Domineque said to me. She looked down at her white

jeans. "And then they put us in the police officer's car, not even the social worker's car. *That* was traumatizing. Then they took us to McDonald's."

The two youngest daughters shared the same father—the sometime-boyfriend Ruben. Ruben's mother had acted like a grandmother to all four of the children, seeing them on weekends, calling to check in, and she offered to take in all four when she got the call from DCFS. But because this grandmother was related by blood only to the two youngest girls, the agency let her house them but not Tad and Javier, who were then driven to a foster family they had never met before. Tad and Javier stayed there five years, until an aunt offered to take in the kids for a while.

Almost on impulse, I asked Christina if she wanted to start meeting regularly, after school or for dinner once a week. Since I had quit Eagles, I had actually been considering becoming an official Big Sister to someone but knew that the success of such a relationship is sealed in congruous personalities, which I couldn't ensure through a corporate matchmaker. Christina was somebody I already knew I liked. She also had needs I thought I could meet.

At that time, I didn't think much about my relationship with my own past and my own biological mother, though the parallel should have been obvious since I, too, left my mother's house forever when I was fourteen years old. But I knew that Christina's mother had been abusive and neglectful, that her mother had thrown her out of the house when she was thirteen. I knew Christina was full of bravado, saying she didn't give a crap about her mom anymore; her mother had lost her chance, and now it was time for "Christina to look out for Christina." She didn't hate her mother; she had just turned off. When I was Christina's age, I told people my mother was dead. I had the same false courage.

And the same guilt. When Christina talked about leaving her sister behind at her mother's house, and that her sister was almost five years younger—the same age difference between me and my own brother—I felt a coil unwinding inside me. More than with any other transgender kid I knew, I felt I understood Christina's killing off a part of herself, the Eduardo part, the mom part. Sometimes I felt if you lined us up, back to back, our edges would blur.

My own mother was silent, ill, mad, neglectful, lost, broken, sad, and gone from me many years before I shut the door. I don't know how much alcohol, or psychological sickness, or men played into her wrongs; kids never know. I do know she was a child in a grown-up's body. When I left her, I went on to live with my father and step-mother. My younger brother followed shortly after, and neither of us ever saw her again. I wrote my mother a letter when I was an adult, and she wrote me back, something about her cats and her dogs and her sister and the ghosts that live in her house. At the top of the letter, she misspelled my name.

Did this history affect me and my choices to involve myself with this particular, adolescent subgroup of the much larger transgender world? It feels almost ridiculous to put the question into words; my mother's abandonment unconsciously drives most everything I do. But I know that when I found Christina and the kids like her, something from my past reached out and held on tight. They were a community of kids whose parents had abandoned them—and who thought it was their fault. This is what, if I am truly honest, drove me to ask Christina if she would meet me once a week for dinner. I wanted to help her, because I wanted to help me too.

Christina at that time lived in a group home run by GLASS, one of the few foster and child services agencies for GLBT kids in Los Angeles. It was a gray two-story house with a sloping roof and a dirt front yard in a rough part of town near the freeway. The inside was clean, if spare, and the living room's built-in bookshelves held a few dozen charity rejects like Michener novels, a baking book from the fifties, and an ancient encyclopedia covering the letter *L*. In the living room was an oversize TV and a few battered videos with a brown secondhand couch and a urine-colored carpet worn down in the middle where people walked. The place smelled like bleach and lasagna. In the dining room, where the twelve or so residents ate dinner together every night, was a large poster of thirty hand-drawn faces showing different one-dimensional emotions like sad, angry, nervous, or pleased. Every day the residents had to place a Post-it with their name on it upon one of these faces—I guess to give everyone else fair warning of their mood. I spoke with Bernadette, who worked the night shift, about taking Christina out once a week.

"That would be nice of you," Bernadette said, leaning on a mop in the kitchen. She looked at me sidelong with her eyebrows furrowed, as though she couldn't figure out why I would willingly choose such a project. "Christina's a very special girl."

Bernadette was older than most of the twenty-somethings who worked for low wages in GLASS group homes. Bernadette was in her late fifties and had teenagers of her own. She spoke with an accent of indiscernible European origin, and the kids called her Mama. Every night she cooked dinner and cleaned the kitchen, oversaw the kids' chores, and searched their bedrooms for weapons and drugs. She pretended not to notice when two or three kids snuck out back for forbidden cigarettes, but she never let the big things, like stealing someone else's body lotion, slide. She could shrivel a guilty conscience with a glance.

Bernadette asked if I'd been Christina's teacher, and my "yes" seemed to satisfy her. She didn't ask for proof, or to see a clean driving record, or ask where I'd be taking her. She just told me Christina's curfew—nine—and said that so few kids had anybody visit them, not even their family members, let alone old teachers. She hinted around about a girl named Melissa, whose mother had died a year ago. Melissa needed someone to guide her, as her depression was making her act out in school. Perhaps I could sometimes take Melissa along to dinner too? Christina, who had been eavesdropping from the dining room, jumped into the kitchen and gave Bernadette a hard look. "Can I take Cris to see my bedroom now?"

Christina shared a room with a boy named Jarvis, who was sleeping on a narrow bed with his face to the wall when we came upstairs.

When I hesitated in the doorway, Christina said, "Oh, you can ig-nore him. He's always like that." Jarvis's side of the room was entirely bare: just a bed with the fitted sheet untucked and the mattress showing and a dresser with a single stick of deodorant on top. Christina's side looked like a prom queen's. Her bed was next to a big window looking out into tree branches, and the windowsill was clut-tered with miniature stuffed animals, like red bears clutching plastic hearts that said "I Love You." There was a bulletin board covered with pictures of Vicki, who was now eleven, coyly posed at photo studios or blowing out candles on a birthday cake. There was one picture of a dark-haired little boy, about ten, squatting on his knees in faded black jeans, in the snow in the San Bernardino Mountains. "That's me," she said. "That's the only picture I have of me as a boy. I keep it so I don't forget."

Christina's dresser was packed with cheap perfume bottles and plastic boxes filled with makeup. She had an industrial jug of hair gel that was nearly two feet tall and bottles of conditioner and aerosol hair spray and fruity-scented lotions.

When Christina first moved into her group home, she hated rooming with Jarvis. He was a light-skinned African American boy who never talked to anyone, was always sleeping, and everyone said he had hemorrhoids. But Jarvis was one of the few boys in the house—the rest were genetic girls—so Christina had no choice. California laws mandate that wards of the state live in same-sex rooms, and they classify transkids by their birth genders. Christina was even a bit afraid of Jarvis at first, because he supposedly was a "288," which means he had been arrested for some kind of sexual as-sault. But then, she said, they started talking at night after the house was asleep. Jarvis whispered that his dad had molested him, starting when he was three. Then, when Jarvis turned fourteen, he himself started molesting his cousin, who was just a toddler.

"At first I was like, 'Gross! How could you do that to your cousin?!'" Christina said. She had cousins the same age. "But then I thought, 'Shit, his dad did it to him, so he didn't know what else to do.' I started feeling sorry for Jarvis after that, 'cause, girl, we had some real talks. And his life was going to suck, no matter what happened. Plus, *ewwwwwwww*, he had those hemorrhoids."

Christina was capable of tremendous compassion, but was also viciously protective of what was newly hers. The first week I came to the house to pick up Christina for dinner, I was spied on by six pairs of eyes as I walked from my car to the front porch. When I knocked on the screen door to no effect because the television was blaring, I heard, in a stage whisper, "We're in back. Come around here."

A wooden gate to the backyard was open. There, behind a thick haze of cigarette smoke, teenage faces stared back at me. I laughed, because they looked so serious, and pushed open the gate. Six girls stamped out their cigarettes and let me through. "You're here to see Christina, right?" one of them said, not quite as a challenge but not quite friendly either. I smiled. "Yeah. My name's Cris."

One by one the kids told me their names. They grilled me like they were parents and I was the date: why was I there, how did I know Christina, where was I taking her to dinner. Then one of them said, "You're coming here every week, right?" Apparently, word had gotten around. A girl with a wide face and tight braids said, "Can I go with you?"

Bernadette heard the commotion and called everyone inside. She held the back door open and pinched her nose dramatically, to show she knew the kids were breaking house rules and smoking. She greeted me warmly. Christina stood behind her, glowering.

"Why were you talking to them?" Christina demanded, as soon as we were in the car.

"Because they talked to me," I said. "Don't worry—they knew I was there to see you."

"They're always in everybody else's business. Damn," Christina said, turning up the radio. She liked Spanish dance music, played way too loud. She shouted, "You're not ever going to take Melissa with us, are you?"

I assured her that no, these visits were just for the two of us. But to make things easier for everybody, we agreed to meet on the corner instead of at the house.

That first night Christina and I went to a Korean restaurant, because Christina had never tried Korean barbecue. She turned the steak over an open flame, saying, "I'll do the cooking." She loved the lettuce cups, hated the kimchi, and consumed more rare smoky meat than I ever would have conceived could fit in her narrow belly. We decided we would make our visits culinary adventures, trying food from a new country each week. Over the next six months, we talked our way through Ethiopia and Eritrea, Vietnam and Malaysia, Brazil and El Salvador. Basically, the spicier and meatier the meal, the higher its points, but Christina was game for most foods. Except sashimi. The first time she tried raw yellowtail in garlic and ponzu sauce, she ran to the bathroom, eyes bulging, to spit it out. She said, "Girl, I'll never trust you again. That was straight-up ocean nasty."

Over one of these dinners, Christina told me the story of how she ended up with an A.T.C. gang tattoo on her arm. It came after a string of bad living situations, she said—a mark of last resorts.

While Christina and her sister had gone into temporary foster care or to stay with relatives here and there when things at home got too violent, the first time Christina called in the authorities herself, she was twelve years old. Her mom was hitting her so much, she said, "I didn't know if I needed a shotgun or not. There was something wrong with her."

Christina-then-Eduardo expected the cops to just talk to the family, but when they arrived, they took Eduardo and his seven-year-old sister, Vicki, out of the house into a police car. "Vicki, of course, was bawling and I was like, 'Oh my god, what have I done?'" Christina said to me. Feeling responsible, Eduardo demanded that they be placed in the same house, which the social worker at the police station groaned about. It's always harder to find placements for siblings than for singles. By what Eduardo perceived as the middle of the night, the social worker found a group home with only three other kids. The parents had room to spare.

The home scared Eduardo, because the parents in charge followed Santeria—a Christian hybrid religion, whose adherents worship the saints and cast spells. "They had a bunch of dolls set up with fourteen-karat jewelry and money by them, and they would pour coffee to them every morning. I thought those people were strange as shit," Christina told me, grimacing. "At night I thought I could hear the dolls' jewelry shaking, and I was afraid to leave my room and go to the bathroom."

Years later it would be a santero that Gloria would consult about her son's transsexuality. During a visit to her mom's house when she was eighteen, Christina found eggs in the corners of rooms and mirrors under beds and knew a santero priest was trying to change her. But back when Eduardo was afraid in a new foster house, he simply wouldn't stay. He'd lived in enough places to know there'd always be somewhere else. At 2:00 A.M. one night, Eduardo and Vicki escaped out a window. Eduardo could run faster, but Vicki kept up a few paces behind, ducking behind bushes and whipping into the alleys, trying to avoid suspicious adults. Vicki had somehow pocketed a cigarette, which she was trying to smoke as she ran. This might have been, Christina thought, what ruined their alibi when a cop finally stopped the kids; Vicki was in first grade and too young to be smoking. Eduardo told him they were just coming home from a friend's house, where they'd been doing their homework. The cop plopped Eduardo and Vicki in his car and took them to their aunt Lina's, where they'd stayed before.

But Eduardo was hitting puberty and was both sensitive and quick to ignite; he couldn't adjust to new people as easily as he could when he was little. During an argument a few weeks into their stay with Lina, Eduardo accused his aunt of taking care of them only for the free groceries (their mother brought bags of soda and milk and chips to Lina's, though Christina said she wasn't allowed to see the kids alone). Lina got offended, and Eduardo marched out carrying a little pillow, two changes of pants, and a shirt. "I was like, 'I know where I'm going. I'ma go with the gangsters.'"

Gangs in Los Angeles are ubiquitous. Membership figures are hard to peg, but the Los Angeles Almanac claims that in 1995, the year Christina joined a gang, there were 203 Latino gangs within the city limits alone, with more than 36,500 members. While weapons and drive-bys are still a part of gang life in L.A., they're really more about business transactions and loyalty. Drug dealing is still a major means of income, and some gangs are heavy hitters, taking their directions from gang leaders in prison, then dealing large quantities of crack or heroin and shuttling the profits back through the penal system. Others make their cash selling fake IDs and passports and through stealing. Still others are more like hoodlums than real gangbangers, selling marijuana and robbing beer from convenience stores.

Eduardo's gang was this milder version. A.T.C. (which is said to stand for "Addicted to Crime" or "All Through Cryin'" or "Alley Tiny Criminals") members commit mostly petty crimes. Eduardo knew this gang from visiting family in childhood, and when he fought with his aunt Lina, he knew where to find them: at the A.T.C.-dominated park on King and Western.

It was afternoon on the Fourth of July, and there was little activity in the park. Eduardo figured the gangsters were probably home with their families, barbecuing. In L.A. whole family trees will be part of the same gang; young fathers will be active members while their sons are just toddlers, imprinting an image of gang life at an early age. Cousins will encourage cousins to join; uncles will encourage nephews. Even a kid that doesn't want to join a gang because he's scared of stealing or getting arrested sometimes has to, because the gangsters will jump him and beat him up, thus making him an official member against his will. Gangsters need numbers to stay strong, and if they can't recruit, they'll use force.

This is what Eduardo was hoping for, as he leaned against the fence at King and Western. He wanted to get "jumped in" to the gang; he wanted to get beat up so then the gangsters would have to take care of him. The trouble was he was only twelve, and a small twelve at that. He just weighed a hundred pounds, his arms were skinny, and his voice was high-pitched, like a girl's. He was still outwardly dressing like a boy, but he felt like a girl inside and knew he walked like one whenever he forgot to be vigilant. A gang's unspoken rule is to never jump a kid who's too young; preadolescents can make the group look weak. Eduardo knew he'd have to get crafty.

There was a time when I would have thought this was an extreme thing to do; choosing between homelessness and gang life seemed a bit like picking the frying pan over the fire. I would have wondered how a twelve-year-old could find such a gang, how a kid would know how to get jumped in. But in L.A., just from teaching in the public schools and living in a city so overrun by gangs, I learned that everyone in neighborhoods from poor to middle class knows how to get into a gang. Being a gangster in L.A. is a normal pastime for many boys. And for Eduardo, the risk of getting hurt when he got "jumped in" was lower than the risks he'd have to take later if the gangsters wouldn't accept him and he'd have to sleep in an empty car.

The day of Eduardo's gang initiation was sunny and hot. In the butter-yellow glow of late afternoon, the area of South Central where Eduardo waited can look quite pretty. The houses are single-story, squat stucco affairs in pale blues and faded oranges, and the neighborhood's a mix of renters and owners. Despite the gang graffiti spray-painted on the houses and in front of driveways, the people are house proud: sprinklers fan front yards, flowers ring front porches, and wooden decorations, like cutesy mailboxes with American flags, adorn about half the homes. The others look more scrappy, with torn screen doors and cars on blocks in dirt front yards, but overall the palm tree–lined streets feel pleasant and friendly during the day.

Eduardo was starting to get worried about where he'd sleep that night when finally he saw an A.T.C. gangster. He was loping across the park, seemingly alone, but Eduardo knew his homies couldn't be too far behind. He waited until the gangster barely passed him and then he stepped in line behind him, a few paces back. The guy stopped, looked back at him, and said, "'Ssup?" Eduardo, in exactly the same tone, his arms dangling in exactly the same way, replied, "'Ssup?" right back at him. The gangster—who was eighteen, over six feet tall, and thick with muscle—cocked his head and narrowed his eyes. He loped on. Eduardo, like a clown, continued behind him, exaggerating his movements. The guy looked back again. Eduardo stopped and stared right back. He noticed, as predicted, more A.T.C. members a few yards off. They started to snicker. The guy, getting mad, continued on. Eduardo had to up the ante, so he added a few curses to his mime act, started to call the tall guy names. The gangsters were shocked.

"Regulate, foo! Regulate!" they shouted. To "regulate" means to put someone in his place, to hit him. Eduardo, excited, started cursing louder, and the gangster turned, red faced, and ran at him. With one hard punch to the jaw, Eduardo soared up, then down, flat on his back in the dirt. The gangster kicked him in the ribs as Eduardo curled, instinctively, into a ball, protecting his head with his arms. Then the gangster's homeboys turned on him.

"Daaaaaawg!!" they shouted. "You're a bitch! That's a little kid!"

He whirled, confused. "But y'all told me to!"

"That's just a kid, dawg!" they said, pushing him away and crowding around Eduardo. The tall guy, hurt and betrayed, kicked at the dirt and walked away. Eduardo looked up at the homies and said, triumphantly, "That's fucked up. What a fucking bitch."

"And that was it. I was in," Christina explained to me over one of our dinners, four years later. Often gangs have strict rules about jumping in new members; they set time limits, like thirty seconds or two minutes, where one or more gangsters beat a new recruit, who's not allowed to fight back, into a bloody mess. A lot of damage can be done in under a minute, which is why so many gangsters have scars or crooked noses or walk with a limp. But Christina was luckier, at least in her version of the story. I didn't question Christina's bravado and bragging, because she seemed so proud to tell it that way. "Because I was a little kid and some big-ass bitch popped me once, I was in."

That evening, after the gangsters cleaned Eduardo up, one of the members gave him his gang tattoo. His name was Bear, and he did the gang's artwork. With a handmade tattoo gun, Bear scripted an *A* and a *T* and then a *C* onto Eduardo's left upper arm, in the same curlicue cursive that all A.T.C.-ers used. The tattoo was about the size of a fist.

This tattoo would later come to haunt Christina when she transitioned into girlhood, as generally only boy gangsters have such markings. When Christina became a teenager and people asked her what the letters meant, she would say, with a kind of sad irony, that they were her mother's initials.

And the gang did, as she hoped, serve as a kind of family. As soon as Bear finished the tattoo, which he made hurt less by providing Eduardo with his first hit of marijuana, Bear invited Eduardo to come stay with him. Bear lived with his mother, and he claimed he always had people crash at his house; his mother wouldn't notice another one.

But Bear's mother did notice Eduardo, and she worried that such a young kid was out on his own. She told Eduardo he could stay there, but only if he didn't do drugs and didn't hang around Bear and his friends. It was a promise Eduardo couldn't keep.

Coming from foster care and his aunt's, Eduardo had entirely the wrong wardrobe for a gangster. Bear, with the money he got from selling drugs, bought Eduardo boxers and white tube socks, shorts, T-shirts, and even the expensive, coveted Cortez sneakers. Just like red or blue Chuck Taylors can indicate Blood or Crip affiliation, Nike Cortez shoes are a general mark of membership into some kind of Latino gang. They made Eduardo look protected. Because he was so young, the other members didn't expect Eduardo to commit any crimes, and they shared their beer and their food and their pot with him, with no expectation of reimbursement. It was a nice summer, Christina said to me, hanging with the gangsters during the day, learning about how they robbed people or stores or avoided the cops on drug runs, without having to do any of the dirty work. But three months into gangster life, Bear's mom kicked him out.

"This lady cared so much for me, she ended up getting hurt," Christina told me, her voice and her eyes dropping low. The woman knew Eduardo was hanging out with Bear, and she could smell the weed on both kids when they came home at night. "She just said, 'I don't want to see nothing happen to you.' And then she told me to leave."

From one of the gangsters, Eduardo learned about an abandoned apartment, and he went to live there. He still had his clothes and the little pillow he left Aunt Lina's with, but the apartment was scary for a twelve-year-old, and he didn't like sleeping alone. Plus, summer was over, and Eduardo started thinking about school again. None of the gangsters cared about it, but he did, for reasons he couldn't entirely explain. Partly, he knew, finishing school was a matter of pride, because his mother had told him too many times that he wouldn't amount to anything. And partly he liked being smart; he was still young enough to enjoy surprising the teachers with his wit and ability to retain facts, even though his school records indicated he was truant for much of grade school. Also he could read some, but he wanted to be able to read more.

So Eduardo started trying to think of someone he could stay with who wouldn't bother him too much and would help him enroll in school. He settled on a cousin named Mario who was older and married. Eduardo looked him up in a phone book and found he lived well outside A.T.C. territory. Mario told Eduardo to come on over.

When Eduardo arrived, Mario explained the house rules: He was to clean the house every day after school before Mario got home from work. This way his wife could take care of their three children, who were all under five. He could sleep on the couch, and he could have his own friends, as long as they weren't gangsters and as long as he wasn't doing drugs. Mario told him he had to get rid of all his gang clothes, the shorts and the baggy T-shirts and especially the sneakers that marked him as a gangster. So while Eduardo appreciated Mario's structure and his proposed relief from actually living the gang life, he pushed the boundaries right away. He whined, "Can't I at least keep my Cortez kicks?"

# 3

## MOTHERS

$\mathcal{E}$VEN WHEN A YOUNG transgender person's home life is healthier than Christina's or Domineque's, adolescence is often traumatic, or at least bruising, without other transgender role models and guidance. There are children whose parents genuinely want to help them, who love them in spite of their change or alongside it, and then there are parents who feel unable to navigate such a confusing state of affairs, though they certainly wish no harm. Whether they're still being parented at home or not, many transgender teenagers will find new parents. These "parents" are called drag mothers or drag fathers, and often they are just a few years older than their "children." They're transsexuals who have already been living in their rightful gender and are in the position to teach their younger counterparts. In New York these drag mothers and drag fathers can actually be heads of household: they'll mentor anywhere from a handful to dozens of the younger street kids, sometimes renting out large apartments as shelter for the more transitory kids. This especially happens in Harlem, where these houses have names like the House of Revlon or the House of Chanel—monikers under which house kids will compete in the underground catwalks and balls (made famous in the 1990 documentary *Paris Is Burning*), winning money for the "family" and helping with bills. In Los Angeles the system is less structured, but, still, drag mothers teach their daughters how to walk and talk, how to pass and attract men. These parents may not live with their children, but they look after them and bail them out when they're in trouble. They'll train them in (relative) hormone safety, connect them with their estrogen suppliers, and often even give them their first shot. Most importantly, they'll intuit a burgeoning transperson inside a tentative teenager, and offer a gentle lesson in makeup application, or maybe buy her some shoes—just a small step in teasing out the real gender.

Several of my students at Eagles had had drag mothers. Domineque, for instance, had Juliana, who, had she been born an insect, would have been a firefly. Juliana's movements were slow and drowsy, like she was perpetually grazing through a sultry heat—but when she wanted to charm someone, she would light up, all phosphorescent magic. Juliana showed Domineque where to buy her first hormone shot, and taught her how to move her body in that lazy way, and to apply makeup in taupes and browns—makeup that accentuated the depths of Domineque's eyes, that sleepy sadness.

Another student, Nina, had a biological mom named Estrella who loved her, but she needed a drag mother too—because Estrella couldn't, or wouldn't, teach her how to survive as a woman.

"It isn't like I don't love my mom," Nina explained to me when I asked her why she chose to live in a group home for gay and transgender kids rather than with her mother, just a few hours away. Estrella was always worried about Nina going out at night—that she would get beaten up, or worse, for her transsexuality. For Nina, who had lived on her own in Mexico for a while and had a Mexican drag mother, this fretting felt stifling. "I left home because I needed to spread my wings. I needed to prove to myself and to my mother that I don't need to depend on her."

Nina was sassy with me, crisp. She was never afraid to tell me what she really thought. I remember one day in class when I had echoed the common belief that a transsexual was "one gender trapped in another gender's body."

"I am not trapped!" Nina retorted shrilly. We were reading a review of the just-released transgender movie *Boys Don't Cry* wherein a
sympathetic writer had repeated this adage to explain the plight of
murdered transboy Brandon Teena. I liked the story, and Nina lit
into me. "It's you all who are trapped. My body is just fine—it's the
rest of y'all who can't deal with it."

Nina had fully transitioned before I met her, meaning she already
lived as a girl all the time. Nina was only seventeen but she looked
twenty, with her floral dresses and flowy pants, strappy sandals, and
pedicured toes. She passed as a genetic woman with ease; she was
trim and pretty, with long, curly, black hair—Nina never wore
wigs—which she would hastily pull back with a clip, so that a strand
or two would fall sexily into her eyes. She was about five foot nine
and, because this was popular at the time, often wore henna tattoos
on her bare arms or stomach but very little other makeup or adorn-
ment, maybe just some pale lipstick and a thin streak of coal eyeliner.
Nina was born Adelio Martez in Mexico but was raised primarily in
California, and said she knew she was a girl from the moment she
could talk.

"I remember being in kindergarten having to go to the bathroom
and just walking toward the girls' room automatically," Nina said,
when I bought her an obscenely tall frothy coffee drink with caramel
drizzled on top at a Starbucks near school. Nina crossed her legs and
casually let a sandal dangle from her right toes. Every few minutes
she scanned the busy café with her eyes, but this didn't make her
seem nervous; she was just constantly observing. "My teacher was
nice and she let me do it, but in first grade they made me use the
boys' room. So I would hold it all day."

Nina said she even looked like a little girl when she was five and
six and had a boy's cropped hair; it was something in the way she
moved and turned and shyly looked up from behind her parents' legs.
Strangers would stop Nina's father on the street and tell him what a
beautiful daughter he had. Nina remembered smiling proudly and
then feeling perplexed when her dad got angry and shouted, "That

is my son!" By eight Nina was sneaking into her mother's makeup drawer and privately doing up her face, and by eleven she was turning her T-shirts into dresses and scampering around the house when no one else was home. When she was thirteen, Nina's father had died and her mother, overwhelmed with the task of being a single parent, sent Nina to her strict uncle's house in Mexico.

Nina told me these stories with the kind of been-there, know-it-all weariness you see in older women whose lovers have left them one too many times. Her style was affected as she leaned back in her chair and made her eyelids heavy, her head shaking slowly back and forth.

In Mexico, Nina said, she lived with her uncle and a few of her older cousins in a small town in Coahuila for several months. The cousins, especially, were critical of Nina's femininity, and they strictly curtailed her going out at night. But during the day, Nina went to school and spent her afternoons shopping and getting to know the small town's characters. One of these was the owner of a bakery, an old drag queen everybody called Grandmother. Grandmother recognized Nina's proclivity and told her if she ever needed a place to stay, she could live above the bakery. He said plenty of stray gay kids from the neighborhood who had been kicked out of their homes stayed upstairs. The offer wasn't lascivious, he promised; it was legit—he knew how hard it could be to be gay or transgender and be trapped with your family. A few weeks later, Nina ran away to Grandmother's, and it was there that she really connected with her first community.

"These gay boys asked me to join a drag contest. It was the first time I wore a dress in public—this cute little green dress with matching slippers. It felt so good; I thought, 'Finally. This is who I am,'" Nina said. She leaned in and dropped the older-woman bit as she told me that it was through these gay boys that she met her first transsexual, an older transwoman named Dulcea. Dulcea knew right away that Nina wasn't your standard gay boy doing drag acts; Dulcea knew Nina was a real girl.

And Dulcea, without any pomp or ceremony to mark the occasion, became Nina's drag mother. She explained to Nina that genetic males could take female hormones, like estrogen, and acquire a woman's shape. In Mexico this is easy; estrogen is sold over the counter as a menopause hormone-replacement therapy. Still, Dulcea made Nina wait before she would take her to the drugstore and teach her how to give herself a shot.

"She wanted me to wait a month because I was only fourteen and she wanted me to be sure. But there wasn't a doubt in my mind. I wanted people to see me for the woman that I am." Nina remembered the shot—a quick stab in the behind—and how it seemed she could feel the liquid flowing through her veins, transforming her. This, of course, was a bit of magical thinking; in reality, no one can feel veins, and it takes about four months of regular shots for the breasts to protrude even a tiny bit. Still, the promise is powerful, and many transgirls talk about the high their estrogen shots give them.

Unfortunately, Nina's town was small, and her family knew what she was up to. One of Nina's cousins, exasperated that he and the uncle couldn't keep this nephew under better control, talked a friend into snapping a picture of Nina running around town in a dress. He sent this photo to Nina's mother, who promptly caught a bus to Coahuila. Estrella found Nina at the bakery. Startled and happy to see her mother, Nina broke down crying and said she'd come home to California and live as a boy.

By this time, Nina told me, her hormone regimen had kicked in, and she had breasts the size of a baby's fists. At home, eager to reconnect to her mother, she strapped them down and signed up as a freshman at her local public high school. She used her birth name, Adelio, and promptly joined the cheerleading squad. Nina said she wasn't harassed for being a fag because she was so overtly feminine that the other boys stayed out of her way, more like she was an untouchable alien than a teasable kid. But she was miserable inside and started trolling the boutiques along Hollywood Boulevard on the weekends—places like Frederick's of Hollywood, which cater to larger sizes.

When Nina had accumulated a sizable stash of heels, corsets, makeup, and padded bras under her single bed in the room she shared with her five-year-old brother, she was compelled to run away again. She headed for Santa Monica Boulevard and called her mother from a pay phone a few days later to say she was safe. She was staying in a motel with another girl, but they would get a real apartment soon, she said. She promised to sign up for high school again next week, and to call her mother each Saturday. Nina's mother cried and cried and said wasn't there something they could work out? Maybe Nina could just dress up on weekends and leave late at night, when the neighbors wouldn't see? Maybe they could work together to hide Nina's girl things from the mother's new live-in boyfriend, who wouldn't tolerate girlie dress-up? This new boyfriend had a decent heart, her mother said, and he paid half the rent so, *Dios mío*, the boyfriend had to stay. This boyfriend helped Nina's mother afford her youngest son's good Catholic school. Everybody has to sacrifice something in this life, and wasn't there a compromise, wasn't there a way? When Nina described her mother's begging, her world-weary expression came back. Nina told her mother no and gently hung up the phone.

For Nina, then sixteen, prostitution was easier.

I met Nina's mother, Estrella—a young, pretty woman who lives in a sunny, immaculate apartment in California's Central Valley—with a translator and sat at her kitchen table talking for an afternoon. Nina voraciously consumed the rice and beans that were stewing on the stove, and her mom looked on proudly, watching her child eat. She spoke in girlish tones, almost shyly, but laughed easily, her giggles seemingly spilling over one another. The one part of Nina's story she argued with was that final phone call. She said Nina never called her; the police did.

"I waited two or three days for him to come home, and I went with my sister to his school to ask his friends [if they'd seen him]. When we couldn't locate him, I felt he had been killed."

At this, Nina looked up somewhat meekly but also with an edge of defensiveness. "I was with the other drag queens," she said, using a term to put herself down, as if she were a man dressing up. "I was afraid to call my mother, because I didn't want her to cry. I didn't know how to tell her."

Nina said it doesn't bother her that Estrella uses the male pronoun or even that she still calls her Adelio. "When she's ready to call me Nina, she can; I want her to feel comfortable," she said to me, then translating into Spanish for her mom. I sensed that there was more tension around this topic than the two would admit; they both acted good-natured, but the air felt thicker when I pressed them on it. Then they laughed about the times in grocery or clothing stores when Estrella called out "Adelio" and Nina, feminine and soft voiced, turned around and said, "Yeah, Mom?" Estrella said, giggling, "People always give a second look."

Nina's brother, displaying the easy ingenuity often found in the youngest kids, calls his sister "Ninadelio" like it's one word and tells anyone who will listen that his sister used to be a man but turned into a woman, just because he thinks it's interesting. This, depending on the company, can embarrass Nina a little, but she's patient.

Nina's less patient with her mother's boyfriend, who Estrella conceded ignores Nina or rolls his eyes at her. Estrella called the boyfriend "a macho" and shrugged with a goofy grin like there was nothing she could do about it. Nina visits her mom about once a month, in the afternoons, when the boyfriend's not around.

The first really great drag mother I ever met is a woman named Foxxjazell. Foxx was twenty years old when she first called me; she heard I was researching young transpeople for a book, and she wanted to be included in the project. Foxx grew up Dwight Eric in

Birmingham, Alabama, and had bused her way to Los Angeles as soon as she graduated from high school and had scraped together enough fare for the trip. She wanted to be a musician or, as she said, "the first really big international transsexual pop star."

"You'd better hurry up," Foxx told me in our initial telephone conversation. "I'm going to be a major star, I'd say, within three years, so if you want a shot at writing my biography, you'd better get to know me now." She was young and confident and sounded more naive than vain when she described herself so I could recognize her when we met.

"I'm very beautiful," she said. "I'm tall and black, with butter pecan chocolate skin and long silky hair." She suggested we meet at the Red Lobster.

I recognized Foxx immediately when she loped through the door. She was right—she was pretty, with silver charms woven through her hair and ripped tight jeans, upon which she had scrawled the words "Latins Do It Better." She moved her tall body slowly, like she was accustomed to being watched, and the men in the restaurant did indeed scroll their eyes up and down her figure while the women tightened their jaws. A waiter stumbled as he led us to our table.

Over a well-done steak slathered with ketchup, Foxx told me the story of her own drag mother, a drag queen named Tatiana, whom she had met only a year and a half before. Foxx had just arrived in Los Angeles, as a femmy eighteen-year-old gay boy, and was staying at a shelter for young adults called Covenant House. While hanging out in Covenant's living room, Foxx watched a young woman with a cropped bob haircut and a summer skirt slip through the door, tossing her head and laughing with friends.

"When I first saw Tatiana, she was wearing high heels and her makeup was so fierce," Foxx remembered. "But I couldn't catch T; I couldn't catch the fact that she was really a boy."

"T" is a letter-word that urban transkids use for all kinds of circumstances. It stands, of course, for transgender, but it also stands for "truth." When a kid says, "Here's the T," she means, Be quiet and listen: I'm about to get real. This, I think, is remarkable. The letter that has come to signify difference—T—also means total honesty. Somebody might say, "I didn't spill my T," which means she didn't disclose her transsexuality. But she might also say, "What's his T?"— meaning "What's the skinny on that guy—what's the real truth about him?" With this question she might be asking all sorts of things: is he gay, is he from here, is he available, and so on. "What's the T?" can also be used as a generic greeting—a sort of "Wassup?" for queer kids.

In any case, when Foxx discovered Tatiana's "T," she said, "I wanted to have Tatiana's face; I wanted to have her body. I just wanted to be her." So Tatiana arranged for Foxx to be her roommate at Covenant, and she shared her girl clothes to dress up in on the weekends. Tatiana taught Foxx how to do hair extensions and gave her countless makeup tips, including how to shade her cheekbones and run concealer down her neck to diminish her Adam's apple. Foxx had been dressing as a girl intermittently throughout her childhood, but mostly, because of her inexperience and lack of access to feminine things, she didn't pass. She dressed up privately in her bedroom; when she went out, she was alone and it was night, and she made sure no one could see her.

But with Tatiana, Foxx told me, she could go further. She no longer had parents to sneak around, and Tatiana hustled on the side so she had plenty of cash to share. Tatiana gave Foxx skirts and shoes and the requisite encouragement to walk around in daylight; she told Foxx she looked pretty, that boys would like her, that she didn't have to live her life as a gay boy. She told her real women could have penises—a radical notion Foxx passes on to her own drag daughters today. "'Cause who are you pleasing if you cut it off?" Foxx will saucily quip. "Your man or yourself? Girl, you got to please yourself in this world, and real women can have a little something extra between their legs if they want to."

This idea was, when I heard it from Foxx, still a little surprising, and I felt a shiver of discomfort run down my spine. I had grown up believing, without thinking about it, that genitals represented sex. That a vagina was female, and that a penis was essentially, inarguably male. How could a girl have a penis? How could a boy not? And if a girl did have a penis, as Foxx suggested, wouldn't she want to, above all else, get it removed?

I'm glad I kept these thoughts silent as Foxx dunked her deep-fried shrimp into little ramekins of ketchup and chattered on. I'm glad I just absorbed the image and let it, over the months, become less foreign. It helped that I met more and more kids who wanted to keep their penises, who didn't want to chance losing all future sensation in a risky surgery—kids who were proud of their bodies and willing to present, or protect, them as they pleased.

A friend named Michele also helped me to adjust my assumptions. Michele was a lesbian fire captain in Los Angeles, a male-to-female transsexual who transitioned on the job when she was in her forties. Now Michele and her partner Janis run transgender-awareness workshops. In their classes they hand out sheets of paper with four lines drawn across them, with an *M* and an *F* at opposite ends of each one. The lines are labeled "biological sex," "gender identity," "gender expression," and "sexual orientation"—indicating that these notions aren't fused—and students are told they can mark a spot on the lines where they think they fall. Most people feel they embody a mix of male and female qualities and will place themselves somewhere more toward the middle on at least some of the continuums. We all float a little.

I also started thinking about accidents and surgeries. A friend had a mastectomy around this time, and while the operation certainly made her feel less sexy, it didn't make her question her sex. I asked myself if a man lost his penis in some kind of accident, would he be any less male—and, conversely, would I be any less female if I, in an odd hormonal surge, grew one? I began to understand that the brain and the heart are the only organs with a gender, and that all genital modification or lack thereof is simply a personal aesthetic choice.

As the confidence Tatiana instilled took hold, Foxx no longer wanted to dress as a girl part-time. She wanted to live, day and night, as a woman. Foxx told me she was working at a telemarketing firm during this period, and when the company announced they'd be initiating casual Fridays, Foxx leaped at the news. That very next Friday, workers showed up in jeans and khakis. Foxx showed up as a woman.

"It all came down for Foxxjazell. She just couldn't take just dressing up at night; she couldn't take just dressing up on weekends. So Dwight Eric had to go," she explained, adding that while she wasn't fired from her job, she was required to use an unmarked bathroom on an abandoned floor of the building. "In a way, it was like I got in the car and I saw Dwight Eric and just ran him over; that's how I looked at it," she said. "For a lot of years, I hated Dwight. I hated his short ugly hair. I hated the way no one understood his pain. Foxx is more courageous, more bold."

Tatiana, unlike many drag mothers, didn't give Foxx her name. Foxx concocted it from combining the name of one of her other mentors, a tall transwoman who called herself Gazelle (after the graceful, leggy animal), with her own favorite animal, the fox. And then she played with the spelling until she felt the name supported her burgeoning starlet identity. Foxxjazell doesn't mind being short-handed to Foxx, but she hates the nickname Foxy.

Once Foxx moved into her own apartment, a grubby studio in the largely Latino east side, Tatiana and Foxx shifted roles. Tatiana needed a place to stay, so she often crashed at Foxx's. Tatiana confided in Foxx, who possessed an internal security born of a high school diploma and parents who loved her. (When Foxx came out in California as transsexual, her parents accepted her.) Tatiana had run away from Detroit and had no such support; over the months she began to lean on Foxx. One night, as Tatiana lay her head in Foxx's lap and let Foxx stroke her hair, Tatiana confessed she was thinking of going to New York for a while, with a new man who was offering to be her sugar daddy. The next morning, when Foxx woke up, Tatiana was gone. That was a year before our Red Lobster dinner, and Foxx still hadn't heard from her. She keeps a photograph of Tatiana tacked to her wall, glued to a construction paper yellow star.

After Tatiana's departure, Foxx decided she was ready to be a drag mother herself. Because she had the rare benefit of a real (nonsquat) apartment, countless kids already flocked to her place to sleep or store their girl clothes. If these kids lived on the streets, they didn't want their so-called friends to steal their boots or wigs. If they lived at home, they were usually trying to hide their burgeoning gender from family. Everyone knew they could trust Foxx; she smiled easily and gave generously of whatever leftover pizza or fruit punch she had in her fridge. She also had a job and had never tried to steal anyone else's man—facts that earned her an air of class and sophistication.

Over the next several months, Foxx and I became friends. I loved her southern accent and her polite generosity, and she liked the way I listened. We started meeting for breakfast and afternoon coffee, though Foxx hated coffee and ordered Cokes instead. I was usually hoping to meet at one of the *taquerías* or *pupuserías* near her apartment, but Foxx would groan, "I like the men, not the food!"

Foxx read a lot, mostly books from the library, mostly biographies of musicians whose paths she thought she could emulate. She studied Spanish at the community college, and she learned whatever she could about the history of transsexuality, all potential bits to be tumbled into her lyrics. She spoke of transgender people once being honored and respected as wise or spiritual "back in the day of Zeus." She was right. There is a rich history of transsexuality—or crossgender behavior—documented back to the pre-Christian era. ("Transsexual" and "transgender" are modern terms, but people have been contradicting gender norms for centuries.) One of the very few specifically transgender history books is Leslie Feinberg's *Transgender Warriors*, and in it she digs up ancient paintings of the goddess Athena dressed as a male warrior and marble sculptures of Heracles in women's clothes. She introduces the Greek god Dionysus (Bac-

chus), who was lavishly served by priests dressed in women's clothing, and priestesses dressed as men. Many other historians write about
the Great Mother, a supreme female goddess with many names,
worshipped throughout the Middle East, northern Africa, Europe,
and western Asia during the Stone Age and beyond. As shown in
Mesopotamian temple records from the middle of the third millen-
nium B.C.E., as well as in records from Assyria, Akkad, and Babylo-
nia, men who worshipped this goddess often castrated themselves.
The Greek historian Plutarch wrote about a Great Mother who was
ancient even then and intersexual (hermaphroditic), indicating a
deity in whom the sexes had not yet been split. In my readings I've
found that when there wasn't such a rigid gender divide among the
gods, people tended to be more open toward human gender ambiguity too. Even in Plutarch's Greece, statues of Artemis were draped
with necklaces made of the testicles of her "priestesses."

By the time the Old Testament came along, sometime between
the eleventh and the seventh century B.C.E., we got the famous verse
that's still dragged out as anti-trans rhetoric today: "A woman must
not wear man's clothes, nor a man put on a woman's dress; anyone
who does this is detestable to Yahweh, your God." In a nearby section of Deuteronomy, there's this less familiar but perhaps more
telling admonition: "He that is wounded in the stones, or hath his
privy member cut off, shall not enter the congregation of the Lord."
This implies that when the Old Testament was written, people were
cross-dressing and, for pagan religious purposes, attempting castra-
tion. These biblical laws may have been in part a product of the
Hebrew battle for dominance, Feinberg suggests, over the goddess-
worshipping, polytheistic world that surrounded them. Just as their
Greek counterparts did, the Syrians worshipped a god named Atar-
gatis, whose religious ceremonies dictated that followers dress in the
clothes of the opposite sex. The Assyrians did this too, with a deity
named Ishtar.

Interestingly, as spiritual deification shifted toward the masculine
and Christianity made its appearance, there became more evidence

of women dressing or acting like men in the Western world—rather than the other way around. As Christianity grew, there were records of female-to-male bishops, several female-to-male saints, and even, some believe, one genetically female pope. Known colloquially as "Pope Joan," a pope named John the English was rumored to have served in Rome for two and a half years during the Dark Ages but was discovered to be female when she became pregnant. As to what happened next, the stories vary—some say she gave birth on a street and either died or was killed, and others say she was whisked off to a nunnery in shame. In any case, a special papal chair was developed and used for centuries after the reign of Pope Joan. Called the "*sedia stercoraria*," this commodelike chair had a hole in its seat, which allowed an attendant to reach up into the papal gowns to feel for testicles and ensure a proper gender.

These are just a few random selections, since most history books don't label certain events or people transgender as a matter of course. One must delicately extract a transgender picture from what historians have often labeled "unusual" or "unnatural" behavior. Still, we have enough hints and shadows to argue that transsexuality, like homosexuality, is both biologically based and culturally precedented—with generations passing down traditions and ideas for survival.

It turned out that plenty of kids called Foxx "Mama," but Foxx favored two above the rest. They were Lenora and Ariel, fifteen and eighteen years old, who knew Foxx from the underage dance club Arena. Ariel lived with her mother and sister, while Lenora ran from group home to group home but often stayed with her sister or boyfriend. Both lived as boys during the day but dressed as girls to go out dancing or just walking around at night. Both spoke of wanting desperately to be real women all the time someday. Foxx was initially drawn to the way these two girls danced at Arena, in their tiny black dresses and knee-high boots. They were young and bold—and cute enough to get pushed to the onstage go-go boxes, to shake their bums and squeal with feigned girlish surprise. Lenora and Ariel attracted the kinds of men Foxx urgently wanted—buff, shaved Latino boys with gang tattoos, who liked their transgender girls to pass as "real fish" on the streets in front of their homies.

But Foxx quickly noticed that Lenora and Ariel played these men, having sex with them and tossing them aside. Foxx thought she should step in and teach Lenora and Ariel manners. This is the kind of tricky emotional territory that can exist between drag mothers and daughters. Because there often isn't a tremendous age gap, mothers can at once be jealous of their daughters' beauty or success with men *and* want to help them navigate the transgender community and the straight world beyond. The transgender population was small, Foxx said, and she didn't want the girls' childish games to wither their reputations before they made it to full-time womanhood. (Transgender girls in this community who don't appreciate boyfriends, when so many women want them, are resented and, if they're in the wrong place at the wrong time, occasionally verbally or physically assaulted.) Foxx also wanted to help Lenora and Ariel buck their families' judgments and live as girls on their own.

So Foxx fed them, counseled them, and took them shopping. Foxx lived two blocks from Vermont Avenue, a major thruway of dollar stores and discount clothing shops—the type with headless cardboard mannequins displaying skimpy nylon dresses. Whenever Foxx got paid, she would trot Ariel or Lenora down to one of these stores (she called them "boutiques") and buy the younger girl a bra or a pair of cheap strappy heels that would invariably fall apart after one night out dancing.

I knew Ariel from Eagles, where she had been a student of mine for a few months. Ariel, as a boy, looked petite and unassuming. She hid her body in oversize T-shirts and baggy jean shorts, with her white tube socks pulled up to her knees, gangster style. Ariel rarely spoke in class and was easily run over by the more verbose and sassy students. She didn't like the daily chaos and noise at Eagles, so she left for another school. I recalled Ariel's ultra-soft street style, with her shaved head atop her tiny five-foot frame. If I looked closely in class, I would notice her eyebrows were plucked and her legs were shaved, and she was usually sucking on some little candy that puckered her lips. Ariel whisper-spoke with a bit of a Mexican accent, and she looked at people from an angle with her head tipped up, like a puppy, or a little girl.

Both Ariel's and Lenora's daytime looks sometimes posed a problem during their shopping trips. One payday, for example, Foxx took Ariel to a small discount shop, where she had promised to buy her a dress. After rifling through the racks and sighing over the choices for the better part of an hour, Ariel picked out a white sundress with lacy shoulder straps and yellow daisies splashed across the front. She found the smallest size possible and walked it into the dressing room, glancing furtively over her shoulder. This particular shop was filled with Latina teenagers, some pushing baby strollers, along with a few women in their twenties, expertly fingering the thin fabrics and checking the seams. No one noticed Ariel slip into the slender dressing room, outfitted with a torn curtain and a "Jesu Cristo Es el Camino" bumper sticker. And no one stared at the young "boy" Ariel when she came out, joyfully twirling in a sundress in front of the shared mirror at the back of the store.

At least, it seemed like no one had noticed. Suddenly, a fat little girl around seven years old, who had been watching the transformation from behind a rack of boa-trimmed blouses, went running toward the cash registers, shouting, "Daddy!" A ruddy-faced Korean man, presumably the owner of the shop, hurtled forward through an aisle of miniskirts, yelling, "No boys in dresses! Get out of my shop!" Ariel looked scared and glanced to Foxx for backup. The man shoved his gaping daughter aside and leaned down into Ariel's face. "Get out of here now! I'll call the police. No boys in my dressing room!"

Unfazed, Foxx slowly rose from the folding chair where she'd been appreciating Ariel's outfit. She walked up to the owner. She stepped between the man and her daughter and said calmly, "This is a paying customer. She will leave when she's ready."

The man took a step back and said, "You're okay. You're a real woman. You stay—he goes. I'll call police."

A crowd had gathered. Ariel looked shrunken, and was inching backward toward the dressing room. Foxx kept her level gaze on the owner as she said, sternly but evenly, "And that is a real woman too. I patronize your store regularly; we pay our money like anyone else. You will not throw out my friend." Softer, Foxx said to Ariel, "Did you have anything else you wanted to try on, honey? Or are you over this dump?" Ariel quickly shook her head no, and the owner stammered and rushed back to his cash register.

Ariel didn't want the dress, but, like a little kid, she didn't want to leave the store without something. So she grabbed a pair of size zero capri jeans (when Ariel dressed as a girl, she liked her clothes tight) with a thick band of white lace at the bottom, as well as a padded bra in purple. Foxx proudly walked the purchases up to the register and passed them to the fuming owner. She threw in a hair scrunchie after he'd rung everything up, just to give him more trouble, and smiled sweetly when she walked away. Ariel and I trailed behind, and the owner's daughter stared from the door, openmouthed.

When the girls became Foxx's drag daughters, they were both staying with their respective families in an especially poor area of South Central. The neighborhood felt more rural than it was, as there were sounds of chickens and goats and roosters cooped up in backyards, and there were no stores, save for a few tiny airy bodegas or the corner stands where dumpling-shaped women cooked tacos out of oil cans. Unlike most of the buildings in Los Angeles, which are stucco, the apartment buildings here are built out of wood and reminded me of tall barns, though they housed some ten or twenty families each and many undocumented single men up from Mexico. Makeshift bathrooms were rigged on each floor, and the hallways often smelled of urine. Still, with Los Angeles' relentless sunshine and the bougainvillea that blooms year-round, even the most dangerous neighborhoods can feel sleepy and lush during the day.

Lenora's much older siblings were raised in Puerto Vallarta by her grandparents. When Lenora's brothers and sisters came to the United States for what Lenora termed a "better chance," they took Lenora with them. But they were poor and Lenora was nine, and she quickly went into the system, shuttling from group home to foster family and even once to juvenile hall, where she was sent for fighting with another group-home kid when he hit her for acting too femmy (even as a boy, she giggled). Still, Lenora regularly went to visit or stay with her sister—the one family member who humored her dressing up. This sister promised not to tell their grandmother, who didn't know and wouldn't approve. She smiled at Lenora's photographs of herself, posing in red minidresses and bobbed wigs, snapped at a cheap photo shop. Lenora's face was more angular than Ariel's, long and thin with a square chin and high cheekbones, and her limbs seemed to dangle from her sockets. If Ariel retreated into corners, Lenora floated out of them; there was something ethereal about her, something unsure but curious. Because Lenora's sister was busy with her own kids in a small apartment, Lenora couldn't stay there long and usually ended up crashing with her older boyfriend when she ran away from foster care. The boyfriend's name was Ronnie and he lived with his parents, but Lenora could sneak into his bedroom window at night without getting caught. The trouble was that Ronnie was gay and didn't like Lenora dressing up as a girl and threatened to leave her if she "went fish." Lenora had to hide her leanings from everyone.

Ariel's family, on the other hand, was small and close and very Catholic. Her mother was ill and stayed home all day, praying. Ariel's sister, who was nineteen, took care of her mom and her own daughter. This sister had once caught Ariel applying makeup in the bathroom and flipped out, yelling, "Mom is already sick; why you gotta make everything harder for everyone?" She claimed God wouldn't approve and told Ariel that the neighbors could kill her. So

Ariel promised she would never dress up again, and stashed her girl stuff at Foxx's.

Still, Ariel said, she worried. She'd been to church every Sunday since she could walk, and she felt she was playing a betting game with God. She thought God was tempting her to dress, as she said, "hoochie," and it was her job to resist it. She had ongoing fears of dying, of being killed in her tough neighborhood, and, she reasoned, if she was still feeling transgender when she died, she would go to hell. If, on the other hand, she had gotten over it, if she had willed herself to be male, all the time, every day for a long-enough stretch, she would have served her penance and could go to heaven.

I had known Ariel off and on for more than a year when we had this conversation. I normally just listened to Ariel's stories without comment, but this time I felt myself wanting to argue with Ariel when she pictured herself suffering in hell. I bit my tongue for a few minutes, but as soon as Ariel started to well up, my mothering instinct kicked in hard and my tone got gentle. I heard myself coax Ariel into imagining a forgiving God—into considering the idea that God wouldn't be so cruel as to make a transgender person and then require her to rewire herself into something different. I talked about a God without human vengefulness, a God that was just an energy or a universal force—but I felt like an idiot. Ariel's Catholicism was much more profoundly rooted than any secular sermon I could cook up, and she looked at me patiently and blankly, like I was reciting a recipe for a dish she'd never make.

Foxx used a different tactic. She tried to disabuse Ariel of this "But it's against God" notion by talking about her own back-and-forth as a teenager. She explained that in high school she also intermittently vowed to give up dressing as a girl, but she could never help coming back. This was normal for a teenager, she said, and most definitely not a sign of struggling with sin. "In high school I would get rid of all my clothes—give them to my cousin. But after a few months, I'd dip; I'd have little panties here, some bell-bottoms there. Pretty soon I was back in the women's section of Wal-Mart,"

Foxx said with a sigh. "After wearing those masculine things for so long, I felt like I was getting out of prison."

One Friday night, before the dance club Arena opened up at ten, Ariel and Lenora were hanging out at Foxx's trying on each other's dresses, warming up their eyeliners over the stove flame, and pulling an astonishing number of go-go boots out of the closet. The apartment was small and messy and often smelled like gas from the oven, which Foxx turned on whenever it got cold. There were papers and CD cases everywhere, and because Foxx had two guinea pigs named Shelly and Fiona that she let run around wild, there were also pellets in the corners.

They had all invited me over because Foxx wanted to play me a new cut of one of the raps she had written and recorded and because Ariel had a special announcement to make. When I got there, Ariel proclaimed that tonight was very important. Tonight, she said, would be the last night all of us would see her in a dress. This was, she asserted, her "retirement." She would go to the Arena dressed as a woman, and then give it up forever. Lenora gasped and ran over to Ariel, clutching her arm dramatically and whispering, "No, girl!" But Foxx just rolled her eyes and told Ariel she'd keep her clothes safe for her, whenever she was ready to come back. She offered the kids some Kool-Aid to calm them down. Foxx never served alcohol.

Then the music came on, and Ariel and Lenora bopped around the apartment, trying on dresses that fell to midthigh on their skinny legs. They spoke Spanglish and shouted at Foxx, who was playing DJ, to put on different CDs or turn up the volume. They leaned into Foxx's mirror, which was bordered with magazine cutouts of Pink and Lil' Kim and graphic porn shots of genetic women, legs splayed open.

"Girl, why you got pictures of pussy up here when you don't even want one?" Ariel asked, wiping off lip liner with a used Kleenex.

"Well, a lot of people ask me that," Foxx said, enunciating as though she were an elementary school teacher. "And I don't really know the answer. I guess it just gives me something to think about."

Ariel turned to Lenora, who was struggling with the bra she'd borrowed. "Girl, you don't gotta make your chi-chis so big this time," Ariel offered. "They look too fake."

When kids have the money for a water bra—a gel-filled bra that jiggles and shifts like the real thing—or for the gummy, flesh-toned inserts, they'll use these. But bras and inserts can cost $30 to $40, so the cheaper options are balloons or condoms filled with water. Water weighs about the same as breast tissue, and it'll feel more real than a pair of socks when a stray hand grazes the surface. Plus the rubber knot can look like a nipple, if it's placed correctly. Of course, a hard jab at the chest can mean a wet front and a ruined image.

That night, the girls were "going ghetto" and using condoms. They splashed and laughed as they filled them and poured them out and filled them again, trying to get the right shape. I knew the girls would soon transform into slinky nightclub women, plucked and heeled and watchful, but at that sink they looked like children at an open hydrant. Foxx just laughed at the mess.

At some point Foxx's friend Tito stopped by, dressed in white pants and a white button-down Guayabera shirt, with a Puerto Rican flag wrapped around his shoulders. Tito was, he said, Cuban and Puerto Rican, and he had no parents; his mom had passed away when he was a young child, and his dad went missing long ago. Tito called himself a "drag boy."

"A drag boy is someone who puts foundation on and certain hair pieces and shit. A drag boy still dresses like a boy, still carries himself like a boy, but is more into makeup, wigs, and fashion," Tito said. Boy George was a drag boy in his mind. Tito was gentle and reedy; he had dark, smooth skin and wore contacts that made his eyes blue. He had a bear claw tattooed on each cheek "for protection," and he looked, to me, like he could be either gender. Tito was an example of the range transgender can be, where people fall out of the rubric entirely and invent for themselves a new place to stand. Kids, especially, devise creative options and even rewrite history without a twitch of accountability. Tito had made up an elaborate origin story for these drag boys.

"My style goes back all the way to 1942 when it was okay for guys to wear wigs—Jheri curl wigs, Afro wigs, and stuff. Before the drag boys, there were rebels. And back in 1940 L.A., that was when the rebel crew was just beginning." Tito waved a hand down his clothing. He was seventeen and lived with a foster father but dreamed of the islands he had been to as a baby with his mother, though he didn't remember. "This outfit I'm wearing is called a '1942 Caribbean Latin salsa outfit,' and most likely you'd catch this in Puerto Rico or Cuba back then, and even still today."

Tito was a singer with a honeyish, somewhat feminine voice, and he often practiced or jammed with Foxx. On this night Foxx put on a CD with just a bass line and a beat, and they both picked up microphones.

"Oh-my-god!" their improvised song lyrics began, Foxx's and Tito's voices blending into a mock–Valley girl persona. "That's a man in a dress!"

Tito sang, melodic and lovely, "That's a maa-aa-aan," while Foxx dropped her voice into a lower register and spoke-sang, like a robot, "That's-a-man-in-a-dress! That's-a-man-in-a-dress!" Within minutes they had created a whole dance routine that involved a lot of fast head turns and dramatic foot stomps. Ariel and Lenora just stepped around them wielding eyebrow pencils.

When Lenora was ready—in a red minidress and one of Foxx's wigs, her lips expertly lined by Ariel and her cleavage shaded with cheek blush by Foxx—she announced she was going to go out for a walk—allegedly to pick up potato chips. Foxx began to lecture. "Don't get in any cars, girl; I know you going out for catcalls."

"Ai, Mama," Lenora whined. "I don't do that no more."

Foxx wasn't sure; catcalls boosted confidence, and a quick trick could score a kid $60 for the night. Foxx didn't know if she'd do it, but the youngest kids garner the most cash, and Lenora was only fifteen with a baby face and coy, pouty lips. But there was nothing Foxx could do; she had done the same when she was younger and new to

Los Angeles. She muttered a deflated "Hold on to your pepper spray," and sank into the couch as Lenora closed the door.

"Now she won't be back for an hour," Ariel complained. She wanted to watch Foxx's bootlegged copy of Madonna's "Cherish" video, with the mermaid. Even though Ariel was eighteen, she sometimes seemed younger than Lenora, fussing to get people to take care of her and sitting too close to the TV with her legs bent back behind her like a cricket. She could genuinely well up at the sight of a mermaid—on a sticker or a video or a key chain. She had named herself after the cartoon mermaid Ariel in the Disney movie and got moony when she described seeing it for the first time. She was eight years old and watching it in a movie theater with two boys from school. She said she wept throughout, but hid it from her friends.

In girlish tones Ariel described the movie's underwater scene and the way, at the time, she just wanted to climb into the screen. "The Little Mermaid went for what she wanted, and got what she wanted, and at the end she was happy—everyone was happy, " Ariel said, between candy sucks. Her eyes were wide, unblinking. Her simple language was slow and soft, and I could sense the frustration behind her inability to express herself quite right. "I want to go through the story just the way Ariel did it. From talking to the guy singing and then going to the wicked witch, and then turning into a real girl and getting the guy. Ariel had to go talk to her father who turned her into a human being for real. It would be like my mom saying, 'Okay, you can be a girl.'"

Would Ariel's mom ever do that, I asked. "No," Ariel said. "That's why I'm afraid. That's why I want to retire."

Lenora finally returned, and the two kids clacked their way out of the house in their high-heeled boots, flanking Tito. Foxx didn't want to go out; she was tired of watching her daughters pick up more men than she could. Foxx felt like black men clocked her too easily; they spotted her Adam's apple more often than other kinds of men (possibly because they looked closer), so she favored Latinos. Still,

Foxx wasn't catty, and she didn't want her jealousy to flare when these Latin men whispered come-ons in Spanish to her younger, wispier daughters at the dance club. Foxx could be prone to bouts of deep sadness, especially when it came to men. While she'd fooled around with plenty, both for money and not, she confessed she'd never had a real boyfriend. Approaching twenty-one, she felt inexperienced and unworthy. She sank back on the couch and said she wanted to be alone, to work on the lyrics she was setting to some new beats. She told her daughters and Tito to have a good time. I wished Ariel good luck on her retirement and a quick wash of sorrow ran down her face. She had forgotten. "Thanks," she said, and bent to tug at her boot zipper.

Ariel retired from dressing as a girl to save herself from God's wrath. In her mind God was an angry male figure who could send her to hell, which was an eternity of liquefied fire and screaming. God always saw beneath the skirt; God always knew. The trouble was that when Ariel was buried under her boy self, Luis, she was nearly mute. Luis couldn't often speak to strangers; he'd look away, casting up a hand to show he was too ashamed or shy to answer. Luis couldn't look at men or flirt with them or even ask directions when he was lost on a city bus. Luis would just mumble down toward his baggy pants, smiling slightly, his eyes misting, while people shoved past him.

Ariel, on the other hand, could talk. She was still a quiet person, but when she needed to, Ariel could saucily boss a man into giving her a ride in his car, 'cause she wasn't in the mood to ride no bus. Ariel could share her makeup, could buy you a Coke if she thought you were thirsty, could say she wanted to be a teacher when she finished high school and went on to college; Ariel could jut her shoulders back and threaten to throw down if someone shoved her homegirl. Ariel could gossip in harsh whisper tones and erupt into squeals of laughter. So I wasn't really surprised when, two weeks after her proclaimed retirement, I ran into Ariel, not Luis, at Foxx's apartment. Ariel was getting ready to go to Arena and was sheepish when I asked her how the retirement had gone.

"I lasted a week. A week!" Ariel spurted, giggling shrilly, but she wouldn't meet my eyes. Turns out some of her friends had stopped by Ariel's house that following weekend, asking her to come to the park with them, all dressed up, to take pictures. Ariel loved taking pictures.

"I had no power. I mean, the makeup, the wigs, those stilettos. The walking around all hoochie. It's wonderful," she said, her voice dwindling into a murmur. Did this mean she failed? Ariel dropped her eyes. "Yes. I failed. I did fail. Now I know I'm going to hell."

I asked her what she ultimately learned from this retirement pause. Helpless, she shrugged. "I learned that I'm a boy. That I'm a woman."

Ariel couldn't let herself settle into a singular definition of herself, so she would float for a while. She thought Foxx would always be there, with her Kool-Aid and her lumpy secondhand couch, to catch her.

# 4

## ARRIVING

*W*HEN YOU SEE an aerial photograph of the United States at night, it looks like light has been poured along the edges of the country. Or maybe like the dark land humped up in the middle has sent the glittery bits rolling down the sides, catching in pockets but collecting most densely in the gutters of New York, D.C., Los Angeles, San Francisco, Miami. The coasts are where the people live, right at the boundaries of where we cannot. And the coastal cities are where so many transgender young people head when they decide, from rumor or knowledge or instinct, to find a home. Coasts are by their nature alchemical, and kids come to their cities to transform themselves—though each metropolis has its own identity and shapes each person uniquely.

Transgender kids come to L.A. for different reasons; often they come because it is the biggest city they can think of or because it has a liberal reputation and they yearn for acceptance. But some, like Foxx, come for Hollywood.

Foxxjazell was cramped up for forty-eight hours on a Greyhound bus from Alabama, with the plan of becoming an actor or, as a backup, a singer. After high school graduation, Foxx cashiered in a Birmingham department store for a summer, saving money for the trip. "The bus ride was really boring," Foxx said. "It seemed like

Texas took forever to get through. I would go to sleep about ten times and wake up and ask someone, 'Where are we at?' and they'd tell me, 'Texas.' 'Where we at now?' 'Texas.'"

The first thing Foxx did when she arrived in Los Angeles was rent a cheap motel room and then immediately she got on another bus—to Hollywood. She wanted to see the Walk of Fame, the three and a half miles (if you count both sides of the street) of brass star nameplates in the sidewalk. One night Foxx retraced that first evening with me, as she shopped for a new dress to wear at an open mic performance she was planning to give.

"I got off right here, on Cahuenga and Hollywood. It was not as glamorous as I thought it was going to be," Foxx said, her southern accent betraying her true disappointment even as her words, well trained toward optimism, were careful. On the corner, garbage overflowed from its can, and a homeless man, looking like a rolled-up tube of oil-covered canvas, slept against a wall half a block up. A storefront sold postcards of the Hollywood sign and of girls in bikinis, but there were more cars than people at that intersection and they honked loud and long as the lights went from yellow to red. "I was expecting to see studios and the Hollywood sign and a lot of upscale places. But it's a bunch of wig shops and clothing stores and check-cashing and electronics places. I wasn't that impressed."

I've always felt sorry for tourists who come to Hollywood. Like Foxx, they stand clustered in bunches on Hollywood Boulevard, the trash blowing around their feet, heads together, confused. But where's Hollywood, they're saying. Where can we take a picture? The boulevard with Mann's Chinese Theatre and all the sidewalk stars is the place to go for drugs and stolen jewelry or $20 shoes—especially when I went to visit it with Foxx. Recently, a real-estate development agency built an outdoor mall full of upscale chains oddly encircling two large white elephants perched on columns, but outside the mall, the same cheap stores hawk their chintz. There really is no special hamlet where the celebrities gather and clink glasses and let people look at them, unless maybe it's Monte Carlo.

Defeated, the tourists shell out ten bucks and shuffle into Ripley's Believe It or Not! museum.

Foxx looked down at the ground. "Madge Bellamy. I don't know who that is. Leatrice Joy," she said, laughing as we walked past star after star she didn't recognize. "To me, it seems like if all these people I've never heard of can end up here—Harry von Zell, who the hell is that?—I can assure and promise you everyone's going to know Foxxjazell. Everyone's going to know her star."

The first nameplate Foxx swooned over upon her arrival was Michael Jackson's, which she found on Hollywood near Highland. Throughout her childhood, Foxx had idolized Michael Jackson and spent many afternoons locked alone in her bedroom imitating him and his sister Janet. Foxx didn't know anyone in L.A. when she first arrived, but she imagined everyone knowing her, and that first day she pictured the name "Dwight Eric" emblazoned there with a television symbol. She hadn't yet met a transgender person or seen one on TV, and hadn't met her drag mother, Tatiana, so she didn't know another incarnation, name, or even life was possible.

"I kind of feel that if I hadn't made the transition to being transgender, I would have been a celebrity by now," Foxx said, but without remorse in her voice. We stepped into a clothing store with garish and buzzing fluorescent lights. She asked the clerk about a pink dress that was pinned to the wall above the register. He told her it was fifty bucks and her smile fell. She wanted to see the $15 and $20 racks. When he told her there weren't any, she just walked out, continuing her sentence as though we hadn't been interrupted at all. "Because I've talked to so many psychics, and they tell me, 'Oh, you should already be famous.' I agree with them—because I'm such a better actor than I am a singer."

Foxx did, in fact, go on several television auditions as a boy but said she has no regrets about this earlier expression of herself. She feels it would have been much harder to transition in the public eye, and that it was a "blessing" that she did it before anyone knew her.

"Millions of people would have looked up to me and accepted me as Dwight—but I wouldn't have been able to accept Dwight. I wouldn't have been able to love Dwight." Besides, Foxx added, once she transitioned, she realized she had a message. She saw, and felt, the discrimination against transgender people and wanted to stem it. This is why she writes music that has lines like "If I was a real girl, would you stay with me, not be ashamed of me."

"I'm still open to acting, but my main priority is to express my personal message through music," Foxx said. "Rapping has a more powerful message than acting. When you're acting, you're portraying someone else, a character."

At this point in her music career, Foxx was performing every two weeks or so at various cafés or open mic or talent nights around the city. When she could save a few hundred dollars, she would record a song at a recording studio in Hollywood, hiring the house musician to mix beats and electronic background music for her. These she was compiling into a demo tape to send around to studios and to hopefully sell at her concerts. Foxx's shows could be anything from a Sabor a Mí act, with its jammed and hooting audience, to a Tuesday evening coffee shop gig, replete with a wheezing espresso machine and three polite fans, all of them Foxx's friends. It didn't matter; Foxx xeroxed flyers and handouts for all of her shows and always marched onstage as though a thousand people had responded to her marketing. She'd plug in her boom box or, if it was a bigger gig, nod at the sound guy, and the electric drums would blast out a kicky dance beat. On top of this, a synthesized keyboard tapped the high notes. Foxx loved a poppy, bubblegum sound.

Foxx smiled as she performed and made eye contact. She reached toward the audience with the hand that wasn't holding the microphone, and she gave small skips when she turned, as though she were traversing a much larger stage. She wore big earrings and jean jackets and rapped passionately for justice, hitting the stronger lyrics with a hard face, but then smiling again when she waited for the chorus. One song she did a lot was called "C'mon Out," and part of it went like this:

> *C'mon out! C'mon out!*
> *Let the words do the walkin', let your actions do the talkin'*
> *C'mon out! C'mon out!*
> *Break down the door; you can't hide no more—*
> *If your friends disrespect, you need to reject!*
>
> *. . . Kids committing suicide*
> *Parents kick 'em out—ain't no place to hide*
>
> *In this fucked-up society*
> *Gotta be real with your sexuality*
> *Don't let their shitty asses call you a fag*
> *You're the greatest asset God ever had . . .*
>
> *C'mon out! C'mon out!*

We got to Mann's Chinese Theatre, which was crammed with tourists. Despite all the disappointments Hollywood had dealt her, despite not having a record contract after paying shady "managers" and "agents" she'd found out of the back of music magazines who made promises and robbed her of hundreds of dollars, a Hollywood fantasy still glimmered for Foxx at Mann's Chinese. The theater itself looks like a cartoon: dragon heads are mounted on apple-red columns, rooftops swoop down and point back up in a parody of pagoda roofs, and so many tourists snap photos, it's like the paparazzi suddenly went mad and turned on itself.

At Mann's there are stars' handprints and footprints pressed into the cement, and Foxx gently set her own hands over the smaller outlines of Judy Garland and Marilyn Monroe. She closed her eyes, as though giving silent homage. For Foxx, entertainment was a world she could take refuge in. Lots of young adults, transgender or no, come to Los Angeles with the same dream of becoming a star. Wanting to be a star had much more to do with Foxx's personality than her transsexuality. Transsexuals—in general—do not want to be flashy musicians like RuPaul; those are drag queens.

RuPaul is a complicated figure. On the one hand, he's a beacon; his music videos buoyed many transsexuals Foxx's age through their early adolescence and provided the first (albeit overly glittered and eyelashed) notion that genetic men could dress as women and look better than your sister, your mom, and the pretty neighbor next door. But on the other hand, RuPaul is a drag queen—a gay man who cross-dresses for entertainment. Because RuPaul is the most famous genetic male who looks female, courtesy of MTV, people think all genetic males who look female are like RuPaul: tall, heavily made-up, and into corsets, wigs, and lip-synching. Far too often I've heard, "But why are transgender people so into glamour? They all wear so much makeup." The truth is they're not, and they don't. Call it the "drag-queen seep"; drag queens are prominent in the mainstream cultural imagination, so we look for transpeople to be drag queens.

Despite Foxxjazell's aspirations to be the "first international, transsexual pop star," an Israeli singer named Dana International actually beat her to it. She's an out transsexual from Tel Aviv who was on the top-ten dance charts in the United States in the late nineties and was a major star in Europe. She also sold half a million records in Egypt, where her music is, because of her gender, illegal.

Dana was born a boy named Yaron Cohen to a poor Yemenite-Israeli family. Like RuPaul, she started working the drag-queen circuit in her teens but made her way to London for surgery and in 1993 released her first album as Dana. Five years later she represented the country of Israel at the Eurovision Song Contest (think *Star Search* meets the Grammys, only bigger) and won—this despite major resistance to her stardom from the Orthodox community in Israel. Then she performed at what's known as the gay version of the

Olympics, the Gay Games, that year in Amsterdam—which was controversial as well, because the Gay Games didn't allow trans-sexuals to compete. Whatever drama clatters about her, Dana seems to slip right through, perpetually singing bouncy, boppy songs in French, English, Hebrew, and Arabic—subverting the criticism of her sinfulness by producing party mixes that are broadly happy sounding and internationally appealing. Still, when I told Foxx about Dana International, she waved it off, unmoved—much the way she treated the brass stars in Hollywood. "How is she so famous if I haven't heard of her?" she said.

Foxx grew up an only child in Birmingham, where she remembered feeling like a girl as early as kindergarten, when the teacher would divide the kids into groups of boys and girls. Like a lot of transkids, she knew she was a boy because that's what people told her she was, but she felt a pull toward the girls' group. She hovered in the middle until the teacher scolded her into place. She didn't necessarily play with girl toys, like Barbies, but she did play with girls and, as she grew into her five-foot-nine height, she even started to look a bit like a girl—she was thin and willowy, and her gestures were uncon-sciously delicate and feminine, so strangers didn't always know which pronoun to use.

"It didn't bother me that much until I got into my teens," Foxx said, explaining that her parents, too, were supportive of her gender ambiguity. They didn't speak about her appearance at home, she said, but she's sure they noticed: they just loved her and let her be. "I started getting attracted to the guys, and I would ask myself, 'Why don't I have a boyfriend? Why can't they walk up to me and talk to me like they're talking to those girls?' It just didn't click for me that I was a boy and they were not going to talk to me like they'd talk to the girls because my appearance was that of a boy. My mannerisms might have been that of a girl, but evidently that just wasn't good enough."

Foxx's boyhood "clicked in" for her as soon as the harassment started; shortly after she realized she was attracted to boys, they realized she was a "faggot" and called her that repeatedly and cruelly. Foxx made four suicide attempts in high school.

While there's no official study of transgender youth and suicide rates, my guess is that Foxx's experience is sadly common. A widely quoted statistic for gay and bisexual kids is that they're four times more likely to attempt suicide than their straight counterparts—and this is due to bullying, verbal and physical abuse, a lack of support and role models, and so on. Intensify this for the transkids, and deepen their silence, and I imagine if we did have real figures, they'd be staggering. Granted, the kids on the streets of Los Angeles were struggling with poverty and gangs and familial troubles and other factors, but when I got close enough to them, nine out of ten had a suicide story. And some still had a recurring fantasy.

At first, Foxx fought back against her tormentors. She tried to be masculine; she toughened up her attitude, threw her shoulders back, practiced strutting. She attempted to have crushes on girls, though they didn't feel authentic. She even wrote a rap, cribbed from a Tevin Campbell album, which she performed for one of the popular girls in school, in front of all the other kids. This was a disaster.

"I inserted my own words to the rap and it sounded so phony," Foxx said, laughing sadly. "I remember it. It goes:

*"I'm hard!*
*I know I'm fifteen—but the dudes you like can't even make you scream.*
*I'll blow your mind, I'm a stone-cold lover—*
*Spend the night with me and you'll never take another.*

"When I finished, the girl just started laughing in my face," Foxx said. "She was laughing at the fact that I was trying to be so hard, and evidently it was coming across that I was just so effeminate."

Eventually Foxx simply surrendered. She realized she didn't have judgment when it came to masculine and feminine; even when she tried to be neutral or noncontroversial, other people read her as pushing gender bounds, as making trouble. She remembered buying shoes, for instance, at a thrift store.

"I bought them for ten bucks; I really didn't think of them as girls' shoes," Foxx said, her eyes earnest. "I was just saying to myself these are some really cool shoes, and I bought them. I found out later they were heels."

Foxx didn't have any real friends then and definitely no boyfriends, but, thankfully, her parents were staunch. They had dinner-table talks about the fact that Dwight was gay, which they accepted but worried about. This was Birmingham, they said, and people don't flaunt their inclinations. They didn't want their son to get any more hurt than he already had been.

The only real altercation came about over a wig. One Halloween, which was Foxx's favorite holiday, Foxx bought a $7 wig at a drugstore. It was black and synthetic, with loose floppy curls sticking out three or four inches from the scalp—the kind of thing you might pick up last minute for a party if you didn't have a costume. The wig had no particular character or distinction, but Foxx loved it and kept it long after Halloween was over. Every day after school, she'd put on the wig to walk around the house, make dinner, do her homework—much the way someone else might don slippers or an old flannel shirt. The wig just made her feel comfortable. Then one day Foxx's father, who had been quietly steaming over the strange and unexplained sight of his son in a dime-store hairpiece for weeks on end, snatched it from Foxx's head.

"He said, 'You don't need to be wearing that wig all the time!' And he took it away from me, and he cut it up," Foxx said. "And I cried. I was so mad at him, I told him I hated him. At the time I meant it, because he really messed with my emotions. That wig meant everything to me; it was my only source of being feminine."

Foxx's father was probably trying to do what he thought was best: curb teenage silliness that could get a person hurt. He withstood Foxx's tears, the name-calling, and the door slamming, in the name of protection. And, compared to the thousands of parents who throw their transgender children out when they "act like a girl," Foxx's father was generous—a trait she acknowledges and appreciates now. Still, laws of teenage nature dictate that when you repress one part of their life, they'll just manifest it in another, when you're not looking. And unfortunately for transsexual teenagers, when their expression gets shut down in the house, they'll take it outside, where things become much more dangerous.

After the wig-cutting incident, Foxx started keeping a stash of wigs and clothes under her bed. Late at night she'd put on her secret outfits and climb out the window and stroll around her suburban neighborhood. Because it was Birmingham, and because it was two in the morning, she never ran into anyone, but she loved the way it felt, being outside dressed the way she was. Now Foxx knows it was lucky the streets were silent because, as she said, "I thought I was the T, but really I looked a mess," and who knows how late-night joyriders would have interpreted her costumes. It was during these walks that Foxx could imagine living somewhere else, though, somewhere like Los Angeles, where she told herself she'd be surrounded by other creative people, where the streets wouldn't be silent, where her bed wouldn't be empty at night. She constantly dreamed of having a boyfriend.

As these wee-hour walks and daytime trips to Wal-Mart's girls' department were becoming more frequent, the name Dwight was becoming more of a problem. It's not that she thought it was a bad name necessarily; it just didn't fit. The answer came from daytime television.

"I was watching *Oprah,* and the artist formerly known as Prince, as he was called back then, came on and he said he made this recent discovery. There were two people living inside of him, and one of those people happened to be a woman," Foxx told me, her voice rising with the memory. "And I just said to myself, 'Oh my god. That is so me.'"

Foxx decided to invent a symbol for herself too. She started with an upside-down pink triangle, because everybody already knew her as a gay boy, but then in the middle of it she drew a stick-figure woman in a skirt, like the kind on restroom signs. Foxx asked everyone she knew to start calling her "the symbol" or "pink triangle" (whichever they preferred), and she started signing all her homework and documents with the image. She carried a pink pen with her everywhere she went.

I asked her if teachers went along with the plan.

"No. I didn't really demand that much from teachers. Dwight was just a name that was given to me that I had no choice over, so I still responded to it a little bit," Foxx said. Whenever boys asked her what the drawing meant, she would eagerly explain, using the moment as an opportunity to flirt. "I would get in a real feminine voice and say, 'Oh—it just means that I'm a woman trapped inside of a male's body.'" Here she'd giggle coyly. "Then he'd say, 'So that means you're gay.' And I'd say, 'Oh yes—I am!' And I would hope that he'd then ask if I wanted to kick it with him, but usually he'd just go on about his business."

That was on a good day. On the rest of the days, Foxx was harassed for her androgynous clothes, her symbol, her effeminate mannerisms, and her hair, which, by her senior year, was dyed platinum blond and stood straight up in a four-inch Afro all around her head. She was never attacked physically, but her notoriety spread far beyond the school grounds.

"I would see people at outside functions, and they would say, 'Hey, aren't you that gay guy from Ramsay High School?' And I would say, 'Oh yeah, that's me,'" Foxx said, leaning forward, imitating the eager way she'd answer—with blinky eyes and an open smile. Then she changed her tone to describe the response. She was grim and disgusted, and her nose crinkled up. "'Oh yeah. I heard about you—you're the one who wears the pink triangle.' And I would feel good because I was making a name for myself. That's when I really knew I was meant to be famous."

———

Los Angeles isn't the only beacon for migrant transgender kids. There are trans youth in any major city, but aside from Los Angeles, San Francisco and New York are two magnets. Teenagers close to the West Coast get to choose between two cities with very different cultures. While there are no official counts of transpeople in any city, the per capita trans percentages might be highest in San Francisco, where some claim that around fifteen thousand fit under the gender-variant umbrella. This might be because of the city's history as an anything-goes mecca—the place where even straight people paint their houses pink. San Francisco is the first—and still only—American city to provide sex reassignment surgeries, hormones, and psychiatric care to its city employees. And while transkids don't necessarily know San Francisco's political particulars, they know its reputation as a happy, gay city.

And there is something playful and fun about San Francisco's transgender community. There's an open attitude and more porous boundaries, especially between the lesbian and female-to-male groups. Oftentimes activism and political organizing will take place alongside karaoke, spoken word, and dance performances for the younger "gender-queers" or "FTMs and their friends." This means lesbians and transmen hang out and forge bonds and have fun, knowing that appearance is performance and therefore worthy of a little sass. Online and in community centers, you'll find invitations extended to gender outlawz, trannyfags, and queerbois (San Francisco, also a literary capital, loves to play with words) for an open mic or interactive, "sex-positive" art opening. The feeling is part university intellectual-cum-artist/anarchist rebel. This is the city with a woman-owned feminist strip club called the Lusty Lady and a pro-prostitution activist organization called COYOTE, which stands for "Call Off Your Old Tired Ethics."

Los Angeles doesn't generally use words like "gender-queer"; it doesn't have the same kind of academic spin to its activism, nor the same whimsy. The activists here are numerous and organized and successful: when they have the choice, transpeople in the know will often move to L.A. precisely because it has developed unusually strong resources. In L.A., HIV organizations like Bienestar outreach specifically to transgender street kids; they know the kids will sometimes shoot the silicone from brake fluid into their bodies, and they warn them of the risk. Drug abuse programs like the Van Ness Recovery House have groups and services designed for transgender clients, and GLASS, the group home and foster care agency originally launched for gay and lesbian kids, is acutely aware of its transgender youth constituency. Top administrators at all of these organizations, as well as at the FTM Alliance and at the Division of Adolescent Medicine at Childrens Hospital, which provides health care to transkids, all band together in various citywide committees and collect data on issues of community safety, drug use, HIV risk, and so on. This is light-years ahead of other cities. In an effort to not only combat the negative elements in the transgender community, the FTM Alliance and Childrens Hospital created the first-ever "leadership academy" for transpeople, and activists all over the city work with "the Village" (the city's name for the main gay, lesbian, bisexual, and transgender center) to create an entire weekend of transgender pride activities each year.

Despite its reputation for being "superficial" and "fake," parts of Los Angeles feel more gritty and more urban than San Francisco, and in that way, its young transgender culture is similar to New York's—though even L.A. and New York are distant cousins in terms of the way kids act or talk about themselves. A year after I left L.A., I taught for a semester at the Harvey Milk School, a high school for gay and transgender kids in New York. Here kids called both the female-to-male transgender boys and the butch lesbians "aggressives." The female counterparts were just "femmes" or sometimes, in the case of transwomen, "femme queens." "Aggressive" to me sounded harsh and judgmental, but when I asked my students why they didn't use the word "butch," they rolled their eyes and said that was old-fashioned. I tried to tease out the difference between a pure "aggressive" and an "aggressive" lesbian, and they got frustrated with my splicing; the only thing that mattered, they said, was that an aggressive couldn't date another aggressive. That would be disgusting. Here they went "*ewwww*" and squirmed around like children looking at worms. So, I asked my New York students, was there any possibility of blending; could a person be a little bit aggressive, a little bit femme? Could a person be transgender and gay? What about me? Here I was, with my close-cropped hair and my lipstick; was I femme, or was I aggressive? "Girl, you're just old," was their response.

This highly sensitized labeling may well be an inheritance from the balls, an East Coast culture of dances and contests that black and Latino gay and transgender people have been throwing since (depending on whom you talk to) the 1940s, 1920s, or even earlier. When transgender kids come to New York, they sometimes fall into the network of houses and the "ballroom scene" because it's the most cohesive and extensive transgender community that welcomes, even caters to, the urban poor. These balls are held roughly once a week, in Harlem, Brooklyn, New Jersey, and Philadelphia, and have spread to the South and the Midwest. Gay men and women will dress in drag, and transsexuals will just dress up and perform—dancing, catwalking, and competing for trophies and money in categories centered primarily on passability and style. Contest rounds are called things like "Thug," "Executive," and "Pretty Boy Face." There's a prize each night for a category called "Realness," which is for best overall passability, and there's a grand-prize winner of the whole event, who can fetch up to $2,000 at a large ball, culled from tickets bought at the door.

Gerard Gaskin, a New York City photographer who has been attending and photographing the balls for the past fifteen years, estimated that there are over fifty houses, some with more than five hundred members, and each with their own distinct style and reputation. Houses are rarely actual locations; they're more like clubs. When a person does particularly well at the balls (or gets her "tens" from the judges), she'll be approached by a drag mother or father from one of the houses, asking if she wants to join their house. This means she'll compete under the house name and gain the house's friendship and protection and tutelage. In return, she'll help boost the house's reputation for getting tens and dominating the balls.

Houses are famous for their strength in certain categories, like Butch Queen Face (which means gay male, handsome face) and are often split along race lines. The House of Ebony, for example, is an African American house, and it's mostly, Gaskin said, a dark-skinned house. Some houses are known for prostitution, others for outreach in AIDS or drug-use issues; as in Los Angeles, the line between engaging in the dangerous behavior and providing counseling or services for the dangerous behavior can be very thin.

The names of the houses have shifted over the decades. In the seventies houses were named after actual people, like the House of La Beija or the House of Christian. In the eighties people made up their house names, like the House of Extravaganza and the House of Ebony. The nineties were the decade of the fashion houses, like Revlon and Bazaar, and now, Gaskin said, people are making up house names again. Even as they shift, though, names and categories are very important in the New York City ball scene; after all, you get connected to a house and a family by winning a contest, which means fitting snugly into a category. This might be why there's less interest, at least on the streets, in blurring bounds, in being "gender-queer," than there is somewhere like San Francisco.

Of course, these are generalizations, and the transgender community in all three cities—like all big U.S. cities—wrestles with tremendous homelessness. Transsexuality is little understood by the mainstream, and young people are underserved everywhere. Laws mandating gender-separate sleeping and shower spaces in most shelters, foster homes, and so on for the two genders mean gender ambiguity is simply spliced out of the equation. But it's not for the services that kids generally come to cities—it's for the hope that that city represents. San Francisco represents acceptance and some sort of happy freedom because of its past as a hippie haven, and New York is still stereotypically a big shiny apple, reflecting dozens of possibilities. There's Broadway there, and Wall Street, and the media, and fashion and the museums and big business. It's an island, so there's a sense if you can root deeply enough there, you'll hit water and bloom forever.

Unfortunately, many kids don't have the luxury of choosing where they want to live. If they get thrown out, they run as far as their money will take them, which means the nearest city. An example in Los Angeles is Lu, a skinny Thai girl with twitchy mannerisms, spiky hair, and a loud laugh. Christina, Foxx, Ariel, and all the others know Lu. Several years ago Lu was living as a boy at home in a wealthy town in the suburbs of Los Angeles and working the late shift at a Tower Records when her father discovered some letters from a boyfriend, along with a few compromising photographs. In the photos Lu looked feminine, her boyfriend looked like a definite boyfriend, and when Lu got home, her father gave her fifteen minutes to get out.

"Everything was broken and torn, and he had thrown away a lot of the letters. He said, 'I don't care where you go, just leave,'" Lu said. Crying and shouting at her dad, she tried to stuff all of her *Xena: Warrior Princess* paraphernalia (she named herself after the *Xena* actress Lucy Lawless) along with some clothes into a suitcase, but she knew she was probably forgetting important things. Her father stared at her stoically. Lu stayed with a friend for a few days, but that didn't last, and she ended up moving to Hollywood, where she, like so many other transgender kids, had heard rumors there were "kids like her." Within days she was turning tricks for money.

This kind of scenario, regionally and historically, hasn't always played out. If Lu or Christina or any of the other transkids I knew had been born exactly as they were, only earlier and in a Mojave tribe rather than the Southern California of today, their parents would have noticed their inclination (as they always do!) to act like little girls. But instead of getting slapped or mocked for dressing up or liking boys, these femmy kids would have been brought before the whole Mojave community at the age of nine or ten. The group would have started singing and then encouraging the boys to dance—as it was believed that song goes directly to the heart, and a person can't deny his true inclination when he dances. If the kids danced, as they certainly would have, in the women's style, their parents would have whisked them home, bathed them, and given them girls' skirts to proudly wear back to the gathering, where they would have been introduced as *alyhas*.

*Alyhas* were (and sometimes still are) genetically male tribe members, who wore women's clothing, adopted women's names, and did women's work. Essentially, they lived their lives as heterosexual women, though even this term doesn't quite translate. In Mojave culture in general, there were four distinct sexes: male, female, *alyha*, and the female-to-male counterpart, *hwame*. Unlike transsexuals in mainstream society, *alyha* and *hwame* didn't transition from one sex to another. They already embodied their own categories.

If any of my transgender former students could have been born into this community instead of their own, I realized, their hallway dancing and voguing would have relieved them of years of explaining and defending and running away. Six hundred years ago, they would have lived a reality even their South Central neighborhood thugs couldn't undermine, because it would have been the thugs who sang them into being.

While the Mojave are known for their humor and teasing, these songs for the *alyha* ceremonies, called *alyha kwayum*, were sung in earnest. In fact, the toughest, most masculine men were often designated to sing them, while braiding the pliant bark for an *alyha*'s new skirt. They sang:

> Roll it this way, roll it that way
> I hold it, I place it,
> It is done, it is finished
> Listen.

After the song *alyha* would be treated as women, given women's work, and ultimately married to men.

Men who married *alyha* were lucky, the Mojave said. For one thing, the *alyha* themselves were lucky, in the spiritual sense, or blessed, and they believed this luck could rub off. For another, an *alyha* wife performed the same chores as a traditional wife, but an *alyha* was often physically stronger and could accomplish twice the work. Plus, without the burden of birthing or raising children, an *alyha* had more time to gather plants and herbs and to keep house. In Mojave culture too, it was the women who were considered sexually licentious and unfaithful, so a man who wanted to settle down might feel better sleeping with a wife who was not genetically female.

Often dubbed *berdache* in the four-hundred-year history of Native American ethnographies, genetic males who exhibited female characteristics lived in all parts of North America in multiple tribes, save for the coastal northeastern rim. (*Berdache* is a pejorative term from the Persian *berdaj*, meaning kept boy or prostitute, and it was the word that French explorers used when they encountered such people.) According to the scholarly literature and explorers' notebooks, *berdache* were common throughout the continent, and while their rituals and styles differed from tribe to tribe, they were generally respected by the community.

It seems that these gender nonconformists had everything to do with performing the masculine and/or feminine role, and much less to do with sexuality. In other words, Mojave men could sleep with *alyha* and not be gay, and men could sleep with men and not be *alyha*. What was important in most Native American marriages before Europeans showed up was that one person performed the "husband" role and another performed the "wife" role in dividing up labor. The gender or genetic sex of these two people was secondary and, in some cases, so was the clothing they wore. Among the Navajo, when a man married a *nadle* (somebody who exhibits the behavior of the opposite sex or is born with ambiguous genitalia), they both dressed as men in the ceremony. A *nadle* performed both the men's and women's chores, so the prudent businessperson realized he was gaining a husband *and* a wife (lucky *nadle*). *Nadle* marriages often proved economically fruitful and thus were widely admired. In polygamous tribes like the Lakota, men who had a few *winkte* (Lakota for *nadle*) spouses among their child-bearing wives had extra helping hands and fewer mouths to feed, because *winkte* bore no kids. Many say the Lakota chief Crazy Horse received his spiritual name from a *winkte* (as did Black Elk), and there's a claim he had a *winkte* spouse among his genetically female wives.

For these tribes, there weren't just two genders posted at opposite ends of a field, with a rule against hanging out in the middle. Today, in the United States, people are expected to pick a single side, and then run like hell to get there: a person who sees herself as both or not quite either one doesn't have a comfortable place to stand.

This is the middle ground that thugs and bullies don't like: a genetically male teenager wearing an electric blue prom dress with off-the-shoulder straps, and slightly scuffed silver sandals, with one heel worn down (I heard a girl lost a few teeth for this). They don't like genetic girls who look like guys, homing in on their Timberland boots and Fubu shirts, and they don't like too-big sports jerseys either, with Ace bandages and three Beefy-T's beneath to flatten and cover up the goods. They don't like ambiguous-looking kids of either gender, but especially ones who wear platform go-go boots with tight jeans underneath a miniskirt and a gray boy's hoodie because it's cold outside, with short fingernails painted a gender-neutral black. "What the hell is *that*?" they ask, before they rip apart the so-called threads looking for answers. Three-quarters of high school–aged transgender kids have been harassed or assaulted for being trans, and about 90 percent feel unsafe in school, when they go. This is why they cycle on and off the streets; the protection they receive from drag mothers and peers there is often much more sensitive and immediate than the care they get from schoolteachers or administrators. Sometimes a kid leaves school before she gets kicked out of her home. This leads to truancies and tickets and bench warrants and angry parents, and, suddenly, the child is on the street full-time.

The most comprehensive study of homeless youth in L.A. is essentially an AIDS evaluation conducted by local service providers and funded by the Centers for Disease Control, which took two years to complete. In 1995, the study determined, there were between 7,000 and 8,000 homeless youth in Hollywood alone. Thirty percent—2,400—were willing to report to a survey intake worker that they had engaged in "survival sex," or prostitution, for money or shelter. (Of this group, incidentally, 24 percent said they were "not at all likely" to get HIV.) Fifty percent had been homeless for a year or more. As for how many of these kids are specifically transgender, there's no official count, but activists and outreach workers have cross-referenced their lists to land in the 300 to 400 range. This doesn't count the kids who don't use services at all.

In Foxx's mind, being homeless was alluring at first. She spent her first four months in Los Angeles being technically "homeless" by choice—staying in Covenant House, a shelter for kids under twenty-one. It was a move she had carefully planned from home. In a Birmingham library, Foxx checked out a book called the *Gay and Lesbian Yellow Pages,* found a listing for Covenant House, and called them up. If the shelter had taken reservations, she would have made one.

"It was exciting because I had seen so many documentaries about people like Madonna and Tom Hanks; they were starving for so many days and years, and then—bam!—they got famous. That's how I thought it would happen to me. It's actually sometimes seen as glamorous to be homeless," Foxx said, adding that she knew kids who definitely preferred homelessness to their prior homes. She also knew kids who relished the accompanying freedom and sense of early adulthood. "If they live on the streets, they don't have to abide by anyone. Some get boyfriends or girlfriends who come squat with them, and then they finally have this other person who cares about them. They're actually living together—it's a runaway romantic thing."

Christina was a more typical kind of homeless transgender girl, the kind who didn't choose it. Christina also had to "arrive" in L.A., even though she had lived there all her life. She had to physically leave her neighborhood and her gang, but more than that, she had to disentangle herself from the cultural markers that had shaped the early part of her life, and find herself new ones. For Christina, this meant hiding the A.T.C. tattoo, which marked her sexually as a boy, and going looking for the places where she could act as a woman. She first made this move when she was living at her cousin Mario's— the one who wouldn't let her keep her Cortez sneakers.

At Mario's house Christina stayed up watching a lot of late-night TV. She devoured music videos after the family was asleep, hoping for a shot of RuPaul, who was popular then and had his own show on VH1. He had a video out, a cover of the song "If You Were a Woman, and I Was a Man," which Christina was obsessed with because of the obvious lyrics and, she said, because "he sounded like a girl when he sang it." At night no one could question her motives or bawl her out for only watching certain stations.

At night, too, there were the infomercials, with their intricate makeup demonstrations or their earnest thigh-thinning exercises. Here Christina learned that genetic women changed their bodies and spent hundreds of dollars a month on pills that promised to make their skin glow or their waists shrink. She also learned about breast enhancements: sprays, lotions, and (the least expensive) gel cups that you could pop into your bra. Christina pretended to be a woman with a mastectomy who needed advice, and she started quizzing the telephone operators about their products. She practiced sounding much older, with a quaver in her voice, like she expected somebody with cancer would probably sound. She asked about which inserts felt most genuine to a grope or looked most real, which gels jiggled properly, and which potions smelled appropriately sweet or fruity. Operators, she told me, sometimes halted at her invariably inaccurate mastectomy descriptions, but they always answered her questions.

"I would say things like 'I want to know if I can get my breast back.' It's funny now," Christina said. The phone that provided Christina such safe passage into feminine anonymity also was her demise some months into her stay at the cousin's house. Despite the free food and rent, Christina came to resent her cousin Mario, she said, because he treated her like a maid. "He would make me clean the whole house, something his own wife wouldn't do, and then his kids would come and screw it up," Christina said, claiming she cleaned for three, sometimes four, hours a day.

This Christina-Cinderella story sounded fishy to me. I was starting to recognize that Christina was prone to romantic reenactments, especially when she got to be the heroine. I narrowed my eyes, suspicious.

"Girl, yes!" she insisted. "Then one day he said some shit about not trusting me. And I was like, 'Fuck you, then. I'm leaving.'"

By this point, months into our weekly dinner relationship, I thought I could tell when Christina was holding back. She never outright lied to me, but she withheld information sometimes. She was more assertive when she edited herself, more high-pitched and fierce. I occasionally laughed at these defenses, because they were so transparent, which of course made her mad. I asked her to take a wild guess and ask herself why her cousin wouldn't trust her, and she said she didn't know. She paused and said, "Maybe the party lines didn't work out."

Party lines? "I was into it then, girl—you know." I didn't, but I do now. Party lines were big in the early nineties, before the Internet allowed for anonymous sex. They were facilitated conversations between strangers (two, three, or more) connected through a pay-per-minute phone service. Christina started calling these lines shortly after the infomercial phone calls to further test her effectiveness as a girl. Once, it turned out, her wiles worked so well that a guy asked where she lived. Christina gave the name of her cousin's wife, along with the address, just to see what would happen.

"So he came looking for the wife! And they knew it was me that had called. I don't know how they knew!" Christina said this with the same genuine teenage bafflement I saw in my students when they couldn't believe I had caught them plagiarizing a paper they didn't have the skills to write.

And while that was the real reason Christina had to leave, she chalked up the experience as yet another example of how men couldn't be trusted: you think you can count on them to take care of you—then they throw you to the street.

In any case, Christina went back to the street with a broader knowledge of all things feminine. So people wouldn't recognize her, she took buses to malls outside East L.A. where they sold gel inserts in the lingerie shops, about the size of a small pancake and as heavy as a juggling beanbag. She found drugstores that sold Natural Curves breast enhancement tablets, and as she explored, she wondered if there were other kids like her. Eventually, a couple of years later, she found them, but even then, at thirteen, Christina knew Los Angeles was becoming a different city.

Ariel also grew up in Los Angeles. She led a somewhat cloistered life in the tiny rooms of her small homes or apartments, as her mother and older sister moved every few years to poor neighborhoods in the Valley, South Central, and East L.A. They didn't have money for entertainment or going out, since her mother was housebound by the medications that curbed her illness and the family was penned in by her meager SSI benefits. The uplift and escape came from church, where Ariel imagined saints and demons and the promise of a heaven, where everyone got to be an angel and thereby vaguely feminine, gauzy, and winged.

Ariel lives almost entirely in her head—possibly the result of a detached, heavily medicated mother and perhaps because she doesn't particularly like the body she sees below her neck. She'd rather have a different body; she'd rather be a cartoon mermaid; she'd rather life were so much smoother than the complicated mess it seems to be. Because of this core and fervent wish, Ariel can come off as simple.

"Wait, what?" Ariel asked again and again the night I took her to her favorite Mexican restaurant in Hollywood. She asked it with a loopy, dazed expression, like someone had just kissed her or she just happily remembered it was her birthday. I'd gently remind her what we'd been discussing. Ariel would look at me earnestly and screw up her face like she had something big and long and important to explain. Then she'd pause, take a deep breath, and give one of her typical one-word whisper answers, with the last letter extended, the helium coming out of a balloon. "Yesssssssssssssssssss." Distracted again, she'd trail a waiter with her eyes, and twirl a straw between her fingers. "Yessssssssssssssssss."

"Yes" was the answer when I asked whether there was a split between her life "in drag," as she called it, and her life at home. Unlike Christina, Foxx, Domineque, or even Nina, Ariel had never moved out of her mother's house, but the psychological divide between her two lives was wide. At that time she was eighteen, and she carried a rolling backpack the size of a large airplane carry-on with her wherever she went, changing clothes, and attitudes, between the different L.A.'s.

"In South Central, where I live—it's a bad neighborhood," Ariel said, adding she'd been chased several times for being—as the neighbors saw it—"gay." "My sister doesn't like it; she gets frustrated with the neighbors, so when she gets mad, she calls me a faggot too."

Ariel's sister is only one year older but is, as Ariel said, "the head of the house." The sister had a child at fourteen, and manages the bulk of the home care for their sick mother atop her child-care duties. She doesn't have much energy left to worry about Ariel who, at the time of our dinner, had a difficult time being home. Often, she just daydreamed or spaced out or simply left.

And wheeled her luggage to Hollywood. Like other transgender girls, Ariel first heard about Hollywood from friends. Older boys and men started flirting with her after she went through puberty, and they slipped her phone numbers, which she called. When she did, they'd tell her about a place called Hollywood, which she privately swore to find. When she was fifteen years old she did, and older girls took her in and told her she'd look pretty as a girl, told her where the good parties were. The first person to do this was Juliana—the wispy Latina who was also Domineque's drag mother.

"She was real bossy—that's what I liked about her," Ariel explained, demurely licking salsa off a chip. "She was like, 'Dress up in drag, Ariel!'"

That first night they went to the Arena dance club, where, Ariel said, her life simply changed. She had been secretly trying on her mom's old dresses in the family bathroom about once a week, every week, since she was four years old, but this behavior only brought shame and confusion. So to go to Arena and dance publicly in heels, laughing openmouthed and with a carefree head toss like she had practiced in the bathroom mirror—this, for Ariel, was close to a literal heaven on earth.

Ariel started making weekly pilgrimages to Hollywood and to Arena, collecting friends and cramming her time there with lots of dates and parties. In her South Central life, Ariel got on buses, went to school, made dinner for her family, and went to church. It was in the space between these two cities that Ariel felt most alone. "In my mind, there's a small passageway, and there's a girl, trapped, trying to get out," Ariel said, elongating her *s*'s. "I've had that idea since I was little, but I get it more now. The girl is running and she's scared."

Foxx, probably because she had parents who modeled both love and work, basically expected people to like her and to hire her, and this expectation allowed her to root once she got to L.A. Employers were concerned that she looked like a woman despite a social security card that bore a male name, so she never was hired to interface with the public. She did get jobs in telemarketing. She was let go from a few places when coworkers complained about a transsexual sharing their restroom. Foxx took the discrimination in stride. "Genetic women will get along with you, share their makeup with you, but, whoa, don't use their bathroom!" Foxx said to me about the time she was made to use a restroom on a floor that was under construction. "I don't care, though. I felt like a star. I got a whole mirror to myself."

After Foxx had been living in her own studio apartment and working at various telemarketing jobs for well over a year, she got a job with GLASS—which, in addition to foster care and group homes, provides counseling, condoms, and medical services to homeless gay and transgender kids. Foxx was hired to do outreach, to roam streets or nightclubs or after-school programs directing young people to the range of assistance they could get in the city. Through this work Foxx was able to meet—and help—various kinds of transgender newcomers to Los Angeles. Some days she set up a table at the Jeff Griffith Youth Center, a community center for GLBT youth that gives young people showers and meals but no beds, and she handed out tokens for the Metro in order to entice them over to her brochures and her lists of contacts. Foxx was a good salesperson for lease holding and clean living; she was able to leave Covenant after just four months of saving money from her full-time work. Now she even had a car.

A small group of teenagers pulled folding chairs up to Foxx's table, affably teasing one another and anyone who approached for tokens or advice. One of the kids, a short, angular gay boy named Mike, with smooth dark brown skin, tilted back on the rear legs of his chair. A lighter-skinned butch lesbian in her late teens who could easily be mistaken for a boy, Frances, pretended to be George W. Bush. Frances wore a baseball cap backward. Her baggy jeans and enormous windbreaker dwarfed her small body. She banged her fist on the table and fell into her best imitation of a hick voice.

"My name is George W. Bush, and I'd like to say all the homosexuals are gonna die. John Ashcroft's the man who's gonna do it— no Jews, no homosexuals, nothing but good southern Baptist people. Because my daddy done paid and bought this election for me." Here Mike howled a rendition of "Home on the Range." Frances shouted over him, warming up. "I have Colin Powell as my attorney general, but it doesn't matter, because I think black people are the ingrates of our society. They're filling up our jail systems! We've gotta stop them!"

At this, all the kids at the table cracked up. Every one of them was black. Foxx interrupted. "What kind of services are you seeking today, George W.?"

"I am seeking to end the homosexual race because I believe it is not a true race . . . and I believe that God can save you because Pat Robertson done fucked me in the ass so many times," Frances said.

Mike broke in, his real southern accent cracking through. He had run away from Atlanta. "You can't be saved if you're a homosexual—you're going to hell in a greasy sliding board with turbo boosters behind you!"

Despite the fact that she was laughing, Foxx tried to do her job. She asked Frances, "George W., are you seeking tokens?"

"Why, ma'am," Frances answered, "if you're a homosexual, I was looking to turn you to Jesus. If you turn to Leviticus . . ."

The kids kept bantering, but I was distracted by the thought of how rare and lovely it was to see gay and transgender kids interacting so peacefully. This happens at crisis points—at the homeless shelters and community centers that give out meals and tokens. Further up the survival ladder, there's more tension—when there's interaction at all. Many middle-class gay people don't truly know what transgender means, and when they do, some feel that transpeople are splitting the movement, that they make the increasingly accepted "queer" community look too weird or perverse. In a way, the frictions parallel those of feminism in the seventies: straight feminists didn't want lesbians latching on to their cause for fear of alienating the mainstream that was just starting to warm to them. Conservative gay people can feel similarly about their trans brethren, putting transpeople in an even more alienated position. But that day at the center, these kids laughed together at their collective notion of the people who hated them.

When a girl who came into the center from the street approached the table shyly, Foxx grabbed her clipboard for intake. Frances and Mike said not to worry, they didn't bite ("we just nibble") and the girl laughed. Foxx asked the girl's name, age, sexuality (lesbian), ethnicity (Asian Pacific Islander), and how she was surviving. To this, the girl said simply, "Working," and Foxx didn't push. Frances was rambling on, saying, "I believe I am superior to everybody, even my wife. I've had so many affairs, Lewinski don't got nothing on me."

Foxx's entire attention was on her client. "I know you're working and everything, but I want you to know that we have all kinds of other services."

Mike said, "And we want to extend you a warm southern welcome!"

Foxx ignored him. "We have medical services and support groups, like lesbian support groups. Are there any that you might be interested in?"

The girl just shook her head and looked at her shoes. "Nah."

"Okay, then, you just want tokens today?" Foxx asked, and the girl nodded. All the kids in there, who were gay or transgender and homeless in L.A., wanted and needed so much more than could ever be offered at a folding table in a youth center on the corner of Santa Monica and Sycamore. Foxx shrugged her shoulders.

"That's cool. That's definitely cool."

# 5

# BODY

*W*HEN I STARTED MEETING regularly with Christina and therefore talking about her to non-transsexual friends, they would often ask, "So has she had the surgery?" This is a very personal question and not my place to answer—as I don't make it my business to talk about anyone's genitalia without permission. Still, it's an understandable question. Everything in our culture pushes us to be "completely" male or female. It's in the language: a transsexual is either "pre-op" or "post-op"—the "operative" being presumed and nonnegotiable. But contrary to mainstream imagination, there isn't one way to be a transsexual—there isn't a fixed trail of body modifications you undergo, leading to the genital surgery. Rather, there's a range of physical alterations you can make, depending on your financial situation, how permanent or temporary you want the change to be, your patience with a lengthy process, your tolerance for risk, and what you want to look like in the end.

For a few months, I ran a weekly transgender youth group for transgender girls at the Jeff Griffith Center, on Santa Monica Boulevard. At these meetings were the regular suspects—Foxx, Ariel, and Christina—but there were also Lu, Miguel, and Joelle, and occasionally other stragglers. They talked a lot about their bodies and what they wanted to do with them, and their visions and plans were varied.

"I want to have implants, I want to be hormoned out, I want to be extremely beautiful, and I want my own hair to grow," said Joelle, a seventeen-year-old girl in an olive skirt and a floppy fisherman's hat on her head who perpetually whined like an exasperated mother. "And I want to wake up in the morning and be thankful and not all horrible and sad."

Lu, the girl with the Xena obsession, only wanted to gain weight and wasn't thinking about hormones or implants or any other surgery: she felt her lack of hips was what got her clocked. "I'm tired of shopping in the children's department," Lu said. "I mean, I know it's cheaper, but it's embarrassing."

Ariel also wasn't interested in any body modification beyond shaving her head so it would be smooth under a wig. Ariel's wigs are her most prized possessions. She keeps them on stands and combs and styles them regularly; when she puts on her hair, she feels most at home in herself. I once went wig shopping with Ariel in Compton; she was looking for an auburn bob that was angled close to the chin, but she spent four hours in the shop trying on almost every style, gazing at herself in the mirror and making small, nearly inaudible cooing and clucking sounds at herself like a bird.

In the group, Ariel told the story of getting her hair snatched twice—by other transgirls. When girls are envious or mad, the first thing they go after in a fight is another girl's hair.

"Our hair is where we keep our power," Foxx said. Foxx's fashion at the time was all about dime-sized confetti glitter, glued to her eyelids and cheeks. She paired this with a baseball cap, which she was wearing to practice traveling undercover, because that's what she figured she would have to do when she became famous. Foxx was growing out her hair and weaving in extensions.

Ironically, while the girls can choose to do a lot or a little to their bodies, they're all expected to look a certain way—at least by one another, at least in Hollywood. "We might say, 'Miss Thing's a brick—she's bricking it up,'" Foxx said, and all the kids went "*mmm-hmmm*" in agreement. "Brick" means a man in a dress, and on the street the girls will clock one another, calling out the ones who don't look feminine enough, especially if she's perceived as a nuisance or a bitch. "We're too shady toward each other."

Ariel leaned in. "Yeah. Sometimes your friends won't want to walk down the street with you because they think you look like a man."

In part to combat this, Foxx and Joelle were taking hormones, and Christina was considering them. Lu just wanted weight. Joelle would have surgeries; Foxx wasn't sure. That left Miguel.

Miguel was someone I had never met before, and he identified as a "plainclothes transgender." He looked undeniably male in a nondescript pair of jeans and an oversize T-shirt, but his eyes were soulful and soft. Plainclothes transgenders, Miguel explained, don't change the exteriors of their bodies at all; they move about in the world as their birth sex, demanding only that their lovers and most intimate friends use the opposite-gender pronouns.

Miguel had grown up a parentless "glue sniffer" in the roving child gangs of Tijuana, but crossed the border when he was sixteen. After landing in an American group home, Miguel recognized a long-sleeping need to become Alison. He folded his broad shoulders into modest, knee-length dresses and bought cheap wigs that he clasped into buns at his neck. "I looked like a librarian," Miguel told me. It was the look of a virginal Mexican Catholic girl, which earned him taunts on the slicker streets of Los Angeles. Miguel couldn't stand the teasing, so he went back to living as a boy but believed—and told anyone he got close to—that he was really a woman.

"That's not what it's all about, transgender," Miguel said, clearly translating his sentences from the Spanish in his head. "It's not about how you look. Being fierce is about being happy with yourself."

———

I would say Miguel is a rarity; for most people, being happy includes being recognized for who you feel you are. And that means altering your physical appearance to align with your inner self.

Christina's best friend, Domineque, wanted estrogen the first time she heard about it. She "caught T" about black-market hormones from her drag mother Juliana and from Shavonne—my student who choreographed the weight room dance from juvenile hall. Juliana and Shavonne were together when they started on street hormones, when they were fifteen.

"I asked Shavonne what hormones do, and she said basically it softens your skin, it doesn't prevent but it slows the growth of facial hair, and it makes you grow breasts," Domineque told me. At the time she decided to go for it, she was sixteen and Juliana and Shavonne were walking Domineque down Santa Monica Boulevard pointing out the girls who were, and were not, on hormones. "When she said it makes you grow breasts, I was like, 'Okay! I want to!'"

Unlike surgeries, which target a single spot, hormones are systemic and can change your overall appearance, and even mood and sensibility. When Juliana and Shavonne got their hormones, they believed the medicines were a race against puberty, and in a way they are: if you can start a regular estrogen protocol before, say, the onset of full facial hair, you can halt its growth—though a beard will sputter forth again if you stop the pills. But once the beard is there, it will never disappear without electrolysis, though it will thin out on hormones. If your voice has already dropped into the male register, there's also no going back (except by surgically tightening the vocal cords, and that often tweaks voices into a Mickey Mouse falsetto). Estrogen, or a combination of estrogen and progesterone administered through pills or shots, will make existing facial and leg hair thinner and wispier, promote breast growth, and redistribute body fat in a more feminine manner—away from the belly and onto the hips, butt, and thighs. On hormones, transgirls become softer and rounder and, depending on how much they're taking, moodier. For some girls, libido drops considerably, and they often can't get erections when they're taking high doses—which means they can't have orgasms. This complicates an already-complicated relationship to sex: many girls are ashamed of what they consider their unfeminine genitalia, and losing interest in sex psychologically distances them even further from that part of their body. All of these effects, save for the extra breast tissue that will forever flap down in a thin fold, are completely reversible if the hormones are discontinued.

And some do go back. For instance, Juliana, who decided to return home to her estranged and religious mother in Texas and live as a boy again. The kids who kept in touch with her last heard she had graduated from high school and was still living as a boy, so it's a good thing her robust testosterone system had only been temporarily repressed.

Still, Juliana is the exception. Most of the kids I met have known for so long that their biological gender didn't match their internal knowledge of self that they stay the course. Many save their money to buy their estrogen from a swap meet in East Hollywood, where a long-standing black market does a brisk underground business in liquid hormones and syringes smuggled up from Tijuana.

The swap meets in L.A. are giant warehouse–type affairs, where vendors rent space and set up tables or racks or crates of goods. Some are fancy, with mannequins and pop-up changing rooms, and some are little more than tarps on the ground with piles of Beefy-T's or knockoff Nikes in plastic wrap. Sometimes the hormones are sold out of a swap meet stall that sells "botanica" and Santeria supplies—candles and soaps that bring about love or cast off curses—and sometimes one that sells CDs, racks of Shakira and Paula Rubio glistening behind their shrink wrap. The locales shift temporarily if someone hears that a cop has been tipped off, but that doesn't happen very often. Still, the sales exchange stays the same. It goes like this: A transgender girl walks up to the stall and, instead of looking at music, she just stands there. A salesperson asks if she can help her. The girl responds, vaguely, with something like, "Um, I was hoping someone could sell me something." As with narcotics, if nobody says the word, nobody gets busted. The vendor usually goes to get another person who handles the medicines, and the transaction will continue like this:

Salesperson: "Are you?"

Customer: "Uh-huh . . ."

Salesperson: "But you don't even look—!" (Flattery makes a buck in every business.)

Customer: "Thank you."

Salesperson: "Forty-five."

Customer: "That's so much! For Gravidinona?" Here, the customer is the first to say the drug name. Gravidinona is a regulated combination of progesterone and estradiol, marketed to menopausal women, generally in a single dose with its own syringe. It can be more expensive than estrogen by itself. The salesperson shrugs; she doesn't have to bargain with these drugs, and she wants to be quick.

Customer: "Prema?" Premarin—or plain estrogen.

Salesperson: "Twenty. Two dollars for the syringe."

At this, money and a small brown bag are exchanged, and the customer walks away. The whole thing takes less than two minutes, and the salesperson is back to hawking Shakira.

The rate of breast growth depends on how much testosterone the estrogen has to knock out, and every body naturally starts with different amounts. In general, a girl will feel a tingling or sensitivity in the nipples within a couple of weeks; in a month or two, the nipple will swell to a bulgy, raised marble with skin that prickles and aches against every brush of fabric. After three or four months, there may be a slight curve to the breast, a little tissue growing beneath the skin, and after that, the breasts continue to develop to their genetic destiny; a teenager on hormones will often end up with a cup size roughly the same as her mother's. Essentially, transgirls on hormones have to go through a second puberty, with all the emotions and pimples and weird breast shapes that genetic girls endure.

As with genetic girls, the whole messy prospect of puberty generally takes about two years to complete. Even though kids like

Domineque or Juliana can rush things by shooting copious amounts of street hormones, their bodies still won't settle into a final shape until they've been at it for a few years. By this time, their hips and buttocks will have filled out, and their cheeks and chins will be less angled and bearded. Their skin everywhere will be plumper and softer, and, some say, the hair on their head will be more lustrous too, though this may come from increased investments in hair products. But the real payoff is the breasts; this is often the main drive behind the cost and the emotional instability and the inconvenience of hormones. It certainly was for Domineque.

It only took Domineque a few months to get breasts, but this is unusual. Her social worker, Andrea Biffle, said Domineque was growing breasts on her own even before the drugs, though this may have been due to the way she wore her clothes or held her shoulders. Domineque is just naturally fleshy, and her body seems to want to ripen somehow into roundness. At the time she bought her first shot, Domineque was living with her brother Tadeo and a foster dad named Johnny. The situation was decent; Domineque claimed Johnny was gay and was understanding about Domineque's boyfriend. He also was willing to foster siblings, which is not always available to DCFS wards, especially to teenagers. Domineque was getting to the age where she was likely to be put in group homes; private families are often saved for younger children. Plus, Johnny was kind enough, and he promoted homework and chores and other basic values that made Domineque and Tad feel homey and loved. Domineque was only dressing as a girl with her drag mother Juliana and with Shavonne; she hadn't yet shown that self to Johnny. She decided to talk to him about the hormones.

Domineque said Johnny panicked. He wasn't comfortable with transsexuality, and if Domineque—then Javier—were to become a girl, she would have to leave. He would keep Tad. According to Andrea, the issue was more complicated: Domineque was a troubled teenager and was acting out in other ways (like running away), and Johnny was upset by the misbehavior overall. In any case,

Domineque certainly didn't want to leave Tad, the one steady element in her flail-about life and the brother she believed she protected. Still, the hormone idea was worming deeper into her brain. She decided to buy the hormones and hide them from Johnny.

It took Domineque five months from the day of her purchase to inject the estrogen-progesterone mix, though she wanted to so badly, her body ached. Then, the first time she tried, it was a disaster.

"I didn't know how to open the vial; I didn't know you're supposed to flick the top until it pops off, so I hit it against the wall and it cracked open," Domineque said, indicating with her hands that it spilled everywhere. She filled the needle as best she could with the small liquid puddle on the floor. The best place to inject is the buttocks because you want to shoot into muscle rather than veins, so Domineque dropped her pants. "I tried to get the needle in, but it wouldn't go in and I got scared, so I pulled it out and I was like, 'I can't do this,' and I threw the needle away. Finally I just asked Shavonne for some of her pills."

Hormones in tablet form are also sold on the street, and prescribed by doctors in special clinics or in private practice. Because transgender culture is unfortunately invisible to much of the larger medical world, many doctors are not specifically trained in gender care at all. Instead, they learn about it on the fly, usually when a patient of theirs complains of conflicting gender feelings or specifically requests hormones or surgical treatment. When this happens, the doctor will discover that there are no codified rules or laws governing how to treat transsexual patients, but rather a list of suggested guidelines, known collectively as the Harry Benjamin "Standards of Care," or SOC.

Harry Benjamin, the man, was born in 1885 and is credited with bringing much of the German knowledge of transsexuality and its accompanying treatments and surgeries to the United States. Before the Nazis shut it down, the bulk of radical sex and gender research in the world was happening in Germany at an institute called the Institute for Sexual Science, launched by the sexologist Magnus

Hirschfeld in 1919. At the institute Hirschfeld studied sexual biology, pathology, sociology, and ethnology, and he also oversaw some of the first experimental sex reassignment surgeries. In 1933 the Nazis burned the institute's library, including 20,000 books, 35,000 photographs, and 40,000 confessions and biographical letters. Benjamin, who had been forced to relocate to New York in 1915 but returned many times to Berlin, studied with Hirschfeld. He went on to write the landmark book on transsexuality, *The Transsexual Phenomenon,* in 1966.

The Harry Benjamin International Gender Dysphoria Association was started in 1979 as a renamed assemblage of another group that was launched a decade earlier, which held talks and conferences on surgeries and therapies or treatments for transsexuals, attended by medical professionals. Harry Benjamin, the organization, was designed to establish guidelines for the increasing number of medical personnel who were coming into contact with transsexuals and didn't know what to do with them. Now the association hosts a major international conference every other year, and its committees dispense ethical guidelines for psychiatrists, endocrinologists, surgeons, sexologists, counselors, sociologists, and lawyers.

The "Standards of Care" was originally written in 1979 by six men—five medical doctors and one Ph.D.—and then approved by the attendees of the Harry Benjamin Symposium. The current incarnation was created by a committee more than three times that size—some women, some men, some transgender, some not, all with a variety of pedigrees—and the result is a twenty-two-page document that outlines what has become the generally accepted transition process from diagnosis to hormones to surgery. The "overarching treatment goal," as defined in the SOC, is "psychotherapeutic, endocrine, or surgical therapy" to create "lasting personal comfort with the gendered self in order to maximize overall psychological well-being and self-fulfillment." Most doctors who work with the transgender population follow association guidelines.

The resulting document is both impressive in terms of the scope of people it addresses and somewhat cautious—likely because it has to cover such a range. The authors recognize that not all transpeople want surgery or any other uniform body modifications, for instance, and they address this. They also recognize that young transpeople reach psychological maturity at different ages, so, I'm guessing, in order to be as safe and general as possible, the "Standards of Care" mostly mandates against treatment for minors, especially without parental involvement. To start hormones, it says, patients should be at least sixteen, with parental consent and a minimum of six months of therapy. On surgeries it's unequivocal: eighteen is the starting line.

One of the most exciting and, some would say, radical doctors treating transgender youth in California—and probably in the whole country, actually—is a man named Marvin Belzer. Dr. Belzer runs a clinic called the Division of Adolescent Medicine in Childrens Hospital Los Angeles (CHLA). Out of a standard-looking medical office with fluorescent lighting and construction-papered bulletin boards, a place with scuffed chairs and big windows, Dr. Belzer prescribes hormones to minors. He has patients as young as thirteen and a waiting list up to six months long.

Because estrogen is a menopause drug and prescribed widely, it's not federally monitored, the way something like Xanax or Vicodin is. It's easy to obtain and, because it's so common, Medi-Cal, the insurance agency for the poor in California, doesn't question the prescriptions for children with male names. (Belzer said that Medi-Cal recently started recognizing transgender care, so the hormone coverage may no longer be an oversight.) In any case, in practical terms Belzer's job is straightforward and legal. But in philosophical ones, it's more complicated. At first glance, one might say it's reckless to give adolescents hormones; teenagers are known for changing their minds and could suffer physically and psychologically if they wanted to revert back to their biological sex in adulthood. But for Belzer, age isn't the most important consideration. Dr. Belzer follows a "harm reduction" model. Essentially, he explained, if kids are prostituting for hormones, if kids are living on the street rather than in foster care to earn enough money to buy hormones, if kids are risking their lives and HIV status for hormones, then for goodness' sake, give them hormones. The equation, for him, is obvious.

In my universe Belzer was something of a hero. He had taken a community of kids with little money and excess baggage and stepped in to help them. His work didn't even start in the hospital; because several of his patients were wards of the state, Belzer had to get permission from a bevy of judges and social workers and sometimes probation officers before he could even treat them. In the process he was curbing the kids' HIV rates, and because he mandated counseling along with his meds, he provided a template for long-term psychological care; many kids would go on with therapy long after Belzer's program. While he started the program in 1991 for the very high-risk kids, he now sees the low-risk cases too, modeling what he calls the "human right to access health care." Simply, and perhaps most profoundly, Belzer showed kids that someone with authority really saw them and then cared.

The day of my first interview with Belzer, amazingly, the movie *Mrs. Doubtfire* was playing on the television in his lobby, and I watched Robin Williams totter around in a dress as I waited for him. His office was dominated by paper piles; three- and four-inch heaps on every available surface made the furniture feel secondary to the journal articles, the printed e-mails, the various studies and grants, which were all quietly demanding to be read or completed. Belzer wore green jeans and a business shirt and tie; he's white and was in his midforties, with thick boyish brown hair and a wandering right eye. With his good eye, he looks at you thoughtfully and listens closely, and all those papers fade away; I understood immediately why the kids liked him. He listens as much as he talks.

"Clinically, we see about fifty adolescents per year, aged thirteen to twenty-four," Dr. Belzer said, though if they had more funding, they could see more. There's always a waiting list. Of these fifty, he said, only about seven are female-to-male, not necessarily because there aren't as many, but because they're so much harder to fund. The male-to-female kids have an identifiable, well-documented HIV risk, and Belzer has traditionally gotten his major grants by citing his HIV-reduction work. But the transboys aren't involved in prostitution or drug use at the same levels, so Belzer can't justify their funding. Men are the prostitutes' buyers, and they don't want the female-to-males. (They're not a common fantasy on the porn racks either.) These FTMs aren't using drugs in the same volume either, perhaps because they aren't generally trafficking in sex work. What Belzer really needs, he said, is someone to simply care about the physical and psychological health of transboys, regardless of their HIV status or risk, and subsidize them too. So far this hasn't happened.

It was through HIV work actually that Dr. Belzer discovered the young transgender community. He was treating HIV-positive patients when one who happened to be transgender mentioned that she was getting her hormones on the streets. Belzer reasoned that he may as well prescribe her hormones, so she could use her money to take care of herself in other ways. Then several more patients requested this service. Soon they were asking him to help out their HIV-negative friends, and "that just released the floodgates," Belzer said, adding that he quickly applied for grants to meet the growing need. "Word filtered down, and we went from seeing everyone from the really high-risk to the fourteen-year-olds with the intact families."

Even now, with the program's popularity, nobody who walks in off the street gets turned away. She'll get an initial appointment with a case manager who'll explain how the program works. "She'll learn what we offer and what our requirements are—we are a program that requires counseling—and if it's a good match for her, then she'll go on the wait list," Belzer explained. The Harry Benjamin standards require that a sixteen-year-old undergo a half year of counseling before being prescribed hormones, but because Belzer's patients are an at-risk population, each case is considered individually. Some of his patients are bruised from familial abuse or time on the street, and some are young and really do need to sort out their gender orientation before they're given shots or pills. Everyone, he reasons, can benefit from therapy, and some of his patients come to CHLA specifically because they want the free talk.

"I would say 90 percent of the time it's clear after the first visit that this person needs hormones. But then there's the 10 percent who go through therapy and they realize they're an effeminate gay male or they're transgender, but they can't cope with the transition process. They may say, 'I know I'm transgender, but it's just too hard. I'm going to live with my body the way it is for now because there's too much prejudice, and I need to be successful at school or at a job or my family's not supportive or whatever,'" Belzer said. For the 90 percent, the therapy can last anywhere from a week to six months before they start hormones, depending upon a child's psychological stability, emotional maturity, and mental flexibility.

On the streets, where Belzer and CHLA are widely known, this translates to "You gotta go through three months of therapy to get hormones at Childrens." This common perception, Foxxjazell said, means a number of kids who might benefit from the free counseling, regular medical checkups, and HIV-prevention education don't even ride the elevator up the four flights to Belzer's waiting room. Like most teenagers, when they want something, they want it now, and they hate to have an adult slow them down.

Foxx herself went to one of the free clinics that would prescribe her hormones right away. The clinics won't treat minors (likely because of the "Standards of Care" requirements and parental consent laws), and patients still have to pay for the hormones out of pocket unless they have insurance—both hurdles that Foxx could leap because she was nineteen and had a job. "I got a prescription for Premarin, the little purple pills, and I was just so happy. I really wanted to swallow the whole bottle," Foxx remembered.

She continued: "A lot of girls are very desperate and can't wait for Dr. Belzer; a lot of us will do whatever it takes to become women, even if it means stealing hormones." She shook her purse so I could hear the faint rattle of pills within. She said that once when she let some young girl who was new to Los Angeles crash at her place, that girl stole a whole bottle of Premarin from her. At that time if you didn't have insurance, a legal bottle cost about $180. Street hormones are now around $50, depending on what you get. Foxx now carries her hormones around with her all the time. "A lot of girls think, 'If I know I'm a girl, why do I have to confirm that with you? Why do I have to sit through therapy for three months, then go through medical exams, then wait for pills to come in, when I can just get street hormones?'"

Belzer is well acquainted with this attitude and can respond with some degree of flexibility when he thinks it's appropriate. "If a kid comes to us and she's been on hormones for weeks or months or years and she's already feminized, then we usually try to bridge that gap; we have a much more expedited way of doing things," Belzer said, explaining that this patient will still receive free psychotherapy but will likely get hormone prescriptions right away to parallel a regimen she's already been on.

The three-month therapy guideline comes from the "Standards of Care," which recommends even adults cross-live or get therapy for three months before they're given any body-altering medication. While this formula might sound reasonable, many critics say the cross-living concept can be dangerous; they're exposed to too much violence walking around as a "man in a dress." Adult transwomen often prefer to take hormones and get electrolysis for several months while still presenting themselves to the outside world as men, until their bodies and features have shifted enough to make the change. Others see the therapy as patronizing; they say it's taken tremendous courage and generally years of internal preparation to make it to a psychiatrist's chair—they don't need to endure more months of mandated talk therapy to get the hormones they already know they need.

Another problem with the SOC's hallmark approach of "safe" and "general" is that it doesn't resonate with teenagers. "The principles are very good, but they're rigid," Belzer said. "You can follow all the guidelines, and you won't take any chances of messing anything up—or you can say, 'Where is this kid at? What are the dangers of starting hormones? What are the dangers of *not* starting hormones?'"

Even when he does start the hormones, Belzer explained, his team of psychologists has to spend extensive appointment time managing expectations. A lot of kids project their visions of Madonna or Britney or Marilyn onto their initial pill or injection and are devastated when their first sign of female puberty is a pimple on the chin.

"Hormones can do a lot for the girls, but just like a relationship, they take time," Foxx said. "You have to be faithful and patient with hormones, and a lot of girls aren't that."

So they'll shoot up and shoot up and shoot up, on top of what they get at Childrens—sometimes as many as four doses in one week. While you can't technically overdose on estrogen or Depo-Provera, you can get intensely moody (like PMS on overdrive)—and for the many kids who already suffer from depression, this can be dangerous. But the real risk is one that's not fully understood, and won't be until these young people are in their thirties or forties or fifties: breast cancer.

"That's the thing that just scares me to death," Dr. Belzer said, leaning forward in his chair. "There's more and more evidence that estrogen has a small but real risk associated with breast cancer, and we are not giving them physiologic doses, but pharmacologic doses. We're not trying to just give them enough estrogen; we're trying to *overcome* their testosterone. And there are no long-term studies on the effects."

What this means is this: Genetic women have between 20 and 80 nanograms of testosterone per deciliter in their bodies; normal males have around 600. Belzer uses the estrogen to push the testosterone levels down to the lowest reaches of a normal female. The few articles in the medical literature suggest staying in the higher female realms, but few kids are satisfied with these effects, and Belzer wants to mimic what they can get on the streets to keep them in his program. A much safer way to bring down the testosterone, Belzer feels, would be to prescribe something that works as an anti-androgen, which blocks the production or effects of testosterone, something like the cancer drug Lupron. Then he could just use estrogen, in much smaller doses, for breast growth and other feminization, much like MTFs with more discretionary income will do. But most anti-androgens are prohibitively expensive, and insurance plans would require a cancer diagnosis to cover the cost.

It's possible, too, that the hormone regime isn't a terrible threat for transwomen. "When you give progesterone and estrogen together, you're converting a patient's risk factor from that of a male to that of a female, so probably overall you're lowering risk [of death]," he said, noting that a person can die of more than cancer. He said that men, in general, have higher cholesterol and higher risk of heart disease, so the hormones he's providing could be protective against some illnesses while boosting risk for others. Belzer has seen girls on staggering levels of street hormones, and he said he's never seen the kinds of troubles that a Women's Health Initiative study of genetic women on estrogen and progestin found, such as strokes or blood clots, but that may be because his patients are so much younger than the postmenopausal subjects in the study. "There are not a lot of people who have been on hormones for thirty years, and there haven't been a lot of reports," Belzer said, but after another few decades, we'll know more about how patients on high levels of hormones fare over the long term. "The guidelines say, 'Be conservative,' but if I'm too conservative, the kids do the hormones on their own and avoid us, so there's a balance."

Belzer said he gets regular calls and e-mails from general practitioners or endocrinologists around the country who suddenly have a transgender teenager in their office seeking help and don't know what to do with her. "I get about an e-mail a month from a doctor saying, 'I was never trained for this, and I don't want to do anything dangerous,'" said Belzer, who will direct people to the Harry Benjamin Web site and to the primer books of Dr. Sheila Kirk, a transsexual surgeon who writes about feminizing hormonal therapy. "There's an amazing willingness on the part of the physicians [to treat these kids].

"I don't think anybody had a youth program before us," Belzer told me modestly. Chicago has a multifaceted adolescent program at the Howard Brown Health Center with case management, support groups, and medical services for up to a hundred trans youth. Unfortunately, Illinois laws make it difficult to provide hormones to people under eighteen, unless they have parental consent. Dr. Rob Garofalo, the director of youth services at Howard Brown, said judges won't generally allow doctors to prescribe hormones to, for instance, homeless minors. Garofalo also started a transgender youth program in Boston, where, he said, laws are similar. Still, programs like Garofalo's are growing, as are the cities around the country with free clinics that offer hormones to teenagers in the mix of their adult offerings. San Francisco, for instance, has this.

And if a teenager has known since early childhood that she needed to change her gender, how early should a hormone regimen be implemented? "As early as possible," Belzer said. "Before they develop depression, before they develop substance abuse, before they run away from home because their parents are abusive and then get involved in sex work or get HIV without getting educated about their risk for HIV from sex."

When I first met Christina, she swore she would never take hormones. Even though she had struggled with far more dangerous drugs, weeping through monthlong spells of crack and crystal meth use here and there, she worried about altering her physiological chemistry with estrogen. She also worried about getting clocked. She knew she was a girl inside, but she'd had enough pain as a child; she didn't want to willingly sign up for more harassment and abuse as an adult. "I would have backed up any minute if I was embarrassing myself; it would have not been worth it to go on hormones if I looked too manly," Christina said, meaning that if her own natural puberty had masculinized her too much, she wouldn't have even tried to live full-time as a woman. She carefully watched the distress of all the transgirls who didn't easily pass. "I wanted to wait and see what my body would look like without hormones."

Christina's father didn't give her much, but he passed along convenient genes. Just after her eighteenth birthday, Christina was still only five foot five, right around the average height for an American woman, with no Adam's apple, and only eight or ten thin hairs teasing her upper lip, which she plucked ferociously, checking for stubble in a compact mirror several times a day. Puberty seemed to only graze her, whereas it throttled other kids, leaving them hairy and pockmarked from acne, thick necked, and broad. Christina was naturally thin with a full face, and since she was really only clocked when she was in Hollywood and people knew to scrutinize details like hand width or shoe size, she decided she was ready for hormones.

Christina signed up for Childrens but couldn't wait: she took her first shot illegally with Luisa, a main supplier for the community who goes to Tijuana several times a year to buy hormones and syringes to shoot up the girls who are too squeamish or simply don't want to do it themselves. Luisa is Mexicana and in her fifties, of average height and average looks. She wears stretch pants and embroidered sweatshirts and mules that clack when she walks, and if you saw her on the streets, you'd never suspect her of doing anything undercover. I first saw Luisa working at a community meeting for transgender women. As the agenda was being read and grievances aired, women one by one got up and strolled to the corner, sometimes still tossing comments over their shoulders as they went. Then they faced the wall and dropped the top corner of their pants or skirt. Luisa swabbed them in the upper quadrant of their behinds and injected them. They handed her a twenty and went back to the meeting, never stopping their train of talk. It seemed a clean operation, and Luisa always used new needles.

Luisa also makes house calls and works at the nightclubs. People like her because she's discreet and respectful and gentle, and, as Christina said, her hormones are strong. Christina said, in general, the shots seem to work most on skin softening and overall appearance, and pills seem to work on bust size. Belzer explained that shots and pills serve the same function and produce the same result, but a body will utilize and tolerate higher doses via syringe because the hormones don't get broken down by the liver or cause nausea as frequently. That first day Christina had the shot, she didn't know the details of where the hormones would go or what they would do; she just felt a generalized joy. She was with an older friend who was transitioning from female to male; he held her hand, and she didn't even flinch when the needle went in.

A few months after that first Luisa shot, Christina was accepted into the program at Childrens. She didn't mind the psychotherapy and believes people need it whether they'll admit it or not. "I think the therapy should be mandatory, because living the trans life, you need ways of coping," she said to me after she'd been taking hormones—both street and prescription—for a while. "Plus hormones can lead to some serious depression for a few days."

The mood swings don't stop kids from experimenting. Foxx, just shy of her twenty-first birthday, was also augmenting her prescription with shots. "My mother has big breasts, and my breasts will be close to my closest female relative—but I'm a size A now, and I wanted something hanging down," said Foxx. "So far they [the shots] have been working wonders. They've made my breasts bigger, my skin softer, and made my face more clear and round."

But other teenagers don't have the patience to still be a size A after nearly two years (though some, like Domineque, can be a B or C) and, if they can afford it, will opt for implants. A $4,000 or $6,000 surgery is no option, so another black-market business has developed, with much more dangerous consequences than the hormones: pumping, or shooting loose silicone directly into the body where you want it to be larger or fleshier. There are cliques of women who pump and those who don't, and they often don't socialize together, as pumping is perceived as a dangerous or sometimes even "trashy" thing to do.

Silicone is considered biologically inert, and because people inject it with immediate and visually impressive results, the girls who do it can think it's reasonably safe. In the medical literature, it's a less reassuring picture. Depending upon where it's injected, the most common sites being the hips and breasts, the silicone can become a mass of infected tissue that can slide into the lower legs or scrotum or cause real trouble if it travels to the lungs. Transwomen have had long latency periods, where their silicone behaved appropriately for up to seventeen years, and then it has suddenly caused a deformity or infection. In the lungs silicone has led to respiratory difficulty, chemical pneumonia, and even heart failure. It has killed several transsexuals over the past few years. In 2004 a few pumping deaths made the AP newswire, though the victims were referred to as men, or the community as transvestites. Even in the medical literature, it's difficult to get a real grasp on how widespread the practice is or how much silicone it takes to cause a problem; the evidence is all anecdotal, and the writing has a startled "Hey, guys, look what stumbled into my office—isn't this weird?" quality to it. What seems apparent is that some women are pumping excessively; in autopsies women have been described as having silicone deposits in their lymph nodes, spleens, livers, and adrenal glands. One was so full that when incisions were made in her body, a clear, brownish liquid flowed out.

Silicone came into vogue post–World War II when Japanese prostitutes found they could inject the substance into their breasts and boost business. It caught on in the States shortly thereafter, primarily among topless dancers but also in alternative circles, and by the midsixties, the silicone breast implant was being medically marketed and surgically inserted. The implant, as opposed to the purely liquid injection, was not supposed to leak, but it did (even through the sacs and foams that contained it), and Dow Corning, a producer of the implants, settled a class-action lawsuit in 1998 for $3.2 billion. Women who have implants do not commonly experience the more serious side effects as injectors (though they can get hardening and shifting and lumps), in all likelihood because they aren't taking in the same quantities. Now silicone implants are banned in the United States, and women have saline implants instead. Silicone has gone underground for transwomen who can't afford other options.

I first heard about pumping parties when I was a teacher and my students would get buzzed up about a "surgeon's wife" coming to town, which happened about twice a year. It was important that she was married to a doctor, the kids said, because she had access to medical-grade (as opposed to industrial-grade) silicone and because she had watched her husband perform surgeries. She knew how to handle needles and was very safe and clean. This mysterious woman flew in from Florida and rented a house in San Fernando Valley, the way porn directors do (at least in my imagination). I was told that eighty to a hundred transwomen would pay her a few hundred for each breast, several hundred for the buttocks or hips, and then extra for the face: cheeks, foreheads, and lips. Some even got shots in their knees to look less bony, little squirts of perfection here and there. The doctor's wife would work from early morning into the late night and sometimes into the next day, and then she'd be gone, off to another city, clearing a cool couple hundred grand or more.

When the "doctor's wife" or someone like her isn't around, many kids, being young and poor and reckless in other areas of their lives, will use industrial-grade silicone found in sealants and adhesives sold in hardware stores. Usually, some member of the community will rise up as a pumping expert, knowing how deep to place the needle, and how much to inject for the desired effect and so on, and the girls will pay her, but sometimes they'll even pump themselves. The silicone is always injected subcutaneously, in the tissue just below the skin, to the place where you can feel the tissue tearing away from the muscle. If it's too shallow, the skin will discolor.

On transgender Web sites and chat rooms, there are all kinds of warnings about pumping. Some are blanket admonitions, talking about fatal pulmonary embolisms, and displaying monstrous photographs of women whose breasts were so laden with granulomatous lumps that they had to be scraped of silicone, leaving them with a concave, watermelon-sized scar. Other sites are more moderate, simply claiming that if you are going to pump, you're less likely to die if you do it in small amounts; even though it's cheaper and more exciting to jump three breast sizes in one sitting, it's safer to go for several treatments. Plus, they say, no hot baths right after an injection; the silicone could ooze from the syringe holes. And then after a few days, go back to the hot baths: they're good for massaging the "silicone bubbles" out. After injections some women feel little knots or lumps that must be massaged and smoothed so as not to permanently harden. This, according to one site, "hurts like a mother."

Foxx finally gave up on the hormones working all alone and went to her first pumping party in 2002. She doesn't know if she got industrial-grade or medical-grade silicone. She didn't know to ask.

"I went to this girl named Michele—she eventually died of gangrene in her foot—who came from another state and went from state to state pumping the girls," Foxx said, adding that she paid $200 for each breast, which took about fifteen minutes each to complete. To make the breasts keep their shape, Foxx had to wear a firm training bra for two months, even while she slept. Afterward Foxx's breasts were a cup size larger, and she was hooked. She now goes to a clinic in Tijuana, where the process is publicly available. Over three sessions she's had her breasts, hips, and cheeks pumped. She now wants to do the backs of her thighs and butt area to look, as she said, thicker.

"I want to master that thickness that a lot of beautiful black women have; I want to look bottom heavy. If my hips come out more, then my shoulders will look smaller," Foxx said, dropping her pants and pushing on her hips to show me what she would look like if her figure were more hourglass. What about the risks, I asked, noting that her shoulders were already pretty small. Here, Foxx's normally safety-conscious attitude took a backseat to her vision of perfection. "I'm mostly worried about the hardness and the lumps," she said. "You've got to bust any lumps and break the silicone down for the rest of your life."

Foxx is driving toward a vision of an idealized feminine form, but she's not driving toward what many people believe is the end goal for all transsexuals—the genital surgery. This is the arena of body modification that's separate from the others: there are the procedures you do for everyone to see (things for your breasts, face, body shape, and so on), and then there's the "bottom surgery," concealed from view. Some need to change their entire bodies; some don't.

I find it interesting that the unadorned penis is, for Foxx and some others, a holdout for identity politics. I think most people would say that the soul resides in the inside of their bodies rather than on the outside, in the unseeable, unknowable blood and organs and cells that keep them alive, simply because they cannot imagine the soul as invisible, antimatter, ether. So there is the physical person that people see, and there is the "real me," that's "on the inside," literally, with the brains or intestines or heart. The genitals are, in a way, messengers from this interior world; like the mouth or nose, they bring forth inside things for us to examine, a litmus for inner health. Like wounds or secrets, we keep genitals covered most of the time, exposing them only to clean them or to show to doctors or lovers. So I understand the reluctance to change them. Breasts, clothing, hairstyle, walk, and voice are the external cues that convince the outside world that transwomen are women, the cues that make that world a comfortable place for her to move around in; a penis is something that's just between a woman and her partners—and if all interested parties are fine with it, then why change it?

Of course, many transsexuals are sure they want the SRS (sex reassignment surgery), and when they are, they enter an even more complicated relationship with the medical industry. Domineque is one person who has known she wanted it since she was a child, which is part of the reason she stayed with the program at Childrens Hospital. She'll ultimately need proof of her long-term care, as all surgeons require letters from patients' primary doctors and therapists saying they've been on hormones and in counseling for "gender identity disorder," or GID. In a way, the requisite diagnosis puts

Domineque in the double bind of being both sane and sick at the same time. This is the law, as set by the Harry Benjamin "Standards of Care," which most every surgeon follows. Gender identity disorder is a mental illness in the American Psychiatric Association's fourth edition of the *Diagnostic and Statistical Manual of Mental Disorders*, the manual all physicians use to diagnose and treat mental disorders of all stripes. (Homosexuality was also "on the books" as a psychological sickness until 1973, when the APA voted to remove it. Such choices are largely more social and political than medical.) To have GID (previously called "transsexualism"), a person must have "the desire to live and be accepted as a member of the opposite sex, usually accompanied by the desire to make his or her body as congruent as possible with the preferred sex through surgery and hormone treatment." In addition, according to the *DSM-IV*, these feelings have to have been present for at least two years, and the "disorder" cannot be a "symptom of another mental disorder or a chromosomal abnormality."

For Domineque, who's felt like a girl since she was two, she'd get a check mark next to all three criteria. That's the "sick" part; SRS is not a cosmetic surgery—it's a medical necessity. The surgery is the treatment, and a patient needs a letter to her surgeon saying she's got this mental ailment that can only be cured through physical intervention. The letter also has to say that the illness is a physical one—that while GID is technically a mental disorder, the patient is of a sound-enough mind to be able to make such a decision. It's her body that just doesn't fit, the letter will say; that's the "sane" part. In other words, to get such a surgery, a patient can't just ask for it; she needs at least two psychological professionals (one with a Ph.D., the SOC demands) saying she deserves it.

The first American to undergo sex reassignment surgery was a transwoman named Christine Jorgensen in 1952. Because the procedure wasn't yet available in the States, Christine traveled to Denmark for the operation, and her transition made international news—in some ways, perhaps, making her responsible for the contemporary mainstream notion that the end goal for all transpeople is surgery. Christine was a quiet person and a former GI, and some accounts say she wanted to transition in private, while others say she relished being in the spotlight. In any case, when Christine returned to the United States, she was mobbed by reporters, and headlines across the country shouted, "EX-GI BECOMES BLONDE BOMBSHELL!" Christine stories ranked number one for 1953 in the *New York Daily News*, and she became so famous that letters addressed to "Christine Jorgensen, U.S.A.," would reach their destination.

In a book called *How Sex Changed: A History of Transsexuality in the United States*, author Joanne Meyerowitz theorizes that part of the reason Jorgensen enflamed the American imagination was her timing: the postwar era was one fixated on gender roles and whether the war-worker women could be coaxed happily back into their homes. It was also the atomic age, and Jorgensen tapped right into the issue of whether science could and even should win out over nature. Her case literally made "sex change" a household phrase. Before Jorgensen, a person's physical sex, psychological "gender," and sexuality were one fused thing determined by a doctor's quick glance in a delivery room; Jorgensen (or what she represented) ripped them apart.

Jorgensen ultimately used her fame to make a living, as she developed a stage act singing and telling jokes, and appealing to her audience's sympathies. She aligned herself with the American ideal of the lonely dreamer who strives to reach her goals despite the odds. Her beauty throughout her life was deemed sophisticated and understated, earning her comparisons to stars like Eve Arden and Lauren Bacall. (Still, Christine wasn't "American" enough to be allowed to perform in Boston, where lawmakers called her tame act "risqué," nor woman enough to get married, as she was denied a license in the state of New York in 1959.) She lived off and on with her Danish immigrant parents in New York and on her own in California until she died of bladder cancer in 1989.

Fifty years after that first operation, there are still only a handful of surgeons in the United States providing transgender genital surgery, which costs anywhere from $20,000 to $100,000 depending on what you get, how far you travel, and so on. It's odd to me that so few doctors do it, because just as with plastic surgery, your patients come willingly and leave ecstatic that you cut them open and sewed them up again. The surgeries are relatively low risk, there are a lot of ways to creatively approach each operation and implement improvements, and there's a certain aesthetic art to them. Also, because insurance won't pay for the job, you can be assured money up front. In fact, there'll likely be a waiting list for your services.

The young people I know can't afford the surgery, though they regularly talk and argue about wanting it—or never wanting it. Often these discussions are in the context of men and whether having the SRS would make their relationship prospects better. Some, like Domineque, don't care about the men at all; she wants the surgery to feel at peace within her own skin. Some, like Ariel, are still struggling with passing in a dress in daylight; talking about surgery with Ariel is akin to discussing college with a preschooler. But most play with the idea of what they would look like with a vagina, what they would feel like, how it would be to dress every day without tucking (wherein they tuck their penis up between their buttocks so as not to show a bulge), what it would be like to date and not be worried. It's a distant dream, they realize. Some talk of putting $2 or $5 a week toward the plan, but few do. If they do save up, perhaps later when they're older or more stable, they may well go to a surgeon named Dr. Toby Meltzer.

Dr. Meltzer runs his practice out of a hospital in Scottsdale, where he has twenty-one inpatient beds with views of the mountains and a staff of eleven—sizable, for one surgeon. Two-thirds of his surgeries every year are SRS; the rest are just standard cosmetic surgeries—liposuction, breast augmentations, and the like. Most transgender patients hear of Dr. Meltzer through word of mouth and, if they can afford it, will visit him in Scottsdale to talk about their surgical options. But several times a year, Dr. Meltzer also makes presentations at gay and transgender community centers, to show slides of his work and speak to potential patients, who line up with questions about tracheal shaves or feminizing nose jobs. Some cry with relief just to meet him. One Saturday afternoon on a chilly fall day, I went to see Dr. Meltzer make such a presentation in New York City.

Forty adults hunched into folding chairs and stared, rapt, at slide after slide of spread-leg genitalia, whispering to their friends and pointing with pencils at particular regions, nodding happily. This was not porn. This was salvation. In the "after" pictures of both men and women, the women looked better; it's easier to construct a vagina from a penis than the other way around. Meltzer explained that there are a few ways to do it, but that the most common is something called "penile inversion." What this means, in lay terms, is that the penis is basically turned inside out and pushed inside the body to form a vagina. "I don't get rid of much," Meltzer said to the group that day. "It's all still there; it's just in a different location."

For the patient, there are several steps to the process. Before she even sees Dr. Meltzer, she has to have several treatments of electrolysis on her testicles so no hair ultimately ends up where it shouldn't. Then, she undergoes the first surgery to construct the basic vulva and vagina. Dr. Meltzer can't do what's called the "labiaplasty," which is constructing the labia minora and a clitoral hood, until a second surgery, because he needs to let the area heal. Some women stop at this first stage, but many don't; the aesthetics can be noticeably off-kilter.

When everything is completely healed after several weeks, a transwoman will be able to have a healthy sex life, with genitalia that's usually indistinguishable from a genetic woman, except for lubrication. Her vagina will have a depth of five and a half to six and a half inches and, because she has a clitoris constructed from the former glans of her penis, she can orgasm.

There's a saying that goes: "FTMs pass on the streets and MTFs pass in the sheets." There's a reason. Transmen, on hormones, look amazing. Even children under five, famous for loudly noting people's differences, don't clock them. Beards, baldness, deep voices, thick necks, everything. But get them to drop their pants, and you'll have a tough time finding a man-made penis that looks quite like the genetic version. They're either terribly small or large enough but the wrong color, or else they're a funny shape and weight because they're filled with tissue that's heavier than a genetic male's penis. And none of the reconstructed versions can get erect without a pump. The science just isn't there yet.

Fetuses are sexually undifferentiated until eight weeks of age, at which point girls begin to get ovaries and males get testes, boys get penises, girls get clitorises, and so on. The body parts parallel one another, so it actually makes intuitive sense to turn a transman's clitoris into a penis, in a procedure called a "metoidioplasty." After Meltzer's patients have had a hysterectomy, oophorectomy (to remove the ovaries), and a vaginectomy (to close the vagina) with some other doctor—because these aren't cosmetic procedures—he sets about constructing a penis. Essentially, this means removing the skin around the clitoris so it can extend from the pubic region and rotating the labia majora to the midline to form the scrotum. He puts expanders into the scrotum, which are later replaced with a prosthesis.

The average-length metoidioplasty penis is under three inches. It looks like a penis, but there's no chance that a date won't notice its smaller size. So the other option is penile reconstruction, which, in general, is slightly more dangerous, often more ugly, and sometimes less sensate. What you've got with penile reconstruction is—*big*.

Meltzer mostly sends patients who want penile reconstruction to Belgium, where surgeons specialize in the practice. To make a penis, you need skin, and you can take it from a few different areas: the thigh, the belly, or the forearm. With all three, a patient will have a brutal scar at least a foot long and several inches wide, and all three have their downsides. Leg skin is good because it's the same color and you can make a big penis, but the skin is insensitive, it's a less reliable blood supply during the operation, it requires multiple operations, and the urethral lengthening is precarious. If you go with the belly, the skin will be a different color. The forearm is sensitive skin and often makes the best-looking penis in the end, but the surgery is technically difficult and there are complications; a good 40 percent have a narrowing of the urethra and have to have it tracked back to their perineum. Plus the scarring on the arm is the worst of all three, and it's the most visible; even several years after healing, it's a shiny mass of pink and white noodles and suture marks.

In the States, average metoidioplasty costs can range from $2,000 to $18,000 (for clitoral release all the way up to urethral extension and testicular implants); penile reconstruction costs anywhere from $50,000 to more than $100,000. Add to that the cost of a hysterectomy, oophorectomy, vaginectomy, and a double mastectomy, and the price tag jumps another $30,000. And the time off work for surgery, bed rest, and the costs for traveling to the handful of surgeons who do the work. This is why relatively few transmen have the bottom surgery at all. For transwomen, a vaginoplasty in the States will cost from $12,000 to $20,000, and labiaplasty can cost an extra $3,000 to $5,000. A typical breast augmentation can cost a few to several thousand dollars, in addition to the hormones. But those are just fundamentals: some women feel they need a tracheal shave (to remove the Adam's apple), which costs around $3,000, or a jaw feminization, nose job, chin reduction, cheekbone augmentation, or forehead contouring, which can obviously add tens to hundreds of thousands of dollars to the total price tag. And while transsexuals are considered medically, mentally ill in the *DSM-IV* and have to be diagnosed as such to even be considered for the most basic of surgeries, no insurance will cover the cost.

Foxx went back and forth about wanting SRS. Almost twenty-one, she still had not had a boyfriend, not ever, and she attributed that tragedy to mere inches of skin and tissue. It didn't have to do with her face or her body; men in cars and malls who hooted or pressed phone numbers into her palms told her that. It didn't have to do with her personality or her voice, which could charm both sexes into buying extra long-distance services or registering for a trip to Hawaii; her countless telemarketing jobs proved that. Foxx passed everywhere but the bedroom. Still, she couldn't decide what was more important: the intense and personal love from one boyfriend (whom she felt would be easier to snag if she had the surgery) or the diffuse love from countless music fans whom she could encourage to respect themselves and the bodies they were born with.

"It changes from month to month. Some months it's like I want a pussy; other months I want to be a transsexual with a big old—" Foxx paused. She looked at her hands. "More and more I want to feel comfortable with what I have, with my own uniqueness, and I'm scared that once I have SRS, I'll no longer truthfully be transsexual in a way. I'll be categorized the way every other woman is, in the way that a lot more men will feel comfortable with."

Here Foxx grew more adamant. "But I don't want SRS because my boyfriend is going to like it or because people in society will finally accept me. I want it because I want it—and if I have it, I feel I won't be the same role model."

One cold January morning I was over at Foxx's place, and she was cooking grits and bacon for me and a twenty-year-old friend of hers named Keandra who had had implants. On impulse Foxx took off her shirt and asked me to feel the bumps in her breasts. They were small, she said, but they were worrisome. She didn't want them to harden any more or grow into anything unusual. I probed around where she told me and felt the normal, sinewy "rice and peas" that any gynecologist tells a woman to feel for during her monthly self-exams. Foxx's breasts hung down with a satisfying weight, heavier at the base, tiny stretch marks shining along their sides.

"Feel mine too!" Keandra said, and implants bounced out of her terrycloth bathrobe. Keandra's breasts were round like globes, the nipples pointing toward her chin, the skin unnaturally taut. Keandra had never felt a genetic woman's breasts before, so I took off my shirt too, and suddenly we were all at a sixth-grade slumber party, comparing size and lift and nipple shape and then lying on the floor to see how they flopped to the side, as the grits burned in the pan.

"Foxx, yours feel just like Cris's!" Keandra said, and she was right.

This only made Foxx more sure about her decision to get more work done. I asked if Foxx remembered how she used to teach her daughters about the dangers of pumping and to have patience with the hormones. "I remember," she said. "But my patience wore out! It's like that Janet Jackson song, 'Let's Wait Awhile.' It's like, 'How long you want me to wait? Till I'm thirty-six and still singing that song?'"

# 6

## BOYFRIENDS

*A*PART FROM BECOMING a musical star, finding a man had been Foxx's singular preoccupation since her freshman year of high school. All her girlfriends, transgender and non-, had had several—as had her drag daughters, which was frustrating. As with many transgirls like Foxx who date straight men and "spill their T"—or inform them of their transgender status up front—there had been a lot of disappointments and a few cruel teases.

While there are as many kinds of relationships as there are kinds of people, it's probably safe to say that transwomen have to endure more rejection and shame and loss than your average genetic woman. One of the common threads that binds the younger heterosexual transwomen is an intense hope for a boyfriend coupled with a quiet sense of despair that no good man will want her.

"Once I paid a psychic $300 to make a wish come true for me," said Foxx. The psychic promised Foxx she would meet a man in three days and offered a money-back guarantee. On the appointed day, Foxx donned her cutest T-shirt and glued extra glitter on her eyelids. She walked to the neighborhood bodega. "As I was coming back, I ran into this guy who said, 'Hey!'" The man was checking her out, and Foxx just sashayed past, expecting rejection. "Most of the time I don't pay much attention, but this guy said, 'So you don't like Mexicans?'

"I said, 'Yes, I do. I don't have any color lines,'" Foxx answered. The man asked her to "hook him up with her phone number," which she promptly did. The stranger said his name was Christopher Columbus. Foxx thought this might be the psychic's offering, but later that day she went to the beach and met another man, equally handsome.

"The second guy was really crazy for me, and when I told him I was transsexual, he didn't believe me," Foxx said. Foxx always told men she was transgender before she even went on a date; she rightly worried that a mistaken identity could inspire blind rage and violence. "He kept saying that I was too beautiful to be a transsexual. When he finally accepted it, he started talking about how he gets really jealous if he sees his lady talking to the other guys and going off on how he wants his girl to be with him all the time."

This, for Foxx, was a major turnoff. She had her career to think of and didn't want anyone telling her what she could and couldn't do. "I could tell he was going to be a dominant," Foxx said, and decided that Christopher Columbus must be, after all, the one her psychic predicted she'd meet. She went home from the beach excited to see him again.

But Christopher Columbus didn't call. A week passed, and Foxx ran into him in her neighborhood, on her way home from work. This time he was with a bunch of his friends. As she walked up, he said, "Can I ask you something?" A chill went down Foxx's back. Columbus repeated his question, and Foxx didn't answer. She instinctively knew what was coming.

"He said, 'That's a man! That's a man! That's a fucking man!' And everybody started laughing," Foxx said. "I just started walking away, and he shouted, 'You're a fucking man and you're fucking ugly!'"

Crushed, Foxx made it to her apartment building, where yet another man was sitting on her stoop. As she fumbled with her keys, he said, "Oh baby, wassup," and she, still hopeful, managed a "Nothing much." This was back before the hormones had softened Foxx's features, and this man clocked her too.

"You'd be really cute if you weren't a guy," Stoop-man said. Foxx, already emotionally flattened by the Columbus fiasco, ignored him and trudged toward her apartment. He followed her in. "Wait, I want to talk to you," he said. "You live around here?"

Could it be that a man could know Foxx was transgender and still be interested? Could it be that he was flirting? Perhaps he just didn't know how to use polite language and that calling her a "guy" was simple ignorance. She decided to educate him.

"I said, 'Yeah, I live around here—you probably don't recognize me because I've been going through a transition,'" Foxx said. "'I'm a transgender person.'"

Stoop-man answered, "You really are a transgender person?" He turned to leave. "Okay, then, I'm straight."

This is, perhaps, one of the cruelest blows to a transsexual woman who likes men. Foxx considers herself straight too—and with one quick word, Stoop-man was not only calling her a man, but a gay man, an identity she'd run from. "This just really broke my heart," Foxx said.

In general, when a man enters a relationship with a male-to-female transsexual woman, the man doesn't think of himself as gay, and neither does the transsexual. The man is straight, because he's attracted to, and sleeping with, a feminine spirit—she looks female, she acts female, she is female—regardless of the genitalia below the belt. Said Foxx, "It just all came crashing down on me. I went upstairs and I started crying and kicking stuff, and that night I tried to commit suicide. I took about fifteen Nytol pills and woke up with a major headache the next day."

To find herself again, and to feel better, Foxx writes music. "Rejection has been the inspiration for five songs," she said. And, somehow, the rebuffs from men have inured her to, or even strengthened her for, the inevitable denials in the music industry.

When anyone suggested that America wasn't ready for a musician like Foxx or that perhaps she shouldn't debut as a *transsexual* artist, she scoffed.

"People said America wasn't ready for *Queer as Folk,* and they were," Foxx said. "And then there's Eminem: if he's a Caucasian rapper and can be accepted by the hip-hop world, then maybe there's a chance that the hip-hop world and the pop world and the mainstream world in general will accept me as a transgender woman."

At the youth meeting, some said Foxx was lucky Christopher Columbus's attack was only verbal, as many transwomen have had violent experiences with men when they discover their status. Lu, the girl who loved Xena, had a whole coding system for how she dealt with men.

"I am provocatively dressed, so I have a lot of instances where men follow me," Lu said. Sadly, after Lu's dad threw her out, she still hadn't stabilized. She was living in motels and prostituting. "If it's a really ugly guy, I'll ignore him. If it's a black man, I'll tell him I'm a lesbian. If he's white or Latino—well, yesterday, I saw this Mexican guy. He's followed me before. He came up to me and started grabbing and groping. I was checking my pager and telling him my boyfriend was across the street. Then he put his dick up on me."

Luckily, Lu got away. Though the boyfriend comment was a ruse, he may have believed her, because he sped off. (Lots of girls who are prostituting work with boyfriends hiding in bushes or nearby cars.) "I tried to get his license plate number," Lu continued. "I called the police, but they wouldn't do anything."

"The police *won't* do anything," Christina said. "They're going to stereotype you. They'll say you're a transie—you were working, so you were asking for it. That's what they'll say."

Foxx added that it's not just the cops that stereotype. When men in general find out she's trans, she said, they immediately think of sex. Whether they're repulsed or intrigued, they imagine her as a sexual object. The part that Foxx hadn't gotten or admitted to yet was that the way she flirted contributed to this dynamic—a sexy come-on yields a sexual response. Still, this is an experience that even the most buttoned-up Wall Street transwomen can go through. "It really makes me mad," she said. "As soon as they know you're a transsexual, they lose all respect for you. All they think about is getting into bed."

This kind of sexual objectification gets internalized, so that many transgender women, especially when they're young, learn to use their beauty or their flirting to get the things they need—to the exclusion of their other skills—much the way exceptionally pretty genetic women learn that their looks are their best asset and begin to doubt their intelligence or internal value. Catcalls and whistles are also proof of passability, so for transwomen, sexiness pays. Christina, in fact, often based her self-worth on the number of heads she could turn in a day. She prided herself on getting any man to fall for her, including, or especially, the least available.

One night, right around the time of the transgender group meetings, Christina and I drove by the Mormon Temple for the Church of Jesus Christ of Latter-Day Saints. It's a temple that always astonishes newcomers to Los Angeles; smooth expansive lawns bigger than a golf course lead up to a gleaming white castlelike tower with a golden trumpeter on top, facing east. The whole place has the feel of a fantasy princess sanctuary despite the Dunkin' Donuts and video shops that flank it. We had each passed the temple numerous times, but when I told Christina that Mormons don't let non-Mormons into their inner sanctums, her eyes sparkled with the challenge and she asked to stop.

It was 10 P.M. (her curfew at the group home had been extended for good behavior), but the temple was lit up and the parking lot was full. We found an open side entrance, where two young white men, barely out of high school, were standing in the doorway, leaning on rakes. They were evidently preparing for some late-night gardening or just coming back. Christina took my hand and tried to march right past them.

"You can't go in there," one of the men stammered, looking surprised and blocking the door.

"The trumpeter on top, that's the angel, right?" Christina asked, stepping quietly out from beside me. She was wearing a pink T-shirt that said "*Baby*" in glitter cursive, stretched tight across her chest, her bra padded. Her blond hair was pulled back in a ponytail, and her lips quivered a little under her lip gloss. I noticed all this because the men, trying to answer her question, couldn't look at Christina the way they had at me, so I checked to see what was wrong. The boys were talking to the ground. Not because she was transgender—Christina was clocked by only about one in a thousand passersby—but because she was beautiful.

"Um, yeah," one managed, scraping at the rake with his thumbnail.

"The one whose horn is heralding the coming of the Gospel?" Christina said coyly, tilting her head. I looked at her, shocked: how did she know this story, much less to invoke the word "heralding"? The boys were trying hard to avoid Christina's chest, which she was stealthily inching forward. I remembered about the Mormon missionaries—young men who swear themselves to virginity and travel the world, proselytizing. These men were probably precisely that—just a few years older than Christina, and certainly not accustomed to being frosted in sticky-sweet flirtation. She continued. "I was born Mormon, but I'm no longer with my family."

At this, the men glanced up with genuine pity on their faces. Christina's eyes misted. How was she doing this? "And my friend, she's never even been to a service," she said, nodding her head at me sagely like I was too far gone for saving.

This was too much. I stifled a laugh. One of the poor teenagers opened his mouth like a fish, but no sound came out. He cleared his throat and glanced at Christina's face hungrily. "Um, I could show you to the visitor's center during the day. I mean, if you wanna come, um, back or something. Like tomorrow."

Christina smiled and said, "Maybe," and we turned around to leave. She waved back at the boys as we drove away.

Using sex appeal is one way to attract men, but it's not always a way to hold on to them. Alexis Rivera works with Dr. Belzer at Childrens Hospital and was a case manager for dozens of girls over three years, monitoring their health care, counseling, and work and living situations. Alexis is now twenty-eight, but she transitioned when she was seventeen and she knows the young Hollywood transgender culture possibly better than anyone: first, she lived it, and now she runs programs to serve it. Alexis is Mexicana with shiny black hair that she generally pulls back into a ponytail, with shorter strands that she impatiently flicks out of her coal-colored eyes. She's pretty, with full lips and high cheekbones and a smile that happens so fast it looks like maybe she was smiling all the time and you just didn't notice. She has tattoos of a dragon and a flower twisting themselves down one arm, and she rides a skateboard to work. Alexis is now part of the Childrens management team, developing and running leadership academies and services for the transgender community at large. According to Alexis, the impulse to look and act hyperfemme stems from a few roots.

"Especially when you see girls transition at a very young age, there's this super high-feminine Britney Spears/Christina Aguilera look where they're always done up," Alexis said. "Through their mothers, non-transwomen were able to see what femininity or womanhood looked like. Transsexual women didn't get that. We didn't get, 'Oh, here, put on your cute little earrings.' Nobody did that for us."

Instead, Alexis explained, transwomen were raised as boys and learned to see women through the eyes of their fathers or other men around them. "They were socialized as boys who were objectifying women, so it makes perfect sense that [as] women [they] would be seen with boobs out to here, wearing skintight clothing, because their fathers made them think women are supposed to be seen as sexual objects," she said. Her own stepfather, who raised her, didn't teach her to objectify women like this—but she knows plenty of kids with dads who did. "Therefore, they turn around and think, 'When I transition, I'm gonna get attention for my cleavage and having my butt come out of my skirt.'"

Even if this external presentation doesn't attract a mate interested in long-term partnership, there's another problem. In order to maintain a healthy relationship, you need to have had one modeled for you. Parental rejection, which so many kids who end up on the streets have experienced, is neither a foundation nor a model for unconditional adult love. Alexis, who has had several healthy two- and three-year relationships, feels she's been able to do so because she learned from her mom. When Alexis came out at seventeen, her mother struggled with the news for a few months, but she never rejected her daughter and the two now talk every day. Alexis's upbringing was stable and loving.

Even so, Alexis said, she at times has felt insecure about men's motivations when they first get to know her. "For me, the question has always been 'Why do men date me? I'm not really a woman and I'm not really a man,'" Alexis said. "But then I understand that it's the spirit that attracts people. It's not what's between your legs—it's about the two spirits coming together."

Of course, some men—no matter how attracted they are to a woman's spirit—cannot get over the fact that she's biologically male. They have trouble with the penis or, even if she's had the surgery, with the fact that she *used* to have a penis. They feel that this fact still makes their girlfriend a man. By extension, they worry that they themselves are gay.

At the other extreme, there is a contingent of men the girls call "tranny-chasers" who are *only* interested in the girls for their bodies. These men, unlike the guys who are squeamish or outright phobic on the first date, are trickier to spot.

Tranny-chasers fetishize transsexuals, and while they may initially put on a good front of wanting a relationship, they only want sex and will generally dump a woman in favor of another lay. This can be heartbreaking, especially for the adolescent girls who haven't yet learned to identify ulterior motives and can have Prince Charming rescue fantasies clouding their perceptions.

"If you have a girl who's not comfortable with her penis, and that's the only thing a guy's going for, how can she not feel like a sexual object?" Alexis asked. It doesn't help that the girls are finding these men at nightclubs and on the Boulevard, where of course these particular men are looking for that particular thing. "But where else do you go? There are other avenues for straight people. You've got the library or if you have an interest—say, golfing—you can join a golfing club, and you'll most likely find somebody of the opposite sex. But there is no such thing as a transgender golfing club."

And if girls do meet a "regular" man at a "regular" place, they're back at the problem of disclosure—knowing that when they tell him, he'll likely freak out and they'll likely lose him. Since many transwomen would rather have their dates know their status from the beginning, they're dressing up for the transgender nightclubs where men want them for sex.

Some nonoperative transsexuals will not tell a date that they're transgender at all—hoping that when they do, he'll be so in love, it won't matter. They'll say, "We can't have sex because I'm on my period," which, if the couple is young and the boy is naive, can work for a few months. I know transwomen who have fooled men into believing that anal sex, in the dark, with underwear on and pulled to the side, is really vaginal sex, and others who have kept things oral or manual or just especially nonsexual for several months, though this is obviously extraordinarily dangerous. Transpeople are killed every year for just such deceit.

Foxx said that were she to get the surgery one day, she'd feel obliged to inform her lover about her biological status—even if he couldn't tell on his own. "This is something a lot of TSs argue with me about—they say, 'What's the purpose of getting a sex change in the first place if I have to tell him?'" Foxx said. "But my thing is this:

some men have a sixth sense. They'll be like, '*Hmm*, you can't have children, you don't have baby pictures, you never talk about your family, nobody knows you from when you were a child, and you have very big feet.' He's gonna sense it, and he's going to feel mistreated because you lied."

Alexis has noticed a cultural shift among her male-to-female clientele at Childrens Hospital over the years: they're no longer entirely focused on getting boyfriends. A man on a girl's arm used to be external proof of her femininity and passability. Heterosexuality was the unquestioned standard for all transitioning women. But now, Alexis said, transgirls are allowing themselves to explore their own sexualities a bit and imagine dating women or even other trans-people. Alexis herself dated a woman for a while, and Foxx, though the opportunity has yet to present itself, said she'd consider it, as long as the woman were butch enough to attract her. It's the masculine energy, Foxx said, not the gender itself, that draws her.

When transwomen do find partners, male or female, there are several issues beyond sex that can complicate the relationship. For one thing, Alexis explained, the paranoia that people are staring at you or that you're going to get clocked is unnerving to folks who have never dated transsexuals. Or the attention to physical appear-ance—rushing home to check a five o'clock shadow, changing clothes several times before a night among strangers—can seem vain or superficial to a mate when really such behavior is an attempt to soothe rising nerves. Also, the issue of "coming out," once the sole terrain of the transsexual, is now negotiated by the partner as well.

Alexis's loving and committed boyfriend of three years, Matthew, couldn't understand why she felt the need to tell his straight friends and coworkers that she was trans. After all, he said, when they all gathered for dinners or parties, nobody else would be talking about their sex lives. True, she countered, but the women would be talking about getting their periods or starting families, and they'd ask Alexis about her plans to get pregnant. She'd feel like an utter impostor.

"If you're privileged enough to pass and be able to get around other circles of women and know what they talk about, you'll see they do this bonding thing. They say, 'Have you been thinking about children? Is your biological clock ticking?'" Alexis explained. "It doesn't feel right and then I kind of retract, and Matthew is like, 'Why don't you want to hang out with my friends?' I say I don't feel comfortable, and he says they don't have to know. But it isn't about people knowing; it's about being able to express who I am." This kind of discomfort can sometimes lead transwomen in healthy relationships to worry that their boyfriends will leave them for genetic women, just because it's easier.

It was while Christina was thirteen and experimenting with being a girl over the phone, on party lines, and with breast enlargement product pushers that she met her first boyfriend. Nicknamed Ruff, he was twenty when she met him at a house party. "Why Ruff?" I asked her when she first told me the story. "Because he was like a dog?"

"Maybe because he looked like a puppy," Christina said, and laughed. Even then, when she talked about Ruff, a gauzy look crossed her face, because he supposedly loved her the best when she was the most desperate. My guess is that if Christina had met Ruff when she was older, she never would have stayed with him for the two-odd years she did; Ruff seemed as screwed up as any of her later boyfriends, but she was too young then to know how to dump him. She said I was wrong and, as proof, told me about the time she felt his one single tear land on her cheek—the night he got out of jail, when the two of them were hiding in her mother's attic crawl space, full of dust and spiders. No man has ever cried for her like that, she tells me still.

Ruff was from Christina's old neighborhood, and she met him when she was still living as Eduardo. Ruff liked Eduardo right away, and when Eduardo left the cousin's place, Ruff suggested they move into an abandoned house together. Eduardo only let Ruff kiss him— no sex—during the three months they stayed in a one-bedroom house with planks for windows and rotting floorboards. Eduardo did, however, let Ruff give him drugs.

"I'd only done weed before, but, girl, that boy got me hooked on crack!" Christina said.

"Come on now, *he* didn't get you hooked," I protested. "You took the crack yourself."

"Well, he put the pipe in my mouth, and I felt vulnerable, because he was the only person I had at the time. I *had* been kicked out of my house, remember?"

With Christina, I was never sure how much to push her to take responsibility for her past, largely because I myself wasn't clear on where exactly the culpability lay. I had no training in helping abused kids, and as our relationship deepened, it became clear to me that I was the sole person Christina talked to about her life. I had heard enough AA-speak from friends to believe that the only way to get out from under an addictive grip is to admit you were hooked, and that blaming others is to be looked upon with suspicion—but what was I to do when the person in question had been thirteen? Was Christina's crack use her mother's fault? Ruff's? The system's? I dropped the fight.

In any case, Christina-then-Eduardo liked the crack and started smoking it every three or four days. Eduardo's saving grace was that his supply dried up after a few months; Ruff got arrested for possession. Detoxing and desperate, Eduardo went looking for another man he thought could help.

Eduardo hadn't seen his dad since he ran off with the neighbor woman eight years before, but Eduardo found him listed in the phone book. Eduardo took two buses to an apartment where a girlfriend he'd never seen before was home alone. The girlfriend let him in, and Eduardo bit at his chipped nails, waiting.

"I started to cry as soon as I saw him," Christina said, adding that when her dad got home, he stared at his only son from the doorway, apparently stunned. "I just started saying crazy shit: that I was addicted to crack, that Mom had thrown me out, that I had nowhere to go, that I had no money."

Eduardo Sr. looked at his son and said nothing. Then he noticed the fingernails. "He just said, 'What's the matter with your nails?'" Christina said, telling me she had black polish on at the time. Then he shouted: "'My son does not paint his fingernails! Shit. Get the hell out!'"

Eduardo Jr. sobbed harder but ran out the door. The girlfriend felt sorry for him and offered to drive him somewhere. Eduardo told her to go to his mom's house, because he was so freaked out and couldn't think of anyplace to go. She drove him there, but he wouldn't say a word. That was the last time Eduardo saw his father.

Back at the yellow duplex in East L.A., Eduardo found that his mom had changed the locks, so he climbed the fence and hung out in the backyard with the family's new puppies. Gloria saw her son out there, Christina told me, but she wouldn't let him in. For a few months, Eduardo slept in the backyard, showering with a hose.

While Ruff was in jail, Eduardo got off crack, primarily through smoking a lot of weed, but he stayed loyal to Ruff. He went back to his old junior high school, the one where his friend Roxie taught him to wear dresses and bras, and tried to study some algebra, even joining the Mensa Club for smart kids. When the authorities caught on to the backyard situation, he went into new foster care for a few weeks, then ran away and went back to living with his mom for a bit, who let him stay inside, then ran away again. He also found out about Ruff's genetic girlfriend, whom Ruff had been seeing on the side. The girlfriend's name was Lily.

At that point Eduardo was just beginning to transform into Geri, part-time. Geri, dressing up with Roxie and taking pictures at the mall, bought gel inserts for her bra and shaded her lips a soft tint of beige, with gloss on top. She sent pictures of herself like this to Ruff in jail, who said he liked them. Ruff, on the rare occasions when he sees Christina now, confident and womanly in their old neighborhood, says, "Damn! You look good!" And then Ruff goes back to trudging alongside his and Lily's young kids with their small sticky faces, while Christina gloats. Christina believes that it was the feminine part of Eduardo that attracted Ruff, as Ruff hated to think of himself as gay. But the relationship subject at the time was taboo between them—Christina transitioned, and Ruff got out of jail and silently approved; Ruff had a girlfriend, and Christina acquiesced. They each had their issues, and they kept them quiet. Still, Christina remembered being afraid Ruff would leave her for Lily, so she invented ways to test him, shooing him away from her when he made advances and so on. She said, "I guess in a way I damaged Ruff because I was too much of a Cancer."

"You mean too emotionally swingy?" I asked.

"Yeah. One minute I lived for him, and the next I was going to make him feel like shit because of the shit he put me through."

And Ruff did make Christina worry. He shifted from crack to heroin, and then got arrested again, Christina's not sure for what. Once again, she stayed faithful, but Lily was already pregnant with Ruff's child—something Christina found out later, which kept her from ever hooking up with Ruff again. Christina's always oddly loyal to mothers.

At the time Christina told me this story, she was seventeen and dating two other boys, both named Dave. One was older and taller and a speed freak, and one lived in a GLASS group home like she did—where in-house dating was strictly forbidden. She liked the group-home Dave better than tall Dave, but group-home Dave had an anxiety disorder and a history of depression, and he kept disappearing. Christina kept tall Dave around for backup.

Both Daves knew that Christina was transgender. Christina, unlike many transgirls her age, didn't seem to have trouble finding or keeping boyfriends for a few weeks or occasionally months at a time, though there were always problems. Some boyfriends were gay and so didn't view Christina as the straight girl she knew she was; they wanted her to be more masculine. Others would act like they were comfortable with her status at first, but then let slip some sort of cruel comment. Such was the case with a recent boyfriend Christina called "the minister" because of a onetime stint at a Christian summer camp. Christina really liked the minister, felt as though they could have serious discussions, unlike the gangster guys she met on the bus. But then, when she told the minister about playing with her younger cousins, he asked, astonished, "Your family lets you around the children?"

"Like I was some sort of danger," she said to me. Her face was pained. "I felt like he kicked me in the throat."

Of course, as for all of us, there's always the hope that a transgender girl will just stumble upon "the one." He'll be straight, he'll be handsome, he won't fetishize, and he won't freak out. It can happen. The day Foxx found her first real boyfriend, she was trying on earrings at a minimall shop. Fernando worked there, stocking shelves mostly, and he caught her pulling the hoops from their display and sliding them into her ears.

"You know you have to buy those before you try them on," Fernando said, not unkindly. It wasn't love at first sight; Fernando didn't remember paying attention to Foxx in particular because, he said, he generally had to stop dozens of women every day from doing the very same thing. But Foxx noticed Fernando. He was Mexican, and very tall, with dimples that carved themselves into his cheeks when he smiled, lopsided and shy. His accent was thick, emphasis landing on every second syllable like a limp, and his eyes were deep brown and sexy. Foxx vowed to come back and get in trouble for trying on earrings again the next day.

When she did, they talked, and Fernando told Foxx he had just made it to L.A. from Texas, and he really didn't have anywhere to stay. He was twenty-five and getting over a bad divorce from his wife, who had custody of their two sons. He'd done some time in the pen but was looking to go straight. Foxx understood being new in town, and lonely, and she was happy when he asked her to have dinner with him at her house. He'd bring the groceries.

Fernando had never been with a transwoman before, but he liked Foxx, and when they slept together that first night, he asked if he could stay. I met up with them three days into the new arrangement. Fernando had bought Foxx a gigantic TV.

"It's really exciting. Because last week I was single, and this week I have a boyfriend and he's living with me!" Foxx gushed. "And he's cooking for me, and I'm falling in love with him, and he's falling in love with me. It's happening so fast, it's like a dream. I even told him, 'I don't believe you sometimes because you're so fine and you can get any real girl you want and yet you're here with me. And I want to pinch myself and wake up.'"

Foxx was sitting on the floor with her elbow resting on Fernando's lap. He absentmindedly drew figure eights on her forearm and looked at her adoringly. He was wearing a backward baseball cap and baggy jeans and slightly dirty tube socks. I asked him what he thought about Foxx saying he could find a "real girl." He scowled, then looked up, trying to make the English come together. "Well, maybe it's true about that, but my feelings were hurt. I can't never find someone like her," he said. Then he showed me the Catholic cross that hung around his neck under his sports jersey. "And I think everything came straight from God."

Foxx got up and went to the kitchen, asking us if we wanted any fruit punch. "No, baby," Fernando said, and I could feel Foxx's thrill at his term, even from across the apartment. Because she had watched so many friends go through so many relationships, she knew what was expected in a love affair, and she wanted to get there fast. She wanted to collapse all those lonely years, it seemed to me, by becoming as experienced as other twenty-one-year-olds in the space of a few days. She gave a world-weary sigh but couldn't hide her bliss. A toothy grin tugged at her mouth as she spoke.

"It seems like since I have a boyfriend now, all these guys that used to ignore me are coming out of nowhere and trying to talk to me—and these are really handsome guys! I'm sure Fernando can relate, because he probably sees beautiful women every day. I think it's really hard to be in a committed relationship. But I'm just an old-fashioned-type person. No matter how hard it is, I'm going to be with that person," Foxx said. She went on to describe how just yesterday some handsome man came and sat next to her on the bus and propositioned her—something she wouldn't have refused a week ago—but this time she got up and went to sit alone at the front of the bus. "I was really tempted for a minute, but being the honest person that I am, I know I would go home and tell my boyfriend. And I know that Fernando is very faithful to me, and I'm very faithful to him. I don't really see him as the type that would cheat on me."

"Is this everything you thought it would be; does it live up so far?" I asked Foxx, when Fernando got up and was out of earshot. "Oh yes," she answered. "It seems like a full-time commitment, and I'm happy with that."

I was concerned, of course, that Fernando was only using Foxx for her apartment; she was certainly soft on such crimes and had been for years. But he genuinely seemed to like her and had the fumbling awe of the love-struck. Foxx liked showing him off. "Fernando was listening to my song 'If I Was a Real Girl,' and he made a comment that just struck me. I forgot what he said," Foxx told me, though I could tell she had likely memorized his every word. "What did you say, baby?"

"I said you don't have to be a real girl to somebody like me, who cares and loves you," Fernando said, piecing his way through his fractured English. "I feel great, me and her. She's a great person."

Foxx then explained that Fernando had introduced her to everyone at his job and also to his aunt, the only relative he had living in L.A. When she wrote the song the year before, she was imagining that no one would ever bring her home to family; men only wanted her for sex, and while she couldn't completely repress her optimistic nature, she had been starting to lose hope. "He said he's not ashamed of me, and he kissed me. It made me feel so—ooh!" Foxx shuddered happily.

Caught up in Foxx's joy, Fernando pressed on. "I consider myself—I am a straight guy. But like I always say, the heart doesn't see—only feels," Fernando said. He got quieter. "In other words, what it means, I don't see what she has outside, only what's inside of her, and that's what I care about, you know. That's the point. That's the view."

# PART TWO

We are all seeds, we are all stars.

—Chris Abani, *GraceLand*

# 7

## LOCKDOWN

CHRISTINA HAD BEEN in her group home for a little over six months when she called me from the Donut Time on the corner of Santa Monica and Highland. It was close to 7:30 on a Friday night, and she was out of breath and panicked.

"Girl! I got thrown out! The cops are after me—can you come pick me up?" Christina was shouting into the phone. I asked her to slow down, to explain, and she said something about throwing a stapler, except it wasn't a stapler, it was only paper, those stupid fucks, and Ramona, the night social worker at the group home, had said she could go to the bathroom, which was really her giving the green light to run because she should be at juvenile hall right now, Ramona was supposed to hold her, and, "Girl! The cops have my picture! By morning all the squad cars will have my picture, because they have it in my file at the group home and that's what they do—they make copies and pass it through the precinct!"

I wasn't going to get a cohesive story from the Donut Time, so I told Christina to stay put and I'd be there in twenty minutes. Driving, I grew confident: I'd bring Christina home, we'd order takeout, and she'd tell the story in its proper order. We'd phone the group home, sort out whatever happened with the stapler, Christina would apologize for running away, and we'd drive her back by curfew.

When I pulled in, nobody was in the donut shop save for an old man clutching a small milk carton and a preteen boy slamming the side of the video-game machine. The light was a sickly, soured yellow. I scanned the parking lot. Transgirls and gay boys were everywhere, laughing loudly and playfully pushing one another, getting ready to start working or go to the clubs. Why would Christina run here? Because it was someplace she knew? Because if she couldn't reach me on the phone, she would have to turn tricks looking for someone to take her home? I had waited ten minutes when she suddenly came running out of the 7-Eleven, which was part of the same outdoor strip mall, at full speed, backpack over one shoulder. She hugged me hard and fast. "Let's go," she said.

"Oh my god," she started in chirpily, as soon as she buckled her seat belt—as though this were any regular night and she was here to gossip. "I just saw Shavonne. She looks horrible! She's out here with her mom—girl, yes!"

"Wait, what do you mean—what happened? I thought you were going to be waiting inside the Donut Time because the cops are after you. But now you're running around parking lots, talking about Shavonne. What's going on?" I asked. I was confused and a little annoyed; I had canceled my Friday plans for this dramatic rescue.

"I was going to be in the donut place, but then I saw Shavonne. Girl, the crack's gotten really bad. But I know why. Because she's out here working with her mom. The two of them are working together," Christina said. "That's some fucked-up shit."

I had to agree. I remembered Shavonne writing that tribute to her mom back in high school and wondered what kind of psychological floor falls out from inside of you when your mom doesn't help you out of hustling, but follows you into it. And I thought about her three other kids, all younger than Shavonne. I patted Christina's leg. "Okay, though. Back to you. Why am I here? What happened?"

Christina had never been to my apartment; that seemed somehow out of bounds during all the time I had taught and then mentored her. She'd met my partner, Robin, a few times, though, and now she relished the attention from both of us, as we ordered Thai food and let her pick her favorite deep-fried, sticky-sweet treats. She seemed relieved that two adults were now going to take care of her problem, which became more and more tangled and worrisome the more she told us of it. It quickly became clear there would be no going back to the group home that night.

Here's what happened: For the past several weeks, Christina had been attending a school for probation and parole kids, on the suggestion of her probation officer or counselor, Christina wasn't sure which. Sometimes "troubled kids" like Christina, who have a history of truancy and school or district changes, do well in a strict environment with dangerous peers—according to a sort of "scared straight" philosophy. Christina however, being transgender, was likely to fail in such an environment. She said students were frisked every day, which made her nervous that she could be clocked. And thugs, while entertaining to Christina one-on-one, were terrifying and unpredictable in groups.

At this school the administrators knew Christina was transgender because her transcripts cited her boy name, but none of the other students were privy to her status. Until, according to Christina, an administrator told a security guard and that guard told a student. Which led to the events that day. Apparently several students, horrified that this sexy little *chola* was "really a guy," told Christina they were going to kill her after school. Christina called her group home and asked them to pick her up, but the one group-home van was already in use that afternoon. She panicked, and explained privately to her teacher that she needed to leave early because other students were threatening to kill her. The teacher, very likely accustomed to student threats of violence but unaccustomed to the reality of transgender hate crimes, said no. Christina, frustrated and afraid, shoved some newspapers, though she said the teacher told authorities she threw a classroom stapler. In any case, Christina ran from the building before the bell rang—a crime in itself at a probation school. The school called Christina's probation officer, or PO, Marcus. Marcus called her group home, and by the time she arrived there, Ramona the group-home attendant told Christina she'd have to spend some time in juvenile hall for "AWOLing" from her school and being violent toward a teacher. So when Ramona turned her back, Christina ran. And now she had a warrant out for her arrest. She had called the group home from a pay phone on the street and they told her so.

"But this is all a huge misunderstanding," I protested. "Don't you think when your PO understands that it was *your* safety that was being undermined at the school, that you were the one who wasn't being protected, that he'll take it all back?"

"Girl, no," Christina said, looking at me like I had asked her something patently simpleminded. "Once you've got a warrant, you've got to get arrested. They don't let you take things like that back. And now I'm worried they're going to arrest you too, for harboring a criminal."

At this, my stomach dropped a little, but I told Christina not to worry. Robin and I made her up a bed on the couch, and we all went to sleep.

Christina's fear of juvenile hall was deeper and more justified than any teenage kid's might be, though most people are afraid of being locked up. For one thing, she'd been there before—at fourteen, for prostitution. She knew that what happens to transwomen is much more frightening, and potentially dangerous, than to genetic women who have committed any type of crime. In nearly every case in every state, transgender offenders are housed according to their genitalia; a nonoperative male-to-female with breasts will be sent to a male ward, where she will certainly be harassed and likely be assaulted. Many transpeople also stop receiving their hormones and other necessary medical treatments while in prison.

The next morning, despite Christina's intensely vocal desire to just ignore the whole situation and watch TV, Robin and I convinced her she had to call Marcus the PO. We practiced what she could say, with me playing Marcus. Christina started in calmly. "Excuse me, Marcus, but you don't know everything. Those kids were going to kill me, because some faggot-ass guard clocked my T." Here her voice grew high and sharp. "Evidently no one cares about that. Evidently no one wants to listen. And then the teacher said I wanted to whoop her ass with a stapler. She crazy. I just pushed some papers when she wouldn't let me get outta there when those kids were gonna kill me. And now howm' I gonna get back to the group home? You told them to kick me out of there before you even heard my story. Whatever. Whatever. Whatever."

Christina, so accustomed to any authority disbelieving her, gave up before she even began. I told her she put the focus on other people—the teacher and the guard—instead of herself. "And maybe 'faggot-ass' isn't the best adjective choice," I said, handing her some coffee. Christina smirked. "If you're trying to garner Marcus's respect."

We role-played some more, until Christina's delivery was more even. This was after she had locked herself in the bathroom for an hour to alternately calm herself down and then cry under the door that she didn't want to put me and Robin through this because she'd just end up in juvie anyway. She wasn't used to fighting for herself, at least not this way, without fists. Christina said she shouldn't make the call from our house, since this was traceable, and she did have a bench warrant. And we shouldn't drive somewhere to make the call from Los Angeles because that was where the cops had her picture; we'd have to go to a different county. The best one, we all decided, the place where they'd least expect her, was Beverly Hills. And where did they have a bank of telephones where we could all settle in, in comfortable chairs, and order cool drinks? With Christina crouched low in the backseat, we drove off to the hotel Peninsula Beverly Hills, with room rates in the $300 to $3,000 range.

Unfortunately, Marcus didn't pick up his phone all weekend long and never left a message at the pager number Christina gave him. At the beginning, we were all nervous and hopeful about our plan, driving back and forth to the hotel, picking up tacos for sustenance along the way, hoping for a message that the warrant had been lifted. By

Sunday night we were tired of what had started to feel like a game, and we were making calls from the apartment.

On Monday, Marcus called, but not until 5:00 P.M. He listened to Christina's story, and Robin and I cheered her mature delivery. He seemed unconcerned about the death threat; the problem now was that the group home had given her bed away. He'd get the bench warrant lifted, but she'd need to go into the halls anyway until a bed opened up. Before she'd hung up the phone, she started stuffing her things—CDs of Destiny's Child and Britney Spears, eyeliner pencils, socks—which were scattered around the living room, into her backpack. She was getting ready to run.

"Wait—aren't you going to even argue with him?" I asked. "There has to be a way around this. You can't just go to jail because there isn't a bed! You haven't done anything wrong."

"Girl, no. I'm through. You've done enough for me. I don't want to put you through more," Christina said. To her, people didn't go to jail because they did anything wrong. The justice system was arbitrarily punitive, but she had an internal barometer of integrity. "I love you and I can tell I'm gonna get you in trouble. And I'm not going back into the halls, so I'm leaving."

"Just wait," I said to Christina, taking a breath. "No sirens are going to come roaring to the door; nobody knows you're here. Let me talk to Marcus."

When I called, Marcus politely told me the same thing he told Christina, that there were no beds and technically she had broken a rule, and because she was a ward of the state, she'd have to be held at juvenile hall until there was a bed available for her. I was outraged; if a nontransgender kid needed a group home, she'd be placed because there were plenty available, but homes with sensitive staff and GLBT tenants were scarce. Then again, a nontransgender kid wouldn't have been threatened with murder in her high school. The stakes were all so high and the consequences so unfair. Still, I had to keep cool, as Marcus was our ticket.

"Who are you, by the way?" Marcus asked me. "And have you had Christina all weekend?"

Christina, who was listening in, mouthed, "No!" with her eyes bulging. "No," I lied. "Though Christina's been in regular contact with me all weekend. She's been very responsible, reaching out to the safe adults in her life and trying to reach you—wanting to turn herself in and explain that it was *her* safety that had been violated. She wants to do the right thing." I then said that I had been her teacher and mentor for three years and asked if it would be possible for her to stay with me for a few days, or however long it took until a bed opened up. Marcus said he wasn't sure; he'd have to check. It was nearing the end of his day, though, so he supposed she could stay with us for the night. We'd talk again in the morning.

That night Christina was bored with playing lockdown. She wanted to go out with one of her Daves—tall Dave, as anxiety Dave had been sent to another home recently, and while she could talk to him from a pay phone after he had group, she found it stressful to think about someone else's problems beyond her own. Suddenly, Robin and I found ourselves discussing curfews and seat belts and "of course we need to meet him before you can get in his car." I didn't really want to deal with potentially more rule breaking; I wanted Christina to sit and watch a movie for the night, quietly grateful for our help. Then again, she had been watching movies—endless rounds of *Girl, Interrupted,* which she kept on repeat all night long until her eyes were dark and socked in by morning. We all needed a break from one another, and this was the first night without a warrant. "Be back by eleven," I said. She was in by 11:05, and she tiptoed in to kiss us good-night reeking of marijuana.

The next evening I drove by Christina's old group home to pick up her stuff. They had indeed given away her bed, and the waiting list for that particular house was so long that Christina would hit her eighteenth birthday before she'd ever be eligible again to live there. Marcus had never called. I took Christina to her former "Living

Skills" class at a community college near the sports arena downtown that the kids in her house attended, so she could see them all and say good-bye. Unfortunately, she was legally no longer allowed to set foot on group-home property. Bernadette, the staff member all the kids called Mama, was cleaning up after cooking everyone pasta. "Why don't you just keep her?" Bernadette said. "She's only got six months to go until she turns eighteen, and then she can be on her own. It's not that long; you won't have to do that much."

I slid my back down the cabinet I was leaning on and sat on the floor. "We only have a one-bedroom apartment, and Robin's in graduate school; we're living off my writing, and money's tight with the two of us—how can we pay for one more?" Even as the words tumbled out, I knew they weren't the real reason for my fear. We'd been broke before; we'd made room before. Out of pure frustration, I started to cry.

"I can't just keep her for six months," I said. "Physically, she might be eighteen, but emotionally, she's—I don't know—fifteen. She's been hurt, Bernadette—you know that. She's been through so many homes. She needs somewhere to really stabilize. For years. Somewhere she can learn that she's lovable and worthy and okay and . . ."

Here I really started to cry, great heaves of rage and grief filling me up and shuddering out all the broken pieces of stories I'd been carrying around these past years. I cried for the parents who threw their kids out to the streets; I raged for the system that was blind to them too, that didn't have enough beds, that sent them to parole schools, that arrested children for having sex with grown men so they could eat food at night. I cried for black-market hormones and for HIV and for the fact that every single transkid I cared about had tried to commit suicide, and I cried for meth and crack and H and smack and crank, and I cried that gender was at first more crucial and then more meaningless than I ever thought it could be because really the only vital life force is love and that seemed to be what was in such short supply to begin with. I took a ragged breath and wiped my nose on my sleeve.

"Okay," I said. "I'll take her in. But it's really more of a lifetime thing."

"It was that already, whether she lived with you or not," Bernadette said, and handed me a paper towel. Bernadette was right, but she didn't know everything, obviously. In the barest terms, I knew I had no choice: how could I abandon Christina as I had been abandoned?

Bernadette told me that Christina's stuff had already been bagged up and put in the basement. A butchy girl with small braids poking out all over her head, who was too young to go to the "Living Skills" class, offered to help me drag the bags to my car. She seemed to feel sorry for me for crying and had apparently been spying on the conversation from the kitchen doorway.

In all, Christina had five Hefty garbage bags of possessions to her name. They were tremendously heavy, and when she opened them later, I found out why: they were mostly full of beauty products. There were some shoes, some clothes, but there was also can after aerosol can of hair spray, tub after tub of gel and lotion and conditioner, shaving foam, and apricot scrub.

When I picked Christina up from her class, she was in a wretched mood. It really hit her that she wasn't going back to the home where she called somebody Mama. At six months, the group home was one of the most stable places Christina had ever lived. She turned up the Spanish pop radio station so loud it rattled my ribs. I let this slide for a while, then I turned the music down. She turned it back up, and we battled with the knob until she threatened to jump out of the car while it was moving, opening and closing the door on the freeway for effect, me screaming, her laughing meanly. We picked up Robin and marched through the Home Depot in steely silence, as we chose stackable bins where Christina could store her things. We were stuck with each other and knew it.

As soon as we had fallen into a kind of rhythm, Marcus called. Christina was depressed and refused to do much but sleep late and watch TV; Robin and I had taken to waking her up with Dolly

Parton singing "Little Sparrow," because the sweetness of the song made her crazy and Christina's fury made us laugh. And at least it got her out of bed. We talked to her about turning eighteen, and about needing to come up with a plan that involved school and work and a vision, but she was shut down. It looked to me like some of the razor cuts on her arm were fresh, but she wouldn't talk about it. She'd leave for big chunks of the day and come home looking red eyed and stoned. I wasn't sure how much to nurture and how much to push, and I was worried. Every night since she'd been with us, we'd light candles and drink chamomile tea and sit together under blankets on the couch, and Christina would talk about one of the Daves or some other past boyfriends. Those were the only constants—the "Little Sparrow" and the chamomile tea. Everything else was hard.

"Christina is going to have to go back into the halls for a while; I've really done everything I can," Marcus said to me the evening he called. "I've been calling and calling about beds, and there just aren't any to be had."

"But that's just not fair," I said, angry and confused. "She didn't do anything wrong; how can she do time when she was the one who was victimized here? She had her bed taken away because her life was threatened, and now you're telling me she has to go to jail for it? What about the kids who threatened to kill her? What happened to them—are *they* being punished?"

"Well, that was never substantiated," Marcus said.

"Are you telling me she's lying?" I yelled, furious now. I felt so powerless, I was ignoring the advice I constantly gave to Christina that respecting authority will get you further than flaunting it. Marcus rankled.

"I don't know what happened. I wasn't there. I don't know how well you know Christina, though"—and here he paused to let the sting settle—"but she has done bad things in the past. Really bad. So she can go to juvenile hall."

"You can't go to jail now for something you were never convicted of in the past!" I shouted. I took a breath. "That undermines the whole notion of our justice system. That's outrageous."

"You also can't have a minor and a ward of the courts just staying anywhere. So she has to go somewhere where we know what's happening to her. Which right now means juvenile hall," Marcus said. Then he paused, seemingly thinking of something for the first time. "Unless you want to be her official guardian."

"Fine," I said firmly, though I was shaking with anger and relief and worry that I was now formally becoming responsible for a kid who was shutting down more by the day. I realized I didn't know what guardianship meant; if she stole something, would Robin and I have to pay for it? Stealing wasn't Christina's style. If she was truant from school, would it affect our chances of adopting kids in the future? If she cut herself up even more with razors, which she was already doing—wait, did she have medical insurance? Could we get her on Robin's student insurance? We didn't have enough money for this. And what about the drugs she was using and not talking about? I didn't know enough about drugs. "I'll be her guardian," I said.

Marcus sounded surprised, but he took down all my information, address and date of birth and the like. We were suddenly civil and formal and polite, like estranged relatives seated together at a wedding. I didn't tell Christina what happened; an expression of love or commitment could scare her more than one of rejection, and I knew she was close to bolting anyway.

Robin was fine with the guardian move. We had already decided to take Christina in; she felt the title was just a formality in a system that largely overlooked the kids anyhow. The state wouldn't be our biggest problem. Besides, Robin has both a generous spirit and a faith in the alignment of circumstance and capability—she didn't think we'd be handed more than we could handle. She and Christina bonded in Christina's quieter moments; Robin doesn't push for talk and for answers like I do, and Christina was grateful for the contrast.

Also, in crisis, people tend to attach fiercely, and they had. Robin was ready, maybe even more ready than I.

What becoming guardians did change was the time and the volume at which we played Dolly's "Little Sparrow" each morning. Despite puppy-killing glares from beneath an enormous tangle of red and brown curls, there was no more sleeping in. Christina kicked at the covers, threw the pillows over her head, but when the song's volume became unbearable, she'd march off to the bathroom, cursing us under her breath, knowing she'd come back to quiet and coffee. And then we'd work on her plan. She didn't want to go to regular school with teenagers; it was just too fraught. She wanted a high school diploma, not a GED, so we settled on night school, for adults. Together, we created a résumé—her first. What she really wanted to do, she said, was outreach—to help kids like her not end up like her. She wanted to counsel and to run programs, or at least rap groups, and to teach kids about safer sex and drug use and not living on the streets. You're not even out of the gates on that one, I thought, but didn't say it. We talked about long-term visions and short-term goals, and that she could build skills in jobs that weren't necessarily directly related to her plans, and she said, smartly, "Okay, girl, I can apply for retail jobs too."

And that's what she did. Every morning she job-hunted, and by the third day she had two interviews and three more scheduled. With a project, Christina started to come home happier. She liked the idea of working. We knew there could be a problem when she actually did get hired and had to show her male California ID to go on payroll. There are no laws protecting transgender workers, and many times, once an employer realizes the woman he's hired has a male driver's license and social security card, he'll fire her. It's a somewhat complicated, time-consuming, and expensive process to get these documents changed, and it's another reason so many young and disenfranchised transgender people have to work off the books. (I was beginning to realize that any encounter with the "system" was generally ten times harder for a transperson. Laws just aren't written with them in mind.) I knew I'd help Christina change her ID cards, but it was also crucial for her to start looking for work right away. She was losing it watching *Girl, Interrupted.*

Christina grew cheerier with her job prospects, but I never knew what could turn her mood. One thing that hurt her deeply was when I asked if she wanted more privacy. I told her we could buy some screens to put around her couch and build her a kind of "room," and she thought I was trying to hide her away. "Why would I want privacy?" she asked angrily, and I realized she had never once slept in a room by herself. Even when she was a baby and young child, there were aunts or parents in the bed. "I want to be with y'all and part of things. But if you don't want me here, say that. I can leave anytime." We had to constantly reassure Christina that we wanted her with us, to which she would respond, "Whatever," and then trick us into saying it once more.

Which is why it was so infuriating when Marcus called again. It was only maybe about a week later, but the psychological changes we had all been through felt momentous. Christina was at a transgender support group meeting at Bienestar, and I was home alone.

"I talked to my supervisor," Marcus said. "And we can't have you as her guardian after all. She has to be with a licensed foster-care provider."

I fell down hard inside of myself; I had done such intensive soul shifting to take Christina in—now he was taking her away? "What do you mean?" I said. And then lamely, "We have a bed for her, and a place for her clothes, and, and she's getting a job." I wanted to shout about all the transkids that had no homes: if we had a home for such a kid, why couldn't he just let us be? But the words wouldn't come. Marcus pressed on.

"So I've had a warrant put out for her arrest, and we'll be—"

"You've WHAT?" I interrupted. "You issued another warrant?!" Now I felt like one of the kids. I understood why they believed the justice system was out to screw them, why they rolled their eyes at me when I suggested trying reason with the authorities who put them in no-win predicaments. "Why on earth would you jump to such an extreme decision?"

"It's not extreme." Marcus was calm, but his tone suggested he was losing patience with what he saw as my hysterics. We simply could not understand one another. "It's again a problem of beds. There are no beds for someone like Christina, so she'll have to go to juvenile hall. She isn't going to want to go, so I put out a warrant. It's just what you do. If she gets arrested, it'll be erased off her record when she turns eighteen. She's a minor."

"But getting arrested is traumatizing for her," I said. "She'll get booked under her boy's name and put in the male ward. You know it's dangerous for transgirls to be housed with men!"

"I don't know what to tell you," Marcus said. "The warrant's already been issued, and there still aren't any beds."

I wasn't going to get anywhere invoking reason or compassion. I tried issuing orders. "Just give me a day," I said. "I'll find her somewhere to stay that's legal. Just don't arrest her tonight, and I'll call you tomorrow."

Marcus told me he wouldn't get the warrant revoked, but he would talk to me the next day, which I took to mean he wouldn't send the police screaming to my door. I called Christina and told her to take a taxi home because Robin had the car. I asked her not to hang out outside on the street, and she started to cry. She knew right away. "They're gonna arrest me, aren't they?" she asked, and my chest tightened with grief. Going to jail when she'd done nothing wrong had become as rational to her as it had to Marcus.

That night I felt like I thought the teenagers must, up against the system. I had been promised one thing, the guardianship, and adapted to that, only to have it yanked away. In fact, when Christina got home, all bleary eyed and mad, I had regressed, in a way, to my teenage self. I was kicking furniture and playing the stereo too loud, and I asked her for some cigarettes, which I had given up long ago. Robin came home shortly after Christina, and I suggested we all go for a walk, to work off the frustration and try to come up with some kind of solution.

"But the warrant, girl—we can't go outside," Christina said. She was looking at me like I had suddenly become breakable or slightly crazy.

"Fuck the warrant," I said, and I understood why so many street kids had given up on respecting authority. It all seemed so arbitrary and so cruel. "We can go outside. We'll just do it in disguise. Christina, how many wigs do you have?"

And suddenly there we were, two adults and one teenager, in platinum and brunette and black wigs, smoking cigarettes and singing at top volume in the cool Los Angeles night. Christina had decided that "Little Sparrow" was now her theme song, and we did our best to completely maim a country accent.

> *Little sparrow, little sparrow,*
> *Precious fragile little thing*
> *Little sparrow, little sparrow*
> *Flies so high and feels no pain.*

The next day I found Christina a bed at GLASS, the organization that ran her former group home, by calling the president of the organization every hour on the hour until she finally talked to me. Unfortunately, this bed was in the home rumored to be for "288s" or underage sex offenders, which terrified Christina, but she went under the promise that we'd find her something better and we'd visit her every day. Marcus could take away our right to guardianship, but he couldn't eradicate the commitment we'd made to her.

All the progress Christina had made quickly deteriorated at the group home. She couldn't go on the job interviews she had set up nor, more importantly, think of her life as something over which she had dominion; movement at the group home followed a tightly controlled script. Because she wasn't yet enrolled in school, she spent all day in front of the television or slicing more lines into her arms with razors in her room. She didn't touch the GED books we brought her. High school seemed distant and stupid.

In the meantime, I found out that it would take months for Robin and me to get our actual foster-care licenses; social work visits, finding a new apartment, and bureaucratic hurdles would put Christina well past her eighteenth birthday before the state would let us be her parents. So we called the only other foster mom we knew: Andrea, who took care of Domineque.

Andrea has a soft voice that belies her fierce will and tidy discipline. She has fair skin and an easy smile and at the time was in her early thirties, with straight brown hair that she usually pulled back in a quick ponytail. She peppers her speech with phrases like "quite honestly" and "quite frankly," so it sometimes feels like she's letting you in on a secret, though her manner is reserved and calm.

Andrea and her husband, a graduate student in neuroscience, were plenty busy with Domineque. After Domineque had run from Johnny, the foster dad whom she said was upset about her transsexuality, she lived with a controlling boyfriend for a few months in a squat apartment on the east side. Then she came to Andrea, who, after being her social worker for several years, offered to foster-parent Domineque. While Andrea and her husband were licensed to care for special-needs and high-risk cases like Domineque, they also certainly were psychologically taxed. They had to think seriously before taking on Christina too.

Ultimately, because Christina was Domineque's best friend, they did decide to let her live with them, under one strict condition: no drugs. One sign of use—a pipe, some rolling paper—and she was out, no excuses. Christina, Andrea, Domineque, Robin, and I all made a formal appeal to the group home and her probation officer, and they released Christina into Andrea's care.

Privately, Robin and I told Andrea we would still take Christina in on weekends, because we had become attached to the idea and because we wanted to alleviate the pressure on Andrea and Domineque and the family they'd established. Christina said she understood the

arrangement and agreed to it. Despite all the effort I'd made to make
her feel loved and wanted, though, the system won in a way. Rational truth and emotional truth run on separate tracks, and once we'd
taken the last of Christina's clothes over to Andrea's, she still ended
up feeling rejected. Within two weeks and just one weekend visit,
she wasn't speaking to me. She hung up on my every call.

When I called Andrea to ask why Christina wasn't speaking to me,
she sounded tired. I could hear the television tinnily shrieking from
the other room and, above that, Christina and Domineque yelling at
each other in their laughy way.

"Oh, I don't know—she said you took her J.Lo poster," she
answered.

I sighed. I never would have guessed that one. The first weekend
Christina stayed with us after moving to Andrea's, she stole a movie
poster that was hanging loose at a bus stop. It was a sexy ad for Jennifer Lopez, whom we both agreed was a mediocre actress with a
great body. She had left it in the trunk of my car when I dropped her
off, and I'd been carting it around for two weeks.

"You know it's not about that, right?" Andrea asked, hesitantly.

"Yeah, I know. She's testing me. She wants to see if she pushes
me away whether I'll stick around," I said, thinking that as the words
came out of my mouth, they sounded like psychobabble, separate
from the much more real feelings aching at the edges of my ribs. I
was attached to Christina, and even irrationally afraid that she might
end up loving Andrea more than me or deciding she didn't need me
at all. Logically, of course, I wanted Christina to get as much love
and support as she could, and realistically I knew she would come
around, but I missed her. Even though I tried to be more mature
than this, I felt rejected. "It still sucks. How is she doing?"

Christina was mixed: She and Domineque had registered for
high school at a local center for adults. Christina was attending every
day but was dressing more provocatively and was becoming more
withdrawn and cold around the house. She and Domineque had

started bickering, and Domineque was getting in trouble for missing curfews and skipping school. I wanted to talk to Christina about these things, to stem the rising danger signs. But I also felt like I had to give Christina the space to want to come back instead of providing her an opportunity to expend all her energy in a game resisting me. I bit back everything I had to say and offered, "Tell Christina I'll keep her J.Lo poster safe."

The reason there's all this trouble finding legal placement for kids like Christina—and the reason so many kids fall through the cracks—isn't a problem with the kids themselves but with definitions. All of our systems—school, legal, penal, and so on—are built on a male/female dichotomy. Institutions (like the Department of Children and Family Services, for instance) siphon the boys to one living space and the girls to another. Transgender people bring up the question: How do you define *male* and *female*? Mostly, the job of answering has fallen to the courts, though they haven't done a great job of it.

Marriage is a primary area where courts have tried, and largely failed, to define gender. A famous case is that of Christie Littleton, a transsexual woman who married a man in Texas in the late eighties. The marriage was legal: Littleton had changed her birth certificate, her name, and had complete sex reassignment surgery. Countless U.S. transsexuals marry like this every year. Unfortunately, Littleton's husband died, and when she suspected medical malpractice, she sued. When the accused doctor found out that Littleton had been born male, he argued their marriage was gay and therefore null in the first place. In 1999 the court of appeals agreed with the doctor. "Male chromosomes do not change with either hormonal treatment or sex reassignment surgery," the chief justice wrote. "Biologically a postoperative transsexual female is still a male."

The problem with this, aside from being terribly sad for Littleton, is that it effectively annulled, or at least called into question, hundreds of otherwise legal marriages in Texas. And not just the transgender ones. About one in five hundred to a thousand people are born with something called Klinefelter's syndrome, which adds an extra X to the XY chromosome pair; some are even born XXXY or XXXXY. Who are these people biologically, if most feel male but some feel female? And there's also Turner Syndrome, which is XO, meaning there's a whole chromosome missing: are these people to marry no one at all? And Swyer Syndrome babies look female but they're purely XY; their Y chromosome is without the sex-determining segment. This means they won't get testes or their accompanying masculinizing hormones, so in utero the fetus will feminize. She'll end up with a uterus but no ovaries. Should these people have to marry someone who, by all outward appearances, looks like the same sex, just because their chromosomes are different? Speaking of which, the Texas law means that a transsexual gay couple—wherein one partner is chromosomally male, for instance, and the other is chromosomally female, but they both look, feel, and act male—can get married in Texas. Gay marriage wins a point, sort of, but everybody's confused. Lawyer Julie Greenberg outlined many of these cases and the conundrums they kicked up in her seminal paper, "Defining Male and Female: Intersexuality and the Collision Between Law and Biology," in the *Arizona Law Review* in 1999.

In Kansas a similar marriage case rolled through the courts in 2002, but this time the judge ruled that gender was based on physical characteristics. A transwoman named J'Noel Gardiner had to sue for part of her deceased husband's $2.5 million estate, after the man's son contested their marriage based on J'Noel's transsexuality. The judge ruled in favor of the son, relying on *Webster's New College Dictionary* definition of female as "the sex that produces ova and bears young" and male as "the sex that has organs to produce spermatozoa for fertilizing ova."

Once again, the trouble with trying to define gender in *any* way is that human beings do not fall neatly into two distinct camps. Plenty of females are unable to produce ova and bear young: some are born without ovaries or fallopian tubes, and there are people with persistent Müllerian duct syndrome, who have testes alongside fallopian tubes and a uterus.

If gender can't be defined by chromosomes or organs, it also can't be defined by our hormones: we all have ranging levels of testosterone and estrogen. And gender certainly can't be defined by external characteristics, as individual nether regions can vary wildly. About 1 percent of all live births are intersex—meaning the reproductive or sexual anatomy doesn't fit the typical definitions of male or female. Some of these people, formerly called hermaphrodites, have both a penis and vagina, or testes and a vagina, or an elongated clitoris that could be a small penis, or variations therein. Others have chromosomal anomalies or genital variances that appear later in life, like at puberty. If the courts continue to splice gender into narrower and narrower definitions, we get more and more people who fall outside the law. One percent is a huge figure: it puts close to three million Americans in questionable territory with any law that concerns gender. Marriage laws, sexual harassment or assault laws, employment laws, welfare laws—even the way we sentence criminals can depend on sex and gender.

There's often a sort of uneasy peace between the intersex and transgender communities. Their issues and needs are very different, but there is overlap and occasional resentment because the mainstream can lump them together. "We were born this way, and they're *choosing* to be transsexual" is a common complaint from more conservative intersex people who want to be considered a medical anomaly and not social freaks. Then again, many transsexuals would argue that they were born that way too; there's a contingent that feels that transsexuality is probably neurologically intersex. (Until we know more about the workings of the brain, no one can say for sure.) In any case, while intersexuality is defined as a physiological mismatch between chromosomes or organs and one's genitalia, and transsexuality is a psychological mismatch between the mind or soul and one's genitalia, the syndromes both produce people that evidence a continuum between "male" and "female." Both necessitate a society that makes room for more than two.

Universities, unlike prisons, are an American institution that's a little more flexible and accommodating. In the past few years, a handful of colleges have been adding transgender halls to their dorms, where trans students can live with one another or with supportive non-trans roommates. Brown's housing questionnaire allows kids to check a "gender-neutral" box, and at the women's college Smith, students recently voted to eliminate female pronouns from the constitution to make their female-to-male students feel more comfortable. At Wesleyan, in Connecticut, transkids can live in a transgender hall. Ohio University is one of maybe a dozen colleges that have specifically been designating and building separate single-stall or unisex restrooms, to accommodate transgender students and staff who don't look male or female "enough" to safely traipse through public restrooms. At the New College of California in San Francisco, every single last bathroom is gender-neutral.

This bathroom amendment is a rarity; the stick figure man and the lady in the triangle dress are ubiquitous, and they signal fear for many transgender people, especially those who don't pass well or don't choose to mainstream their look. The San Francisco Human Rights Commission surveyed 195 transgender people about their public restroom experiences, and they all wished for gender-neutral bathrooms in common areas. A large portion also wrote about their experiences, which ranged from glares and stares, to shouts of "There's a man in here," to beatings, to interventions by police or security. People also reported damage to their bladders and pressure on their kidneys from "holding it" too long, and even kids I know actively limit their water intake throughout the day just to avoid having to go to the bathroom. Considering that most people urinate an average of six times a day, that's a lot of mental stress to repeatedly face. There are now at least two public advocacy groups fighting to create more unisex bathrooms, in public spaces of all kinds. One is the Sylvia Rivera Law Project in New York (named after the transwoman who kicked off the Stonewall riots), and one is the San Francisco–based People In Search of Safer Restrooms (PISSR).

Another institution that keeps people locked into one gender or another is the government: any driver's license, social security card, or passport has a clearly stamped *M* or *F* on it. Presenting these papers and cards to employers or border agents can be humiliating and self-defeating, and getting these documents changed can be difficult, something I would discover when I helped Christina switch her California ID from Eduardo to Christina—later, when she had resumed speaking to me and was once again visiting on weekends.

It was a Saturday, and Christina and I were a number in a long line of numbers at the Department of Motor Vehicles. Babies were crying, teenagers were talking on cell phones, and adults were fanning themselves with the driving instruction booklets. It was hot. Christina had worn a silver sparkly blouse I had bought her, and her hair was piled on her head in an updo. She wanted to look good for her picture.

To get a name and gender change on a license or identification card in California, you have to obtain a special "change of name and gender" form called the DL-328, along with a letter from a doctor saying you are indeed transsexual. Christina had the form and a letter from Dr. Belzer. When her number was called, she presented them at the window.

"I need a new ID card," Christina said, a little defensively but mostly rushed, to the DMV attendant. The woman looked tired and had permed, dyed black hair that sat in tight curls against her scalp. She wore a green polyester top and had pictures of her kids taped to her workstation.

"Okay . . . ," the woman said, thumbing the documents, "I see you have a name-change form here—but did you go before a judge?"

If a person is going to formally and legally change his name in California, he must make an appointment with the county courthouse and place an ad in the classified section of the local paper stating his intention. He then goes before a judge, and if no one has protested via the newspaper ad, the request is granted. Because of the transgender-specific DL-328 form, transgender people are spared this nuisance. I tried to explain this to both Christina and the DMV woman, but Christina had already burst into tears and run out the front door shrieking, "See! I told you it wouldn't work!" Tight-curls was waving the next customer to her window.

"Wait," I said. "She has all the proper forms here. My client is transgender. All she needs is the DL-328, her old male identification, and the letter from her doctor."

I had no idea where the words "my client" came from, but there they were, sitting between me and Tight-curls like a rock. The next customer, an older man with a cane, breathed impatiently at my shoulder.

"Well, I've never heard of this," Tight-curls answered. "When people change their names, they need legal name-change documentation. Let me talk to a supervisor."

The woman called over a few other DMV employees to a central desk. I overheard her tell snippets of the story of "Eduardo's ID" and "wants a new one" and "doctor's note." A blond man shook his head. Tight-curls walked back to me.

"I'm sorry, ma'am, but my supervisor says this is not possible. We don't process this form here, and if Eduardo wants to get a name change, he'll have to do it the normal way."

"Actually, you do process this form here," I said, emboldened by what I knew was right. I had researched the law before we arrived and, after the "my client" slip, decided to press my luck. "Every DMV in the state of California processes this form. I am an attorney with the ACLU and that was my client. As you can see, she is very upset by this process."

At that moment Christina appeared at my elbow. She smelled like cigarettes. "The DL-328 is a form that protects and serves transgender citizens and was legalized in 1997," I said. I realized that I sounded like a complete buffoon (wasn't "protect and serve" a military line?), and I was making up facts. I didn't know anything about the year. I reined it in. "Is there someone I could talk to at your DMV headquarters? Could we call Sacramento?"

Tight-curls nodded and went back to her supervisor, who, miraculously, put through a call and handed me the phone. I gave the attorney line again with Christina nodding solemnly by my side, and this time the person knew everything about the DL-328. She said Christina should be processed right away, and repeated that to the supervisor.

"I'm so sorry, ma'am," Tight-curls said to me. She was nice, actually. She tried to get Christina to make eye contact. "And I'm really sorry to you. I just didn't know."

Christina gave Tight-curls the tiniest of nods and then practically skipped over to the photo area, hugging me and whooping. There, she couldn't stop grinning. The photo on her ID, despite the smudged makeup from crying, looks like she just won an Oscar.

It's tougher if you want to change the gender on your passport: for this you generally need to have had sex reassignment surgery. If you can't afford it or don't want it, it's likely that you'll have to travel with the wrong gender marker on your passport and risk questioning at borders. If you are scheduled to have surgery within a year, you can usually get a passport with the correct gender marker on a temporary basis, but you'll have to provide a surgeon's letter at the end of the year or your passport will be reissued.

There are similar requirements for changing your birth certificate, though it varies state by state. California, for instance, allows you to change the gender on your California birth certificate if you have undergone "surgical treatment for the purpose of altering [your] sexual characteristics to those of the opposite sex." What "surgical treatment" means, however, can be open for interpretation, and a carefully worded letter and a good judge can sometimes equal a new certificate without all the expensive surgeries. Other states are more explicit: they demand proof of a physician's physical examination of the "sex-change operation." And in Tennessee you can't change your birth certificate, no matter what you've done to your body.

This idea of trying to "fix" what went wrong at birth can go the other direction too: sometimes when parents see their children acting like the "wrong" gender, they'll take them to doctors for help. Parents can choose to have kids psychologically treated for gender identity disorder (GID), since it's listed in the American Psychiatric Association's *DSM-IV* as a mental disorder. Some of the criteria for a childhood GID diagnosis are: the repeated desire to be the other sex; in boys, the preference for cross-dressing or simulating female attire; in girls, insistence on wearing only stereotypical masculine clothing; intense desire to participate in the stereotypical games and pastimes of the other sex; and strong preference for playmates of the other sex. Interestingly, GID rarely manifests in a pure form; rather it shows up as behavioral difficulties in relationships with peers or parents. In other words, the kids don't have problems with themselves—they have problems with not fitting in.

Pathologizing what's societally unacceptable isn't new; in the late 1800s, women were classified as sexual inverts if they had "a dislike and sometimes incapacity for needlework" as well as an "inclination and taste for the sciences." Men could be inverts if they "never smoked," were "entirely averse to outdoor games," and "liked cats." The perception of what counts as gender-appropriate behavior is entirely dictated by one's culture and time. There's been some movement, in the published literature and among GLBT organizations, to revoke GID's disorder status for children and adults, but so far GID is still on the books.

Because the treatment for GID is handled privately in therapists' offices or school counseling rooms, there's no way to quantify how often parents are bringing in their kids, but a common therapeutic response has been to set limits on cross-gender behavior, encourage same-sex friendships and sex-typical play, and make the child "correctly" identify himself as a boy or girl. Thankfully, this kind of treatment may be shifting somewhat, since the American Psychological Association released a statement in 1997 saying so-called reparative therapies that "fix" gay people and make them straight do more harm than good. While treatment for GID is not designed expressly to tamp down homosexual tendencies, many gender-variant children do turn out to be gay (while fewer end up transsexual), and some parents are looking to cure them of potential homosexuality. In the end, "curing" these kids of GID does have an anti-gay, reparative therapy-like effect, so these programs may be on the decline.

The kind of treatment a family or cross-gender child receives from their community probably depends a lot on where they're living. For instance, I know a woman in Arizona whose toddler son was fascinated when he saw her painting her toenails. He asked if she'd paint his and she did. The other parents and administrators at the boy's day care, however, were so upset by this display that they asked her to remove the polish before he returned the next day. The boy was two.

A more famous case involved a biologically male kindergartener in Ohio. This child, who chose the name Aurora after a character in a Disney movie, believed she was a girl since she was two, her parents claimed, and wanted to wear girl clothes and be called by the female pronoun. The parents explained this to the principal, when they enrolled Aurora in the fall of 2000, and shortly thereafter an anonymous caller tipped off Child Services. Claiming that Aurora was "suffering from illness" (gender identity disorder) that wasn't being properly treated, a magistrate ordered Aurora into foster care, where she was called Zachary and made to dress and act as a boy. The parents, fighting in the courts for custody, were allowed only supervised contact.

The case was further complicated by the fact that the parents had various mental health issues, so it wasn't as simple as "good parents, bad school." Still, the child was removed from the home for being allowed to attend school as a girl, and now there's a gag order on this case, so there's no official word about its conclusion. The parents divorced shortly after Aurora's removal, and there's some indication on the transgender message boards that the mother currently has custody, but there's no real verification. Still, the gag order itself is interesting in its implications: first, that parents should not allow their children to experiment with gender, and then, if they do, they should certainly not talk about it.

This all makes me wonder what would have happened to Domineque, to Lenora, to Christina, had their parents been better equipped to raise them. If they had been supported fully and allowed to express whatever inborn "nature" they felt, would they, too, have been Auroras as children? And then would they have just ended up in the courts and foster care anyway?

When she was fifteen, Domineque actually contacted her birth mother, Inez, again. Inez was clean, and had been for a number of years. She was still with Ruben, the stepfather that Domineque knew, and the two of them had become sober largely through the support of their church. Inez had custody of two of her biological children, both Ruben's. All of the other five kids were wards of the state. Inez was living in South L.A.; she was thirty-three years old.

"When I saw her, she started crying and told me she was sorry she wasn't able to take care of me, and I was like, 'Oh my god, don't!' I didn't want to cry," Domineque said. Seeing her firstborn son as a woman was a nonissue for Inez; her own past misdeeds and desire for forgiveness overshadowed any judgment that might have billowed up. "I got a pass," Domineque said, laughing wryly.

That first day at her birth mother's place, Domineque stayed for five hours. Inez looked the same physically, Domineque said, but she felt different, almost as though she had a different aura about her. Domineque mentioned this at the beginning of the visit, and Inez said it was because she was off the drugs. She told Domineque that she and the children attended church and church events probably three times a week. She then called over the kids.

"She said, 'Meet your big sister. Her name is Domineque.' I was shocked when she said that, and could tell that she was accepting me as a girl and not a confused young boy," Domineque remembered. Her siblings were three and four. "I reached down to say hello, and they automatically stuck out their arms to hug me. I started to cry. Even though it was my first time meeting them, I had so much love for them."

Domineque, however, couldn't emote as easily to her mom. She couldn't say she loved her—only that she missed her and had thought about her every day—and she didn't offer her forgiveness, because she wasn't sure she felt it. Years later, Domineque explained it like this: "I don't blame her because I understand the craving [for crack], but I don't completely forgive her either."

Domineque understood the craving because by her late teens she was deep into drugs on her own. She was fourteen the first time she tried crack. She was with friends in a motel room, and she was thinking about her mother the entire time. In fact, for Domineque, the hit on the pipe was more of a psychological experiment than a physiological one.

"I wanted to know what could be so good about a drug that could make my mom give up her kids for it. What could make you buy a rock before putting shoes on your child?" Domineque said. "And then when I tried it, I knew: I was the happiest I'd ever been in my entire life.

"You can get hooked the first time—and I want you to underline that," Domineque said to me once when I was taking notes on our conversation. "Crack feels like heaven."

Crack continued to have a special lure for Domineque because of her mother's dependence on it, and Domineque continued to use it even when she was living with Andrea, who was helping her feel stable and loved.

"To me, Andrea will always be my mom," Domineque told me, even though she only lived with her continuously for two and a half years. Andrea was the first person to call Domineque her daughter, and she stuck by Domineque through five or six rounds of juvenile hall and detention camps. On the sixth of every month, which was the date that Domineque first came to live with Andrea and Richard, the family celebrated Domineque coming into their lives. Often Andrea and Domineque went to get their nails done on that day. Domineque got long white tips, and Andrea got airbrushed daisies on her toes.

Their actual beginning wasn't so sentimental. As her social worker, Andrea knew Domineque had depleted her resources: the kid had failed at a traditional group home, and she had failed with a single parent caring only for Domineque and her biological brother; foster agencies were going to throw up their arms. While she realized she herself was one of Domineque's few hopes, she actually had to trick her into an offer of living together. Andrea called Shavonne to help.

Shavonne asked Domineque to hang out in Macarthur Park, but didn't tell her Andrea would be there. "Domineque was not too happy with Shavonne; she felt she betrayed her," Andrea recalled. So she kept the interaction short. "I just gave Domineque my cell phone number and said, 'Call me when you want something different.'"

Four weeks later Domineque called. She ran away from the boyfriend when he was out of the apartment. When Andrea picked her up on a street corner, Domineque only had a backpack to her name.

No matter how much Domineque may now think of Andrea as her "real" mom, and no matter how much Andrea tried to be that when they lived together, there was always an impossible roadblock between them. And that roadblock was the "real mom." "I think Domineque's drug of choice was crack because that was her mom's drug of choice; that had more of a linkage to her," Andrea says now. "She was working out 'Why did my mom make the decisions that she did? Why did my mom let everything go?' And she found out the hard way."

Lenora, Foxx's drag daughter, had also been abandoned by her birth mother—but this mother left an infant Lenora and her older brothers and sisters with the children's grandparents, who raised the kids in Puerto Vallarta. There was no foster care in the early years, no shuttling around, no drugs. Lenora calls her grandparents Mom and Dad. Lenora's adult siblings couldn't support her financially when they moved to the United States, so they let her go into the system but still saw her regularly. Lenora's grandparents called every week; they missed her, but believed she would have a better life in the States.

Domineque and Lenora were both foster kids, both transgender, both of Mexican descent, both experienced with poverty and the streets of Los Angeles. And yet, at seventeen, Lenora was working every day after school and sending money home to her grandparents in Puerto Vallarta. Domineque was doing drugs and going in and out of juvenile hall. Their behavior had nothing to do with being transgender. It had to do with whether they had a constant loving family in their early years. Domineque was looking to fill what had long ago been scooped out of her.

I saw this pattern again and again. The transgender kids that did the best were the ones who had an interior well of confidence to draw from, a sense that they were worthy and lovable, formed by family—formed somewhere before their gender was even internally articulated. The kids like Ariel, Lenora, Foxx. The Christinas, the Domineques, may have blamed their pain on being transgender, but the roots were nestled somewhere deeper. And no loving too late could take that hurt away completely.

# 8

# SKIDMARKS

$\mathcal{C}$HRISTINA RESUMED SPEAKING to me about four weeks after she had stopped. Domineque had gone into juvenile hall for violating probation, and Christina was bored. She called abruptly, like nothing had happened, wanting to know what I thought of Gwen Stefani's new CD. We talked about Domineque and how it was hard living with Andrea and Richard without her. I asked about her month of silence, and she didn't say anything about the J.Lo poster, only that she had needed time. She admitted that she missed me and Robin and that she wanted to see us, to stay with us for the weekend. I suggested we do something simple first, like go to the Museum of Contemporary Art. She said she'd never been to a museum.

The day I picked her up at Andrea's, she was the only one home. She had her own room, with a single bed and the clothes bins we had bought her at the Home Depot and bright girly things like a puffy bedspread, a glittery tiered makeup box, and a lamp with a ruffle. Andrea was trying to make her feel welcome, I could see. Still, the place was a disaster—clothes everywhere in twisted, scrambled heaps, CD cases and keys and lighters spilling off the bedside table, and dust already thick on the windowsill and bureau.

"Are you going to get dressed?" I asked Christina after she barely hugged me and I told her how glad I was to see her. She was wearing silver jeans so small that the seams on the thighs were strained and the front would neither button nor zip and was splayed open as a wide V at her crotch. Here she wore lace G-string panties, the lace showing the shaved pubic area beneath. On top she wore only a bra, stuffed full, so her then-minimal cleavage, taped and strapped for maximum effect, could spill up as though in some kind of prepubescent Victorian undergarment. Her makeup was drag-queen harsh, all greens and golds and black liner. Makeup was Christina's "DO NOT CROSS" warning sign, the flares she put out to prevent oncoming traffic from colliding with her. She normally wore only lip gloss and a little mascara.

"I *am* dressed," Christina said shrilly, checking her eyebrows in the bathroom she and Domineque shared, which was cluttered with beauty products and smelled like raspberries, gardenias, and mold.

"I'm not going out with you dressed like that," I answered.

"That's so fucked up," Christina said to the mirror. "I don't tell you how to dress. I don't criticize you."

I tried a different tactic, one that failed. "You'll be embarrassed, once we're out there. You don't want your entire crotch shining in the sun. You know the men will harass you."

"No, *you'll* be embarrassed. I don't give a shit what no man thinks. I'm not looking to get with no trade. I'm only looking out for me now—Christina is it. Ain't nobody else looking out for me, so I gotta do it myself."

I took her bait. "Christina, you've got a lot of people looking out for you—me, Robin, Andrea. We all love you. Now put some clothes on."

"Fuck!" she shouted, and shoved past me. Her shoulder jammed into mine like a limp, though intentional, punch. She came back wearing a gray sweatshirt, zipped up to her bra line, the bottom part covering her unzipped jeans. Fine, I thought, and we drove to the museum, Christina blaring the radio and leaning on the car horn when I couldn't swat her hand away fast enough.

At the museum, the only art Christina showed any interest in was a mountain of pillows, probably fourteen feet high. Visitors were told they could climb the mountain, as long as they took off their shoes, and it was mostly being scaled by eight-year-old boys, who stealthily whacked one another with the pillows before being reprimanded by attendant guards, and then they slid down the other side on their bellies. Christina's eyes gleamed. While a few adults giggled as they slipped their way up the slope, cameras swinging around their necks, arms clutching at silky pillows that only glided away, Christina strode up the mountain like she was a giant in cleats. She took it in four big strides and stood at the top, pelting pillows at the boys, a little too hard.

"Miss, the pillows aren't for throwing," a guard intoned, leaning in.

Christina glowered and jumped down onto her butt, crashing her way to the bottom of the exhibit. She pulled on her shoes and took my hand as she sashayed out, flashing a mean grin at the guard.

In the next hall, Christina continued to hold my hand nicely for a few minutes but then dug her long nails into my palm, leaving welts, laughing showily. I told her we had to go. She marched away, unzipping the sweatshirt, exposing herself. I cursed myself for going to the museum anyway, for thinking the sweatshirt would be enough, and waited for the guards to throw her out. She came back to me, sweatshirt off completely now, smiling toothily at the men that stared at her in her bra and unzipped jeans. "What?" she snapped.

In the car I tried to get her to open up. We picked up Robin, who had been at work, but Christina wouldn't talk to her either.

"Is something going on at Andrea's?" I asked. No response.

"Are you missing Domineque?"

"Are you mad at me or Robin?"

"Can you please tell me what's behind all this?"

"Do you have to be such an impossible shithead?"

Christina was entirely silent; she kicked her boots into the dashboard and refused to speak. We drove her home to Andrea's, and she slammed the car door hard.

The subsequent weekends were filled with such conduct, spotted with hopeful bursts of lucidity, where Christina would talk about her plans to graduate from high school and work as a counselor or social worker for kids like her, or she would talk about men and the ways she needed to love the bruised bits of herself before she could hope for them to treat her with respect. But mostly our weekends looked a lot like the one at the museum, where Christina was punishing us and testing the limits of our love.

I remember a trip to the movies where a sickly sweet smell kept wafting up from the seats between Christina's bursts of "*Eww!* What *is* that?!" People turned around to stare, and Christina would say loudly, "Ma'am—would you please go wash off your perfume? It's disgusting." I couldn't catch her, but I could tell what she was doing from the smell: she was squeezing a bathroom air freshener shaped like a purple hippo that a friend had brought back from Korea. By the time the movie reached its emotional crisis point, the people sitting around us were gagging. I grabbed Christina's wrist, but her hands were empty, her face staring placidly at the screen. When I finally glimpsed some purple plastic in her purse and made a lunge for it, she screamed at top volume. "*Aaaa!* She's trying to molest my hippo! Mr. Hippo! Mr. Hippo!" We had to leave.

Christina smoked weed in our apartment's parking lot to see what we would do, and stayed out past the curfews that we set, and threatened several times to jump out of the moving car, and was rude and sulky and stormy and mean. Screaming scenes were common, especially while driving. She loved to yell inflammatory remarks like "Nigger! She wants to suck your cock!" to passersby while I was behind the wheel. Sometimes she'd duck so they could only see me. Once, after we caught her with Mike's Hard Lemonade under her bed and threw it away because she obviously wasn't allowed to have alcohol in the house, she ran away for a few days. She couldn't even keep a straight face when she raged against our "unfairness," though; it was like half of her knew she was being ridiculous, and the other half had to follow through on the act.

She was especially difficult when we picked up her biological sister, Vicki, from their mother's house so the girls could spend an evening together. Christina desperately wanted the time with her sister but was jealous of any attention we gave to Vicki, and any familial love she wanted to dole out was scrambled and choked by the fact that Vicki was allowed to live at home with their mom. While Vicki had done her rounds with the aunts and with a few foster parents, she always got to come back. For the past six years, from Christina's perspective, Vicki had been the wanted child while she herself had been consistently shunted off to group homes, foster care, or the street. So while we often brought the kids together for movies or meals, it always felt like punishment. Christina would revert to a ten- or twelve-year-old version of herself, pinching Vicki in the backseat of the car, trying to make her scream. Or she'd put on her headphones and ignore Vicki entirely, yelling lyrics to drown out her sister's answers to our questions about school or friends. Still, she'd frequently beg us to pick up Vicki whenever we were out.

Christina wasn't doing much better at Andrea and Richard's, though her storms manifested differently. There she was just silent. She didn't consider them parental the way she did me and Robin, so she mostly just stayed out until her curfew and then burrowed in her room, not answering Andrea's questions about her well-being or responding at the dinner table. She felt that she was a charity case—taken in because she was Domineque's friend. But with Domineque gone, Christina's place was more tentative, and her reaction was to ice over.

When Domineque got out of juvenile hall, Christina had a purpose in the family again, and that was to keep her friend off drugs. She'd initiated a few positive changes—she picked up an after-school job—but she started skipping school to be with Domineque, so she could lead her away from temptation, encouraging her to at least stay home and watch Angelina Jolie movies again and again. This was Christina's story to me; Andrea wasn't sure who was leading whom into dangerous territory—but both girls were turning up truant and coming home possibly high.

Christina and Domineque were always climbing into cars with boys they didn't know, who didn't know about them. They would kiss guys they had just met—guys who were teenagers, and guys who were full-grown men. They would drink Cisco. Christina said she would smoke pot, and Domineque would smoke anything else. One particularly terrible night, they partied with some guys they met on the street who offered them some weed and probably speed, though Christina doesn't like to talk about that night now, so I'm not entirely sure. They started out just driving around, and they ended up in a motel room. Christina got nervous as the drugs got more intense and the pressure on the girls to put out escalated too. Christina knew, as all women know, that the risk of rape goes up when you mix drugs and strangers and a late hour and an enclosed space with only one exit. She also knew that the risk for transwomen is even higher: when men feel duped or tricked because they thought they were partying with "real" women, they can blow up and become violent.

Many transwomen are beaten or killed for such deceptions, or raped for revenge, though on a national scale, this is only anecdotal— no one's officially keeping a regular count. The government compiles data on hate crimes based on sexual orientation, though their numbers are unequivocally low. (I, for example, have been verbally threatened with rape in my neighborhood "for being a dyke" while walking hand in hand with Robin. This technically is verbal assault, though I've never taken the time to report it.) The FBI tallied 1,406 sexual orientation hate crimes in 2004. They don't have a category for anti-trans crime offenses, so we have to look to more local statistics and extrapolate. For instance, the San Francisco Department of Public Health conducted a survey in 1997 and found that of 392 male-to-female transsexuals, 37 percent had suffered abuse within the past twelve months, and 59 percent reported a history of rape.

Christina tried to get Domineque to go home with her, as the men didn't know their transgender status, but Domineque wanted more drugs. Christina got scared and went home. Domineque stayed and was gang-raped by four men in the motel bathroom. Her head was smashed against the sink.

Every time I've tried to ask Christina about that terrible night, she's gotten furious—demanding why I always have to bring up the past. She feels responsible. I don't want to make Domineque dredge it up again, so I don't really know the details of what happened— what part of town they were in, what time of night it was, or whether the men were even caught. I do know that Domineque's drug use intensified after the rape, and her attitude about consequences or juvenile hall deteriorated. She seemed to stop caring about everything.

Before Domineque went to jail again, Christina turned eighteen. We had been planning the party for weeks—it was going to be at our house, with Domineque and Andrea and Christina's sister, Vicki, and maybe one of Christina's friends from her old group home. Three days before the slated Saturday, Vicki called. Could we have the party at her house instead? She had talked to her mother: it would be fine. Vicki said Gloria would even be there, and that would mean so much to Christina. Vicki, who was then thirteen, would handle all the decorations if we would bring the food.

The walls of Christina's mother's house are covered in pictures. The living room showcases oversize photographs of Vicki. There are none of Christina. In the hallway that leads to the bedrooms are the older family photos, and here are pictures of Christina as a baby, as Eduardo. He is fat and drooly, hair slicked back with water, one new tooth shining its way out of a fleshy gum. There is Eduardo as a ten-year-old, sitting in a wicker chair in dress pants and shiny shoes, his eyes far away and his jaw set, and there is another with him as a first grader all dressed up with other relatives in gowns and suits; he's squirming to get away. Even though the photos are from the late eighties and early nineties, they are already yellowing, making them seem from a different era, which in a way they are.

When Robin and I pulled up to the house, Vicki was taping yellow crepe paper to the yellow door frame. Nobody else was home, so the three of us dragged a table out to the backyard and set up all the sodas and chips and snacks and tried to rig the stereo speakers out the window. Gloria was supposedly out buying a birthday cake, which both Vicki and Christina, who had had a brief telephone conversation with her a few days prior, assured me she would do. I was dubious but hopeful for Christina's sake.

Christina and Domineque arrived in top-to-bottom black, as though they were going to a nightclub in Manhattan. Christina rushed through the house in leather stiletto boots and silver dangle earrings, waving one arm and happily shouting "Heyyyyy!" as if friends and fans were running toward her. Her makeup was mild, I noted with relief, but her real hair was hidden under an iron-straight black wig, pulled back with a headband. She looked about twenty-five. Vicki stared up at her adoringly.

For a while we all sat around outside, listening to Domineque's brother Tad, who had come along with Andrea, tell funny stories about the punk rock band he was starting. Tad was fifteen and still lived with Johnny, the foster dad Domineque had run from. Then some cousins arrived, the children of Gloria's sisters—many hadn't seen Christina for a few years and were curious.

Gloria herself arrived an hour late, with one of the aunts. She was all smiles; she hugged me and Robin and Andrea as though we were mere guests in her home, as though we hadn't been appointed the guardians of her child. She nodded at Christina, and Christina kissed her cheek. Gloria's English is poor; I pretended I spoke less Spanish than I do, and she went back inside when communication proved difficult.

Christina, however, was thrilled. Here she was, with all of her variations of "mom" collected in one place for one afternoon. She laughed easily and at everything, and kept jumping up to hug her three-year-old cousin or to repeat a song on the stereo so she and Domineque could crack up over a line they made dirty by transposing a few of the lyrics. Pretty soon Gloria came back outside with the cake. We all quietly gasped when we saw that it was made for girls: on top was a knockoff Barbie and mounds of pink roses. The name, however, was wrong. In loopy cursive a clerk had iced: *"Happy Birthday, CHRISTIAN."*

Even that couldn't dent Christina's buoyant mood. She winced but brightly blew out her candle. The Barbie was triumph enough. Her aunt handed over a card addressed to Eduardo, full of messages about Jesus helping her through, and Vicki gave Christina a solar-powered radio, so if ever she was stuck without batteries, she could still have her music. Robin and I gave Christina a camera, so she could take her own pictures with which to someday fill her own walls. Christina pronounced it the best day of her life.

Within a few months, Domineque would be back in juvie, this time for stealing Andrea's car. Andrea herself called the police when she realized what had happened, knowing that Domineque was driving without a license, knowing that she was likely driving high.

It wasn't the first time she had called the police, though this string of arrests wasn't Andrea's planned trajectory for her foster daughter. When Andrea first brought Domineque home, she thought the high drama was behind her. "I thought, 'It'll be okay—she's in a safe place. It'll get better now,'" Andrea said. She had originally attributed Domineque's bad behavior to her run of bad luck. "But then it didn't get better."

So while Andrea's love for Domineque remained abundant and sprawling, her own rules had to become more rigid and corrective. Andrea was forever teaching "personal choice." Whenever Domineque would threaten to break curfew or go out when she was grounded, Andrea wouldn't get angry. She would simply say, "That's your choice. But then you'll be grounded next weekend too, and you can't go to that party next month." If Domineque threatened to cut off her ankle bracelet tracker when she was under house arrest, Andrea would calmly reply, "That is your choice. But you will get a warrant, and you will be given more time."

But the message never got through. Somewhere inside, when Domineque heard that her latest stunt would yield more punishment, she thought, "Good." It was, to my mind, an extreme form of Christina's cutting: if Domineque could make the pain of her outside reality match the pain of her inside reality, then her worlds aligned and she could relax. At least that's the way I saw it—too much love and decency is hard to take when you think it's not deserved.

I saw a similar tendency to push love away in Christina, with both me and Robin and with her boyfriends. For instance, several months later Christina met a boy named Francisco on the bus. A few years older than she was, Francisco worked in a factory that made party supplies. Francisco was gentle and soft-spoken and when Christina told him right away that she was transgender, he asked what that was. Most men, at this point, turned away, with varying degrees of disgust or shock or confusion, but Francisco's response was measured. He sat there quietly for a few moments and then got her pager number and asked her to the movies that next weekend, along with his female cousin and her friend. Christina was stunned that he'd introduce her to family so fast. In her diary from that time, a green journal with a photograph of a wolf on the cover, Christina wrote, "Fuck, he's so cute. And heavyset too." She always has liked chubby men, men she can pillow into, men who can dwarf her already smallish frame. She went on, "Even though we were in public, he was great with me. Kissing me and holding me. I was loving it."

Francisco was one of the few boyfriends Christina brought home to me and Robin; the rest she knew were too thuggish to pass our scrutiny. Francisco was like an adoring pup, always wanting to be next to Christina, appreciating her fierce humor—the way she would turn a term like "an administrator" into "an ad-menstruater" when she asked to see a female official, or how she could reference three movies and a Britney Spears song in a single sentence when talking about the groceries. Francisco brought Christina home to meet his parents, who lived a few hours away, and Christina called us in a panic; she didn't know how to cook—how was she supposed to bond with his mother and grandma? She also wanted to make breakfast for the family in the morning, to thank them for their hospitality, but she'd never even cracked an egg. This is a problem for many transwomen; they may have felt female since preschool, but they were still raised as little boys. They were never taught the things genetic women take for granted, like how to cook or take care of small children. Robin told Christina to buy some instant pancake mix—the instructions would be on the box—and Christina didn't even burn one.

Francisco didn't tell his family about Christina's status; he didn't think they'd understand. But it seemed there was never a flinch or second thought on his part about being with a transgirl, even when they started having sex, some few months into the relationship. But this was right around when Christina started to get bored. Francisco was too nice, she complained, not exciting anymore, and she sounded like the countless genetic women I knew who, despite protests to the contrary, wanted only bad boys.

So, just as Francisco was committing himself more passionately, talking of moving in together, and starting to save some of his paycheck each month to help her pay for the surgery if that was what she wanted, Christina met a guy named Loco.

Loco, like most of Christina's paramours, spotted Christina on the street or, more specifically, in a park where she was rolling a joint and drinking a beer trying, as she said, to relax. Loco liked this in a girl and came up to Christina and asked her if she wanted to kick it. His parents were away in Tijuana, he said; they'd have the house to themselves.

Unlike Francisco, Loco was stocky and tough looking; he had tattoos and had lost the baby fat that made Francisco still get carded for cigarettes. Loco immediately brought Christina to his bedroom, where she should have known he was a player. He had dozens of girls' numbers taped to his bureau mirror. Christina got defensive and asked him why he wasn't calling one of them instead, but he charmed her by pulling out a coral necklace he had lying beside the bed. Then he kissed her.

Christina kissed back, but she was worried. She always worried at this point in a date; Loco didn't know she was transgender, and she wasn't sure how he'd react. She let him pull off her shirt, and together they noticed they had matching tattoos on their biceps. In Olde English script were the black letters *A.T.C.* Loco was from her gang.

"How'd you get that?" Loco asked.

Christina's stomach clenched. The moment of reckoning. "I got jumped in."

A flicker of disbelief went over Loco's face. Only boys were in A.T.C.

"That's impossible. All of the homies are guys."

"I know," she answered. "All of us were."

"What?" Loco answered, screwing up his face. "What?"

Christina bit her lip. Then Loco got it. He looked closely at her face, and her body, and then simply went back to kissing her, more gently this time. He knew what she was and he accepted her. It was perhaps because of this—a sort of sign of recognition from a past Christina felt had spurned her—that made her fall in love so fast. They slept together that day, and as they hung out afterward, they realized an amazing coincidence: Loco was the gangster who had jumped Christina into the gang and then disappeared.

This link was intoxicating for Christina, and Loco, unlike Francisco, prompted a kind of hunger that didn't have her writing in her diary about how cute he was, or about how he held her or kissed her. She wrote, "It's about time a man can do me like a man should." What she meant was aggressive, dominant, and rough. She stopped talking to Francisco the week she met Loco; she simply didn't return his calls. When he finally stopped leaving messages, she convinced herself that he hadn't wanted her anyway: her empty pager was proof of his inevitable lack of interest.

Christina was in love with Loco, more so, she said, than she'd ever been with anyone else. He was from her male childhood, and he accepted her. Sort of. Loco didn't like Christina hanging around his homeboys; he got paranoid that they might pick up on her status. Even though she floated around the gang's old neighborhood quite a bit and was never clocked, Loco was afraid other gang members might remember her from their shared past, might think of him as gay. So he didn't always return Christina's phone calls, kept her crying on the phone at night with me or Robin, bemoaning men and their withholding ways.

But Loco also gave Christina a chance to be mean too, which Francisco never did. "When he'd get mad at me, I'd be like, 'What, are you going to hit me?'" Christina said—to remind him that she was once a boy, to play with fire, to tease him about his own violence, which was the part she said he didn't like about himself. When Loco protested that he would never hit her, she would push, "'Why not? You've done it before.' I would always throw that shit in his face."

But Loco's real insecurity wasn't about violence. After a few months of dating, he told a friend from the gang that he was dating a transsexual and asked if that made him gay. The answer came in the form of a phone call. To Christina.

"I was at the swap meet and Loco called me. He put this guy on the phone—who called me a faggot and said he was gonna jump me. Then Loco got on and said we were through," said Christina, who immediately started crying. She wanted to see Loco, to talk it through—but she was also afraid, because she knew he really could show up with his friend who really would beat her up. "I knew the type of people Loco went with. Back then I always put myself in dangerous situations with dangerous people, because I was looking for a way out of this world."

Christina's boyfriends often mirrored her mother's behavior: short bursts of decency followed by long stretches of denial, which were spotted with outright cruelty. It always surprised me that Gloria never inquired about where her child was living, never asked for the phone numbers of her various foster parents or caregivers, even though we came to pick up Vicki and had met her several times. Gloria's attitude toward Christina, from my perspective, was one of a disinterested neighbor. She wasn't angry when she saw her first-born, though Christina was generally rigid with anticipation whenever Gloria walked through the door; rather, Gloria would glance her direction as though there were a worker in the house nailing in carpet, and then she'd say hello to me. After the birthday party, Christina's mother went silent again for several months.

At the same time, Christina started pulling back from Robin and me. When she did let us see her, she was either manic or vaguely strung out, but she refused to talk about drugs. She was clearly using—I thought it was probably speed—and she wasn't going to school very often.

One day, I got a call from Andrea. She had come home from work early to find that the kids had been there before her: they had been skipping school and, judging by the number of beer cans lying around the living room, they hadn't been alone. Everyone ran out the front door when they heard Andrea's car in the driveway.

"Can you just come over? I need to talk," Andrea said to me over the phone. She said she found a pipe with marijuana in it on the back porch, right next to Christina's makeup bag. I could imagine it; I'd seen it before. Clear blown glass with swirls of red and green and orange held a small bowl, enough for just two hits; the pipe was short enough to hide in a fist. I remembered Andrea's rule: one sign of drug use and Christina had to go.

Andrea and Richard lived in a two-story town house with three bedrooms and a small den that Richard used as an office. There was a long narrow table when you first walked in that was covered with photographs of Domineque and Christina, and another one, built in beneath the living-room window, also jammed with frames. Andrea and I sat on one of her two overstuffed couches, her fluffy white dog Bianca, who was the size of a guinea pig but five times as happy, curled on her lap.

"I don't know what to do," Andrea said. "They know that drugs are the limit. And she left her pipe—right on the porch. Where I had to see it. "

"You can stick by the consequences you set up," I said, thinking Andrea needed to be reassured. "You were perfectly clear about what would happen if anyone used drugs in the house. And besides, they broke a lot of rules. They were skipping school. There were men in the house. They were drinking beer."

"Who's buying them beer?" Andrea asked.

"When do you think they'll come home?" I asked back.

"Who knows," she said, and asked if I wanted one of the beers—there were plenty left. We laughed; they were cheap, bad-tasting beers.

It wasn't a question that Domineque would get to continue living with Andrea and Richard; she was still a minor and they were her legal parents. She would just have to suffer the consequences of breaking house rules and be put on a tighter watch. Christina was the one on the line.

Because the girls came home that night and because Christina, out of sheer fear of another bout of rejection, apologized profusely, she got to stay. She also lied, saying the pipe was dropped by one of the boys. Andrea likely didn't want a scene—everyone was home; everyone was sober—so she just went to bed.

The incident got me and Robin talking about what we'd do if and when Andrea asked Christina to leave. We didn't have to wait long to find out. It was less than a month later that Christina and Domineque got thrown out of the alternative high school they were both attending; they got into a fistfight with a couple of other girls at school, and everyone was expelled. After that, Christina started using the house entirely as a crash pad; she claimed that she had "some job" in Hollywood, but Andrea didn't believe it—another teenager informed Andrea that Christina was doing some small-time drug dealing, which Andrea wasn't sure about but didn't put past her. Both kids, when they were home at the same time, were bickering like children. Domineque was using heavily. While no one can remember now what exactly the trigger was, Andrea and Domineque got into a tremendous argument, and Andrea hit her wall: she wanted both kids out of the house. Now. Within a few hours, I found out later, Andrea calmed down and told both girls that they could stay; they just had to respect the rules of the house. Domineque knew she'd been impossible and accepted the offer. Christina wouldn't touch it.

Robin and I were in San Francisco visiting family the day I got this message: "Girl! It's me! I just got thrown out!" Christina was sobbing and furious at once. "Can you please call my cell as soon as you get this? I didn't do nothing to those people! I wasn't even home! So I just spent my only $40 on a hotel, but I don't got no more money and, fuck! Can you please call me, girl?!"

I called her. I told her to use her key to our apartment and to stay there. That we would be home in three days. Somehow, even though Christina was using drugs, I trusted her: I knew she wouldn't let strangers into our house; I knew we wouldn't get robbed. There were years of love running between us now; we were family. She wouldn't let harm come to me like I wouldn't let harm come to her. Still, as soon as I hung up the phone, I felt sick. I wanted to rescue Christina, wanted to blanket her flailing limbs and soothe her night terrors and tuck her in to our little house, where she'd be safe forever. But the truth was that Christina was a train wreck. She was on drugs and on a self-destructive, self-hating spin. If she couldn't do well staying with Andrea, I didn't know how she'd do better with us. Now she was, technically, an emancipated adult. An adult with no money and nowhere to go. I had recently read that of the thousand foster kids that age out from foster care in Los Angeles each year, 45 percent are homeless and on the streets within six weeks of their emancipation.

Still, much as I hated myself for it, I didn't want her to move in. I suppose this was my inheritance—to wrestle with these ideas of rejection. I wouldn't let her go. But if Christina took up permanent bedship on the couch, I knew it would end up breaking all of us somehow.

When Robin and I got home from our trip, Christina was parked on the couch watching television. She had a bedspread wrapped around her and the shades drawn, and the kitchen was cluttered with fast-food bags because the trash was full and she hadn't bothered to take it out. She shuffled up to hug us smelling like socks and honey and the warmth of too much sleep, and she leaned into our bodies, but she didn't lift her arms because they were strapped down in the comforter like a mummy. I was hoping she'd be hungry for conversation after so much time on her own, but the days alone had only shut her down. We dropped our bags and asked how she was. Christina just looked at the TV and plopped backward onto the couch, steeling her eyes into slits.

"Okay," I said. "You can have a little time to be quiet. But I'm going to take a shower and make some tea, and when the tea is done, we're all going to talk. We need to come up with a plan."

Christina gave no response.

"Okay?" I asked.

"Okaaaay!" she said, too loud and annoyed, as though I'd been pestering her for many minutes, instead of just one.

Robin and I had done some research while we were away. There were two shelters she could stay at in Los Angeles that catered to people who were newly adults, and that were sensitive to transpeople's needs. One was Covenant House, where Foxx lived when she first moved to L.A. from Birmingham, and the other was a shelter run by the Gay and Lesbian Center. Both places offered job training and placement help, as well as connections to high school and GED classes. The mission of both shelters is to be a sort of urban incubator linking adolescence and adulthood. Residents enter the programs on a tight leash: there are early curfews, room checks, frequent counselor meetings, and so on. As they successfully clock their time, they earn their freedoms—eventually even qualifying for independent, subsidized apartments. The rooms are free, as long as residents are in school or working, and if they're working, the bulk of their paychecks are saved for them in a hands-off account. This way, when they leave the shelter, they're assured of a nest egg with which to kick-start their autonomous adult lives.

Christina was resigned when we told her she couldn't stay with us for more than a few weeks; she even pretended she saw it coming.

"I know, girl, I know," she said, though there was panic in her eyes. I could see the old abandonment anxiety welling up inside her and worried there'd be no way to explain that that wasn't what we were doing. "I know you ain't got room here."

"It's not just about the room," Robin said, reaching out to put a hand on Christina's knee. Christina was wearing Robin's old red flannel pajama bottoms, which she wore every time she stayed at our place. We always teased her that she looked like a lesbian in flannel, that maybe she should listen to a little more folk music instead of all her glitter pop and hang out in the granola section of the health food store to find herself a girlfriend. "It's that the shelter has all the services that we don't have. If you take advantage of it, you can have them help you get a job and get back in school. And you'll have counselors there—"

"And rules, which I think you need right now," I interrupted. Christina made a sour face.

"It's true, though, Sparrow," I said. We had taken to calling her Sparrow ever since the Dolly Parton wake-up days. What I didn't say was that I was afraid—afraid that I couldn't, or wouldn't, be enough for her. Christina needed a team of helpers: she was hating herself; she was using drugs; she was climbing into cars with gangsters and strangers; she was cutting herself, thin razor marks appearing each morning like fresh sprouts. I felt like my own arms weren't long enough to contain her, to hold her in and make her still. Yet, I felt weak and worried that this choice was the wrong one, that it could make Christina worse. Of course, I couldn't say these things.

"Robin and I have to work," I said, lamely. "You need help getting back into school and getting a job. And you need to stop doing drugs. The shelter has people who are professionals for these things."

"I'm not doing drugs," Christina said, glaring at her teacup.

I looked at Robin. The clock ticked. I didn't know what to say.

"Just weed," Christina said. "You already knew that."

"Christina, you have been doing some speed—you told me that. And with Domineque—"

"*Don't* talk about Domineque," Christina said, her tone fierce and low. This conversation was feeling all wrong.

"Fine," I said. "Look, we don't have to talk about drugs right now, but we will have to talk about it sometime. The point is, Robin and I aren't going anywhere—we're still your family. We're still here to support you with everything—getting jobs, school, homes, just like always. But you're an adult now, so you have the adult version of family—which means you stay with us when times are hard, like now—and then we help you get into your next place . . ."

I could feel myself stammering, struggling to express both love and firm expectations so she wouldn't be let down. I had no idea how to parent in this moment, and she knew it. She interrupted me.

"Can I be excused now?" she said in a nasty singsong. She shoved her chair back from the table and stomped off toward the bathroom, the cuffs of the pajamas tucked around her toes like Gumby feet. In five minutes she was dressed, striding out of the house, slamming the door.

Sometimes I hated her.

Christina came back to us that night and agreed to go to the shelter. As the next day went on and bled into the next, however, I think Christina imagined we'd cave and let her live with us again. As it became increasingly clear that we would not, Christina grew increasingly furious. She refused to talk about her future plans and refused to admit that she was using drugs, even though she had dropped ten pounds and her eyes were both sunken with exhaustion and pulsing with energy. When a bed opened up the following day, she wouldn't let me drive her to the center, and she left behind a mess of dirty dishes, a cluttered and filthy bathroom, and sheets and blankets impressively tangled on the floors of two rooms.

Whenever things were particularly difficult with Christina, Robin had this vision she would conjure for both of us. It came to her in a dream one night. The three of us were on a rooftop in some undefined city. Christina was about thirty, and she was wearing a cute black dress. She was laughing at something one of us said, then we were all laughing. We were all comfortable, older, and easy around one another. Christina was healthy and self-assured. In the dream, Robin believed that Christina had some kind of steady job and comfortable home and felt proud and happy about her life. When things seemed impossible in the present, Robin and I held on to this rooftop picture of the future Christina, believing it would all be worth it in the end.

"I left the shelter," Christina said to me flatly, between bites of a bacon cheeseburger, two days later. She was calling me from her cell phone, using day minutes, which she didn't like to do.

"What?" I said, startled but not surprised. "What do you mean? Where are you going?"

"To my mom's. I'ma stay there for a while."

At this, I was shocked. "Does she know? Have you asked her? Have you thought about this? Why didn't you tell me?"

"Girl, yes," she said. She sounded irritated and had that tone that I knew meant she would hang up soon. "She just wants the money. She's gonna charge me three hundred dollars a month to sleep on the floor."

"Wait—what?" I stammered, but Christina interrupted me.

"I already told you. Just don't look for me at the center." And she hung up.

I wasn't sure how to understand Christina's move at first: Was she trying to make her life as difficult and wrenching as possible? Was she attempting to impose some sort of backhanded guilt on Robin and me? I knew that while shelter programs have to be strict to work, the rules are often too rigid for kids accustomed to the haze and flow of the streets, and they can't take the scrutiny. But still, two days? Christina hadn't even tried.

I finally realized that however broken, unpromising, and drug-addled her outreach might be, Christina had unfinished business to reconcile. Even though she effectively had to pay her to spend time with her, Christina needed her mom. She had been on the streets or in foster care since she was twelve years old; now that she was an adult, she could pay rent and come back on more equal terms—essentially to ask the plainest of questions: you didn't see me then, but do you see me now?

Paying rent, however, was a problem because Christina didn't have a job. She hadn't prostituted since she was a young teenager and knew the stakes were higher now because she was an adult: an arrest could mean jail and a record. Still, the friends with whom she was hanging out and doing drugs were hustling, and they didn't make it seem so bad. They told her she could make $300 on a good night, $100 on a bad one. A couple of nights a month, maybe five or six, would be all it would take to pay her mom and buy food. She could still look for a legal job during the day and stop hustling as soon as she had earned a few real paychecks.

When Christina prostituted before, she was homeless and fourteen, living intermittently as a girl. It was then she got arrested and sent to Los Padrinos for a few nights, one of three juvenile detention facilities in Los Angeles County. So she was already wise to the

"Bully," or Santa Monica Boulevard, already knew how to spot the cops. She knew that cops usually travel in pairs, so as long as you get in a car with a single guy, you're probably okay. Though more than once, the police have hidden their colleagues under blankets on the floor of their unmarked cars. These sidekicks will pop out with handcuffs, reciting the Miranda rights, as soon as any mention of cash comes up in the front seat. That's when a hustler can be arrested—as soon as money is discussed or exchanged. So Christina knew not to set a dollar amount herself, to let the john do it first. Such offers would be considered illegal baiting if the john were indeed a cop, and an arrest would be implausible.

Of course, this rule of thumb presumes the street vice are ethical, which, Christina claimed, they're not. Several people I know told stories of getting raped by men who flashed their badge; others described cops planting drugs and then arresting them, to meet their quotas. I don't know how true this last claim is, but I do know that many of the girls on the Boulevard use drugs, especially speed. Speed, often crystal meth, gives one the feeling of being invincible, powerful, strong. Sometimes the girls will work for drugs, but those are the ones who are addicted, who look strung out, whose clothes become dirty and torn. Most of the kids use drugs primarily while they're working, to get through. Speed makes the night easier, more like a party and less like pain.

Because I lived so close to the Boulevard, I often drove along it to get home. So many kids cycled through that culture—when they lost a job or a home, or went out with friends who did it—that I was usually sure to see a kid I knew or at least recognized. Sometimes I liked driving by; kids would call out to me, and I'd buy them a taco, find out how they were. And sometimes I'd discover that someone had been hurt or arrested, and I'd get discouraged and overwhelmed and avoid the street for a few weeks, inventing various circuitous routes to my apartment.

On a main hustling corner like Santa Monica and Highland,

there'll be ten to fifteen kids clustered together on any Friday or Saturday night. One block down, in front of Benito's "Home of the Rolled Taco," it's the same thing. On all the other corners, on both sides of the street, there'll be one or two kids and young adults hustling, usually sitting at bus stops, usually looking bored. This makes a grand total of about forty people working on a regular weekend, which shrinks to half during the week. Their ages range anywhere from twelve to about twenty-four, and the youngest ones, predictably, garner the highest wages. If you have a baby face and a cute manner, you can get $80 for giving a blow job, $60 for a hand job, and $100 for anal sex. "Brick" hustlers, the ones who look more masculine, make $10 or $20 less per service than their more feminine counterparts, but every job is negotiable. The Boulevard is the best street to work in town; two blocks north, on Sunset Boulevard, is good too, but that's for genetic women. Kids who pass easily will sometimes work there, because the flow of cars can be more steady, though, obviously, they're taking a safety risk. Also, on Sunset they have to contend with pimps. (For a reason no one can explain to me, there are no pimps for the transgender hustlers.) When kids look too drugged out or desperate, they stop getting tricks on Santa Monica and they'll be forced downtown, to what's actually called Skid Row, for work. Here, crack is the drug of choice, and a blow job can pay as low as $8.

The men who cruise the Boulevard are as varied as you can imagine. Eddie Murphy made headlines in 1997 for picking up a transgender prostitute in the neighborhood, though neither was arrested and Murphy swore he was only giving the girl a ride home. Kids say Murphy is not the only celebrity they've met (Hugh Grant was arrested just off the Boulevard with a genetic woman two years earlier), and they say that most of their clients are straight men with wives and kids. Many are rich and many are middle class and many are return customers. Few identify as gay, because gay men can pick up boys on Santa Monica a few blocks west; most johns simply want the titillation of knowing that the girls are trans.

Black girls on the Boulevard complain that the white ones pick up more rides, white girls say the Latina kids are more popular, and the Latinas, depending on whom you talk to, agree with both. Watching the action from a Mexican chain restaurant across the street, it looks like an equal-opportunity operation. As a car slows at a corner, the girls will glance at one another, and one or two will step forward. There seem to be the same unspoken rules operating for prostitutes as there are for surfers; if you've been out in the water the longest, you're entitled to catch the next wave. One of the most interesting things to watch is when an undercover cop pulls up. One of the older, more experienced girls will recognize him from prior arrests, and she'll make some indication that she knows what he's up to: like marching away from the corner briskly and with intention. This signals to the other girls that cops are around, and within what seems like seconds, the street for a full ten blocks will be clear of all prostitutes. They'll walk into the pizza joint, they'll order Chinese food, they'll ask to use a bathroom, whatever—but they'll get off the Boulevard. There have been times I've driven down Santa Monica and seen no kids at all, only to return ten minutes later and see dozens. Communication between the kids seems to move like electricity.

Christina briefly considered trying the safer way to prostitute, which everybody called "working the papers," meaning advertising in one of the free sex weeklies. The largest and most widely distributed of these papers is called *L.A. X... Press*, a tabloid that has four pages of "news" (meaning single-paragraph blurbs on random world events) and twenty-eight pages of ads for prostitutes. Looking through this paper is discouraging; on an average week, I can spot three or four kids I know under the "specialties" section where transsexuals go, all purporting to be twenty-one, all claiming to be "new in town" and "fully functional." And these are the ads with pictures. The cheaper ads—and there are hundreds—are just names, physical descriptions, and phone numbers.

Working the papers is safer in terms of getting arrested, as the police are more focused on street prostitution. But it also requires more money and stability, as you need your own phone and apartment or hotel room out of which to work. Moreover, it necessitates a level of psychological commitment to the *idea* of being a prostitute, and Christina hated the work, liked to think of it as a passing necessity.

Of course, very few transsexual girls overall live on or work the streets, just as very few genetic, heterosexual girls live on or work the streets, percentage-wise. It's salacious and misguided to uphold the transsexual-as-sex-worker stereotype, but such work is a reality when you have little money, no parents, and an underage ID.

Having grown up in the *Pretty Woman* early nineties, some kids nurture the dream that they may meet a Richard Gere look-alike on the Boulevard—someone who'll see their golden hearts and fall in love with them and take care of them forever. They're teenagers, and prone to fantasy. They can also be drawn to it because, on top of the money they earn, it cements their femininity.

Foxx told me that prostitution, at times, has boosted her confidence. "A lot of times you'll have these really gorgeous men, and you'll sit back and say, 'Oh god, he's paying to have sex with me?'" she said. "It makes you feel really hot."

Alexis Rivera said that some of her young clients at Childrens Hospital will prostitute because that's what their mentors have taught them. "Girls who got thrown out, whose parents didn't want them, are getting raised by the street, and if you get raised by the street, you're gonna work there," she said to me once. "It's not like people will tell you where to go to college; they'll teach you to stand on this corner. That's the kind of education that happens in some parts of our community."

But none of this was why Christina hustled when she moved back to her mother's. For her, it was about the money. She could get it fast because she was cute, and she didn't mind being pushy or foul-mouthed to drive clients away from the more vulnerable acts, like intercourse, and toward the ones she could be done with quickly and mindlessly, like hand jobs. She'd encountered so much danger in her life, she wasn't afraid to climb into cars or to use the knife she always carried in her purse if she had to. She also carried pepper spray and an iron key chain that we gave her that was shaped like the outline of a cat's face. The key chain was probably illegal because it was more dangerous than brass knuckles: the pointed ears were at the perfect width for gouging out an attacker's eyes.

Because I was afraid for her safety, Christina didn't tell me the story of her one assault as an adult until nearly a year after it happened. She was working where she always did, alone in front of the Shakey's Pizza restaurant, when a cop pulled up in his unmarked El Dorado. Christina usually has a good radar for cops, but maybe she was high, I don't know. In any case, she said that when she suggested a good side street for the service, the john instead flashed his badge and turned onto the freeway. He pronounced her under arrest, and she slumped in her seat, presuming they were heading to the station. At the off-ramp, though, the cop pulled over and handcuffed her, then drove into an unfamiliar neighborhood. He marched Christina, still handcuffed, into his apartment, and molested her. The cop threatened that if Christina snitched, she'd only be admitting her own crime of prostitution in the first place; plus it would be the cop's word against a teenage prostitute's. Whose would hold up in court?

I only saw Christina on Santa Monica Boulevard twice in the nine months she worked there. I purposely avoided driving that street at night because I didn't want to see her. Or, more accurately, I didn't know what to do about it. When we got together, she'd mention "clocking coins" or "getting her work on," but she wouldn't talk about it. When I pressed, she got angry.

"Girl, what do you expect me to do when I've got to pay my mother three hundred dollars to sleep on the floor?" she'd ask.

"There are other places to sleep," I'd retort.

"I'm not going to stay in a shelter."

"Fine. Let's get you a roommate like millions of other eighteen-year-olds."

"I can't live with anybody. I hate people," she'd say.

"You hate prostituting."

"Cris!" she'd yell, nostrils flaring, eyes wide, furious that I'd called her out so plainly. The word "prostituting" sat between us like some roadkill we'd suddenly encountered that we didn't know how to remove.

"You could get another job," I'd say, and I'd remind her of the places she'd applied when she was staying with me or with Andrea—employers with whom she could follow up, job boards she could check.

"It's too hard," she'd say. Or, "Whatever, girl." Or she'd pull her classic and most transparent move: she'd talk about the latest plans she had for her hair. "Maybe braids—the tiny ones, or brown again, with red undertones that you can see in the sun. I'm getting tired of blond."

Sometimes I threw her terms back at her.

"Whatever," I'd say. "When you can imagine your life past tomorrow, I'm ready."

Christina didn't care about the World Trade Center bombings. September 11 happened during her worst period, and when we talked a few hours after the attack, the first thing she mentioned was her hair. Robin and I had lived in New York before moving to L.A.; we hadn't finished the head count on all our friends, and we called Christina to make sure she was okay. I couldn't stomach her response. "Why do I give a fuck what happened to some buildings? They shooting up East L.A. every day."

"Because people I love live there," I said. "Because not everyone's been accounted for. Because I'm scared."

"Oh," she said, softly. It was so hard for her to see beyond her own life.

———

Thanksgiving that year was quiet. A close friend and her six-year-old daughter, Gemma, had driven down to Los Angeles. Dinner was just going to be the four of us, along with Christina, who, up until the last moment, wasn't sure if she'd come. Just as we pulled the turkey out, in she marched, made up like a drag queen with a cheap blond wig that clotted together in sticky strands. Oh no, I thought. This is what she dresses like when she wants people to clock her, when she wants to feel terrible about herself.

As soon as Christina saw Gemma, though, she softened.

"Can I wear your wig?" Gemma asked.

Christina laughed. "Now everybody be knowing it's a wig!" She put the tattered thing on Gemma's head and styled the front tresses behind her ears. Gemma, who has dark hair and eyes, ran off toward a mirror, shouting, "Look, Mama! I have yellow hair!"

Christina told us that the rest of her family had gone off to one of the aunts' houses for Thanksgiving dinner and she hadn't been invited. Lisa, Gemma's mom, is a chef, and she made Christina a perfect bite of roasted turnips and parsnips and fingerling potatoes that she'd cooked in a roasting pan she'd brought with her all the way from northern California. Lisa didn't trust our cooking tools. "*Mmm,* these are weird potatoes," Christina said, waving steam from her mouth. "They're good—they taste like the earth."

Gemma was staring at Christina's exaggerated makeup; she had likely never seen anyone so done-up in person before. Christina excused herself and went to the bathroom to wash up. When she came back to the table, she was scrubbed clean of all makeup, her dark hair pulled back in a plain bun. Gemma was still wearing the wig.

"How do you spell your name?" Gemma asked, a colored pencil clutched in her fist as she hovered over a stack of paper she had carefully folded into fourths. Gemma had decided we all needed place cards at our seats, and Thanksgiving dinner couldn't begin until she made them all.

"X-t-i-n-a," Christina carefully spelled, and then she went over to help Gemma write it. Gemma happily climbed onto Christina's lap when she suggested they tackle the project together to speed things along. Gemma drew the pictures, and Christina wrote the names. Christina looked happier than I'd seen her in months.

When the turkey was finally cool, we all went around the table to say what we were thankful for. "I'm thankful for these girls," Christina said, looking at Robin and me directly one at a time, tears spilling openly. She didn't wipe them away. "They're my only family. They sort of saved my life."

The next night, when Robin and I were driving around with Lisa and Gemma, we spotted Christina working on Santa Monica. We were coming home from a restaurant and chatting so much, we forgot to take a different route.

"Isn't that Christina?!" Lisa shrieked, in horror. "Stop the car! That was definitely her!"

In a flash, I saw Christina's—and now my—world, as an empathetic but not entirely familiar person would see it. Prostitution was an alien, exotic, and horrible thing: a dirty crime of desperation. A sad and terrible act—something nobody you know does—and if you do know someone or, worse, love someone who has to hustle, you do everything you can to stop them and help them. This is how a visitor to this environment saw streetwalking, which was exactly what Christina was doing at that very moment.

Robin was calmly turning the car off the Boulevard and onto a side street, Lisa was getting upset about how we had just had Thanksgiving with Christina and how she was just a kid, and Gemma, her voice rising to a confused pitch, was saying, "What, Mama, what?" I put my arm on the windowsill and leaned my head into my hand, closing my eyes.

"We have to pick her up and take her home—she can't be out there like that!" Lisa, my dear friend, the reasonable one, the real mom, said. Yes, of course, you're right, I thought. That's the child I love out there, prostituting herself. What on earth have I been thinking?

"Lisa, she won't come with us," Robin, my wife, the other reasonable one, said. "She'll be too embarrassed that you saw her. We can't help her until she's ready to help herself." Right, I thought. That's right. We do help her. She knows we're here. Oh god, I thought. Which truism was true?

"What's Christina doing?" Gemma asked. Everyone ignored her.

"Well, then, we have to give her money to go home so she doesn't work tonight," Lisa said, stuffing $30 into my hand. "I can't stand it."

Robin drove farther down the block so that even if Christina walked along the Boulevard, she wouldn't see our car. I wasn't sure what I'd say; I figured I'd be plain and tell her that I wanted to help her get a legal job—now here's some money, go home.

"Cris!" Christina screamed when I turned the corner. She was embarrassed and she was high. I could tell her pupils were dilated, though she wouldn't make eye contact. She laughed a laugh I'd never heard before, a distant, echoey laugh, like she was in a cavern. "Look at my toes! Girl, can you believe I'm showing my feet?"

Christina was wearing open-toed sandals with espadrille-style wedge heels. Her toes, which she considered thick and ugly, were bare, as were her legs—all the way up to her skirt, which was actually a bandanna tied around her waist in a triangle. On top she was wearing a second bandanna, like a halter top. She was about 6 percent covered. The rest was skin.

"Yep, your feet look pretty cute," I said, looking into her face.

"No—I mean, look at them!" she said, laughing that laugh again and staring at her shoes, one foot twisting around in display. She clearly didn't want to meet my gaze. "Don't my toes look so fishy? You know I never go out in public with my feet showing. And look how much I can show in these shoes! These sandals are the bomb."

"We were just driving by," I started.

"You were driving?" Christina said, suddenly startled. "Did Lisa and Gemma see me? The little girl?"

"Yeah. It's not a big deal."

"Shit!" she said. "Cris! Where are they?"

"They're around the corner," I said. "Don't worry. They can't see you now. And Gemma has no idea what's going on. It's mostly Lisa who saw you."

"How embarrassing," Christina said, slumping against the wall of Shakey's Pizza.

"It's okay. Nobody's judging you." I noticed Christina had goose bumps all over her body. It was late November and probably forty degrees. "Are you freezing?"

"No. I'm fine," she said.

"Look, if I give you some of the money that you'd make tonight, will you just go home?" I asked. "And borrow my coat."

"No—I'm not taking your money," Christina said, slipping her arms into my old leather jacket. "You know I don't like to do that."

That was true; Christina had always been uncomfortable taking cash. She'd let Robin and me buy her clothes or books or other necessities to a point, and then she'd argue that she didn't want to take advantage or that she had plenty already. Actual bills were even more touchy; she would rather get by on a $10 week by living on $1 tacos and 59-cent bags of Doritos than ask for money. If she was particularly hard up, she would usually "borrow." She kept a running tab of what she owed us.

"Sparrow, I don't like to see you out here any more than you like to be out here. You keep saying you want to get a job. So go home tonight and take care of yourself, and we'll talk later about what kind of job you'll get," I said. I handed her $50, and she looked at me warily. I knew I couldn't tell her that half of it was Lisa's. She would have been mortified. "You're tired of this; I'm tired of this. The money is just the faith that you can do it."

"Okay," she said. "Just this once."

"You'll really go home now?"

"I'll really go home."

The irony in Christina's hustling to pay her mother was that Gloria was disgusted by it. Christina never left the house in her trampy clothes—she'd change in a restaurant's bathroom and hide her regular jeans and T-shirts in the bushes—but she said her mom knew what she was doing. Christina claimed that Gloria never once asked about what kind of work her child was doing but accepted the $50 bills and the late-night hours without comment. Christina said she told her mother that she was a terrible parent; that she was neglectful and abusive; and that she hoped she didn't screw up her younger sister as badly as she had her firstborn. Her mother, Christina told me, said it would be better if she would just die of AIDS than to bring this kind of shame upon the family. I never heard these conversations firsthand, so I can't vouch for their validity, only their aftermath—which consisted of Christina calling in tears followed by a few days of self-loathing so deep it astounded me. She'd cut her arms with razors and call herself a man as she was applying her makeup in the mirror. She'd pick fights with her sister and with strangers on the street. Once she smashed her head against another transwoman's head outside a nightclub for some perceived slight, and another time she purposely threw rocks at boys from her old neighborhood who knew her when she was little, to get them to harass her for being a "man" and a "faggot." When her mother hurt her feelings, she did whatever she could to make someone else hurt her more.

Christina and I never did talk about another kind of job she might find. Instead, a few nights after the incident outside Shakey's, I got a call from Andrea.

"The girls stole a car," Andrea said, her voice even and resigned. It was 11:00 P.M. "The police haven't caught them yet, but you'll probably get a call from Christina from jail later on tonight. I just thought I'd warn you."

"How did you know already?" I asked, amazed. Andrea seemed to possess the supernatural ability to stay a step ahead of Domineque, despite Domineque's erratic self-destruction.

"They knew the owner of the car. Really stupid," she said, anger edging her voice. "Apparently they were all hanging out together, and somehow Christina and Domineque got him to get out of his car and they drove off. He called the police, and the police called me."

"So what do we do?" I asked. Andrea was only a few years older than I, but her longer parenting experience often made the gulf seem wider.

"We wait. Call each other when one of us hears."

We hung up. Robin and I boiled tea and we waited. We lit candles and, because we were afraid to say them out loud, offered silent wishes that there wouldn't be an accident, that the kids weren't too high or drunk. At 1:00 A.M. Robin and I went to bed and pretended to sleep. At 2:00 the phone rang.

"This is a collect call coming from a Los Angeles County Jail. Will you accept the charges?"

"Yes," I said. Robin and I both cupped our ears to the receiver, as we owned only one telephone.

"I got arrested," Christina wailed. At least that's what I thought she said. After that she was sobbing and sputtering and breathing so fast, it was hard to tell. We let her cry for a few minutes. When she slowed down, she said, "Domineque stole a car. They pulled guns on us! There were so many guns. We crashed into a building!" And she started sobbing again.

"Sweetie, try to take a breath," I said. I took an exaggerated in-breath so she could hear it. She tried to follow along, but she was hiccuping and hyperventilating. She sounded like a fish tank. "It's gonna be okay, whatever happened. Just breathe, and then you can tell the story."

"No it's not!" she wailed. This started the sobbing again. I was a little scared but mainly relieved; I knew she wasn't dead, for starters, but I still didn't know if she was hurt at all, or what happened to Domineque. Robin tried talking to her.

"Christina, we're both here. Are you hurt physically?"

"No, I'm fine," she said, her voice smaller. "The car was totaled. We crashed it into a building in Beverly Hills. We were going eighty."

"Is Domineque okay?" Robin asked. I knew it was impossible for them to be going eighty.

"She's fine too," Christina said, trying to catch up with her breath. "We both walked away."

Suddenly I was furious. All my fear from the past three hours warped and twisted itself into a column of rage running through the center of my body. I got off the phone and slammed through the apartment. My bookshelves were blurry; my kitchen was blurry; my couch was blurry; my mind, especially, was blurry. When I got back to the bedroom and put my ear to the receiver, Christina was calmer and explaining how Domineque had tricked the car's owner into running inside his apartment for some snacks, leaving the girls outside alone, with the engine idling. I interrupted.

"You-are-so-STUPID!" I yelled. Robin jumped back from the phone.

"I know," Christina whispered. "I'm sorry. I'm sorry. I'm sorry."

"How could you do this? And don't blame it on Domineque! I heard you just saying that she tricked the guy—but you could have gotten out of the car. This is your life, and you are fucking it up. You could have died!"

"That's what we were trying to do!" Christina yelled back. Then she started sobbing again. "I'm sorry. I'm so sorry."

Robin, who had been holding her head in her hands, was back on the phone. She said, "You were pulling a Thelma and Louise."

"Who's Thelma and Louise?"

Robin and I looked at each other. It was the first time we smiled, the tiniest of smiles, all night.

When the story finally tumbled itself out in a reasonable order, it went like this: Domineque and Christina, who had been drinking and doing drugs with the owner of the car, made a suicide pact that night. They had been talking about their collective unhappiness, and when their friend left them with the keys, they saw their opportunity. They wanted to broadcast their misery, and they were inspired by Madonna's recent video "What It Feels Like for a Girl," in which a tattooed Madonna goes on a crime spree, swallows a bunch of pills, and then crashes a car, in an apparent suicide attempt. The only creative addition in Domineque and Christina's case was the car chase; they had hoped for a dramatic cat-and-mouse that would land them on television and end in flames. (Unfortunately, in Los Angeles everyone's enamored with the high-speed chase: you see one every night on the six o'clock news, the ten o'clock news, and interrupting regularly scheduled programming at all hours. This thug-life glamorization is its own self-fulfilling prophecy; once an outlaw realizes he's being pursued, he'll hit the gas for a shot at fame.) What happened to the girls, miraculously, is that they were pursued down only a few empty residential Beverly Hills streets until Domineque turned a corner and lost control of the car. She crashed into the side of a brick storefront, crumpling the car's front end and sending the girls hurtling into the dashboard. Several police cars surrounded them, and Domineque and Christina climbed out, arms raised.

For three days, Christina was detained in the West Hollywood police station. She was held in a cell by herself and was called by her girl name and treated with respect by a deputy we talked to daily. This deputy had worked with several transgender inmates before, and knew the discrimination they usually faced. West Hollywood is known as a "gay city"—more than 40 percent of the population are gay men, and the mayor and council members are usually gay and definitely gay-friendly. It was only a matter of luck that West Hollywood was the closest precinct to the crime.

"I don't wanna die," Christina said the morning after her arrest. "I think this was God saying I'm supposed to live."

"Good," I said. "I want you to live too."

Christina cried and cried from the jail, perhaps partly from the detox, partly from fear, and mainly from letting go of death. Dying had always been part of her plan, she said. But now, she felt some kind of inner click, a release from that fate. She felt she had been saved by an outside force she couldn't name—because she wasn't sure she believed in God. What she was sure of was she could no longer just wait for the inevitable bad things to happen to her; she thought she had a kind of duty to start building a life.

"I probably can't manage starting everything at once; it's too much for me," Christina said thoughtfully. This was the first time, ever, that I had heard Christina make manageable, bite-sized plans, and I thought it was a major breakthrough. "So I can't go to high school right away. I'll get a job, and I'll move out. Or I'll move out and then I'll get a job. Or both at the same time. I can't stay with my mother anymore. It's not good for me. I can't change her, and I can't make her love me."

It was funny, and gratifying, to hear words I'd said several times echoed in Christina's speech. I didn't want to be the reality check, but I had to. "Sparrow, you know you might get some serious time," I said. I had been talking to Andrea, and heard the cops found speed in the backseat of the mangled car. "This is grand-theft auto we're talking here. And you're an accomplice."

*"Accomplice,"* she said. "Domineque did it. And she's still a minor, so she'll be okay. I can just say that I didn't know the car was stolen. I wasn't driving."

The courthouse in Beverly Hills, the closest to West Hollywood, is a two-story construction of glass and stone. The grass in front is neatly manicured, with lollipop-shaped trees and tidy signs directing traffic to underground parking. It's not as imposing nor as dirty as the courthouses downtown. The interior is light and airy, thanks to the oversize windows, and lawyers and clients alike carry lattes and gourmet sandwiches from the fancy delis nearby, as there are no fast-food restaurants. On the day of Christina's hearing, Robin and I arrived early and sat in the hallway next to a cop who was waiting to testify against a hit-and-run.

"What do you think will happen to her?" I asked the officer, once I explained the barest details of the theft and crash.

"Unfortunately, you might be outta luck," the cop answered, leaning back in his chair to ease the obvious furrow his thick black belt was making in his large stomach. "She might walk."

"What do you mean, 'walk'?" I asked, thinking this was police talk for some kind of elaborate or lengthy punishment.

"Well, if she was only in the passenger seat, they might not be able to get her on anything. A judge'll usually drop a case like that without even hearing it," he said. "There's no way to prove intent, because she can always say she didn't know it was stolen or she didn't know what was happening or whatever. Was it your car?"

"Oh no," I said, realizing that he thought I was hoping Christina would be punished for the crime.

"Then why are you here?" the officer asked, clearly confused. People come into the Beverly Hills courthouse to fight the criminals, not to support them.

"Because we're her pseudo-guardians," I answered, gesturing at Robin.

"Oh," he said. "She shouldn't be stealing cars." And he walked away.

It turned out the police officer and Christina were right; the judge did drop the case against her because she was a mere accomplice and her level of participation couldn't be proved. Domineque, because she was still a minor, went back to juvenile hall. Christina was released the next morning, as it took the remainder of the afternoon and evening to process her paperwork. She paid for a taxi to her mother's house, took a shower, and changed her clothes. She called Covenant House, was accepted, and went out looking for a job. By the next day, Christina had scored an interview.

Christina called me ecstatic; two days out of jail and she'd been offered a job at Ripley's "Odditorium" on Hollywood Boulevard, enticing tourists to drop ten bucks to see the world's largest tire or a statue of John Wayne constructed entirely out of laundry lint.

"Yeah, girl," she said. "Believe it or not."

# 9

## VIOLENCE

*I* KNEW THE DYNAMIC between Foxx and her boyfriend Fernando had been deteriorating, knew it from the night they took me out for beers and Fernando asked, in his sweet way, tipping his head and raising his eyebrows, if I would be their "couples counselor." I laughed, and he quickly blanched, wounded.

"I'm no therapist!" I sputtered over the top of my bottle. We were in some over-dark dive bar off Sunset Boulevard, where we had gone after watching Foxx perform two songs at an open mic at a nearly empty club. Foxx's songs and stage fashion were getting sexier—the last few times I'd seen her acts, she was wearing skimpy bralike tops and making lots of those heavy-lidded ecstasy faces at the audience, breathing deeply into the microphone. She was singing less political songs now, and more about love—with lots of rhyme schemes on the order of *hips* and *lips, thighs* and *sighs*. Her dancing was incredible: she could jump onto a chair with both feet in four-inch boots, and then kick one leg up into a full split, only to land on a half beat, syncopating different parts of her body to the different tiny internal rhythms of a song.

Fernando was starting to mimic Foxx's style; he now had hair extensions running down his back, the plasticky glue at his scalp covered by a red bandanna. He was also newly branding himself a musician, and while he didn't perform at the open mic with Foxx, he carried around a guitar, which he was teaching himself to play. The two were writing a song together about how rough it is to be in a relationship, but how love would get them through.

"Yeah, but you know us two," Fernando protested. "And we've been having troubles."

I looked over at Foxx. She was drinking lemonade and talking to a woman in a wheelchair.

"What kind of troubles?" I asked.

"We been hitting each other," Fernando said earnestly, his English broken and strained. "And me, I love Foxx. And she loves me too. I don't want to do that no more. But we get so mad. Can you help us?"

Fernando's unblinking sincerity was disconcerting. "Umm, I'm not the best person, because I *do* know you both. I think you're supposed to have somebody neutral and trained for these things," I said, grasping. "But it's so good you want help, and that you love each other so much. The Gay and Lesbian Center has free therapists, though. Have you talked to them?"

This clearly wasn't the answer Fernando was hoping for, because he thanked me and loped over to nuzzle in Foxx's neck. Perhaps he wanted something easier, more direct.

When I talked to Foxx about it later, she agreed; their fighting had gotten ugly, and they were both hitting each other, though Fernando did it more. Fernando loved Foxx, but his internal wires scrambled when he felt frustrated or angry with her; he thought he should feel happy with her all the time. She first witnessed his temper flare about two weeks after he moved in. They were arguing—now she can't remember what about—and she smashed a dinner plate on the kitchen floor to get his attention and to make him stop yelling. Fernando swooped down on the broken half and smacked her with it, cutting her cheek just a little. At the time, Foxx said she wasn't concerned.

"It didn't strike me to worry," she said. "I was hysterical crying when it happened, and he apologized and apologized."

Each time they fought, Fernando apologized, and the making up was intimate and rewarding. Months later Foxx would read books and attend groups about domestic violence that taught her, she said, that "violence is not love; accepting it is not love; and a person can only change if he wants to." But back then she didn't know how textbook her case was, and every time an argument got physical, she believed Fernando when he said he would change. Even when he stabbed her with a knife.

"On or about May 14, 2001," the court transcripts read, Fernando Juarez did "willfully and unlawfully commit an assault upon Foxxjazell with a deadly weapon."

Fernando was already in jail by the time I got the call from Foxx; the police had arrested him the night of the fight when Foxx got scared and dialed 911. He had hit her with a chair leg and stabbed her in the thigh with a small knife; her injuries didn't warrant stitches, but the escalation in weapons made her afraid that Fernando didn't have any limits. At first, she was relieved to have him gone. By the third day, though, she regretted pressing charges because she missed him. She called to tell me she was going to have to get creative to help get him out.

Foxx knew Fernando was slated to be locked up anywhere from one to three years, and she hoped her appearance could reduce his sentence.

"I didn't put on any makeup, and I wore a lot of baggy clothes," said Foxx, who hadn't gone anywhere dressed as a man for three years. "I did that to make my case look weaker, like I could have defended myself—as if it were two men involved in domestic violence instead of a man and a woman."

Foxx was right in a sense; throughout the country there is a sentencing disparity in domestic violence cases, though no official mandate exists for such treatment. Simply, men who attack women get more time than men who attack men. The Gay Men's Domestic Violence Project in Massachusetts points to a prevailing myth that two men in a fight must be equals, in both size and weight and sensitivity to violence. There's also a misconception that violence in the context of a gay relationship is some sort of consensual S&M scenario or, in any case, better left to the bedroom. In a study jointly conducted by the National Institute of Justice and the Centers for Disease Control, researchers found that of the more than 4.5 million acts of "intimate partner" physical violence against women in a year, 55,000 partners went to jail. Of the nearly 3 million violent acts against men, however, fewer than 5 partners were convicted or sent to jail. The study doesn't specifically break down whether the partners were the same or opposite sex but does claim that "intimate partner violence is perpetrated primarily by men, whether against male or female intimates." So, it made statistical sense for Foxx to be a male.

And her look worked. Fernando was sentenced to the minimum 365 days in county jail. But at what price, I asked Foxx. What damage did such "performing" as a male do, when she'd worked so long to establish herself as a woman?

"It didn't do anything to me psychologically," Foxx answered, annoyed by my question. "I'm an actor, so I'm used to doing things like that. I could step out of myself and say, 'This is a role I'm playing for the benefit of getting him off.'"

For the entire year that Fernando was in prison, he wrote Foxx letters. He promised he'd change, said that he was very sorry, that he loved her even more now that he was away. Foxx held out; she told him he needed to attend domestic violence classes upon release and learn to feel his feelings before they roiled up into an attack. She said she'd consider dating him when he got out, but it would only be dating; he'd have to prove that he was working on himself, and she couldn't promise that she wouldn't see other men. This of course made Fernando furious, but Foxx thought that was a good test—a controlled way for him to learn to manage his temper. Under no circumstances, she said, would he be allowed to live with her again. He'd have to score his own place and his own job. Still, she missed him terribly.

Christina, during this time, was having her own run-ins with violent men. She did stop prostituting and keep her legal job, but slipped back to her mother's house once more when the shelter rules overwhelmed her. And her newest strategy for surviving at her mom's was to stay away as much as possible: she tiptoed in the front door after everyone was asleep and left before anyone was awake. This self-imposed exile made her feel unwanted and unloved, so she repeatedly hopped into cars with unknown men to get some attention.

Sometimes Christina just wanted a joy ride or someone to flirt with for a while, but often she wanted them to drive her somewhere completely across town—to a nail shop for a manicure, to Papa Jim's for some weed, to see another guy with whom she'd exchanged phone numbers. Usually this was all fine; the men were amused to be bossed around by a young, hot woman in their car for an hour or so. And as soon as they started asking if she wanted to go kick it back at their place, she'd start inquiring about their wives or soliciting pictures of their kids, trying to catch them in a cheat. To Christina, it was all a game: getting men to pick her up affirmed her femininity; riding around with them was dangerously exciting enough to pass the time and make her forget her home life; and then leaving them to feel bad about themselves for picking her up in the first place asserted her rightful superiority over the kind of dirtbags that hit on teenagers.

Usually this mix of sexy, cruel, and smart left a driver's head spinning enough for Christina to jump out of the car at her stated destination. But sometimes men anticipated repayment for their chauffeur service—some men asked to kiss that quivering lip she used to lure them in; some men expected more.

After Christina had been staying at her mother's for a couple of months, she got into a car with one of these expectant types. He was going to the nearby city of Pasadena, and because Christina had nothing better to do, she went along. She figured she might make him drive her to a house of some people she knew there or else drop her in Hollywood on his way back. But just inside the Pasadena city limits, the man started kissing Christina, pinning her shoulder back against the seat so she couldn't squirm away. She resisted, fighting him with her free arm, but he was stronger. He went right for her crotch, squeezing her through her jeans, Christina scissor-kicking her legs and yelling for help. But he felt her and immediately knew.

The shock of feeling extra flesh when he wasn't expecting any made the man release Christina for a flash second, enough for her to throw open the car door and start bolting down the street. Rage is a powerful chemical, though, and the man quickly caught up to her. He had grabbed a broom from the back of his hatchback and snapped it over his leg, screaming the whole time that she was a "fucking man." He punched Christina in the face, and when she went down, he lashed at her neck with the broken end of the stick. Christina, terrified, punched him in the nose. He grabbed at his nose, giving Christina enough time to jump to her feet. As she started to run again, he caught her arm, yanking it out of joint and beating her forearm with the stick, cracking the bone. She somehow jerked herself free and ran into a small deli that, thankfully, was just yards away.

I've always thought that Christina has a fierce guardian angel, and possibly more than one. The owners of the deli, a husband and wife who had likely been watching the assault from their window, immediately shot into action. The wife pulled Christina back behind the counter to check her bleeding neck. The husband stood in the doorway and screamed at the man to get out of his store—he was calling the police. Miraculously, this worked; the man shouted a few threats at Christina from over the deli owner's shoulder, but at the mention of cops, he ran. The wife, comforting Christina and giving her water, called 911, and Christina was zipped away in an ambulance.

When Robin and I got to the emergency room at the Huntington Memorial Hospital in Pasadena, Christina looked sunken and small. She was wearing an oversize gray sweatshirt, given to her long ago by one of the Daves. Apparently, we had just missed the police who had come to the hospital to file a report. Unfortunately, Christina didn't describe the attack as a hate or bias crime, which it certainly was, because the cops interviewed her in front of a nurse.

Hospitals, like all other institutions that make gender assumptions or inspect bodies, can range from unnerving to downright terrifying for many transpeople. The emergency-room triage nurse, while taking Christina's temperature and blood pressure and doing an initial swab on her cuts, asked her the standard battery of intake questions. Could she possibly be pregnant? When was the last time she had her menstrual period?

The cops waited patiently while Christina answered no to the first question and "um, sometime last month," to the second. Having just been assaulted for being transgender, Christina didn't feel comfortable telling a nurse about her status; she wanted to be taken care of and not gawked at or judged. The young transgender community, including Christina, all knew the story of Tyra Hunter, the Washington, D.C., transwoman who died in 1995 at the hands of emergency medical technicians who stopped administering care once they cut off her clothes and realized her birth gender. Transpeople all knew instinctively not to trust the police and not to trust doctors, and here Christina was in an emergency room confronted with both.

To the police, I'm sure the crime just looked like a typical lovers' spat; Christina simply described what the man looked like and the type of car he drove and stayed mum about everything else. The cops even teased Christina about looking like Popeye, as her forearm had swelled to three times the size of her upper arm. This enraged Christina since she was vain about her arms already and didn't want them to look masculine, but the cops had no idea what tender territory they were probing.

At the hospital, we sat in the waiting room for three hours watching tinny reruns and eating stale M&M's before a doctor would see us. Christina's whole body was aching from the spent adrenaline and the bruising, and aside from the welt on her neck, she had a cut that curved around her brow, temple, and cheekbone, just missing her eye. She couldn't unbend her swollen arm, and I had to help her unzip to go to the bathroom. We tried to play hangman and other distracting games, but then Christina just wanted to lean first on my shoulder, then Robin's, always maintaining contact with both of us at once.

In a way, I was quietly thankful for the scare, hoping it was serious enough to stop Christina from luring men at stoplights and yet not so traumatic as to register among her worst experiences or to make her feel she deserved it. I was musing on this when we finally got called in at 2:00 A.M. Christina perked up for the X-ray, interested in the science and making jokes about the housewives that would wear a "heavy metal apron." The doctor at the light box pronounced her arm broken, but said she'd have to come back in a few days for a cast, once the swelling had subsided. He prescribed her painkillers and sent us off to an empty office.

The pretty nurse who wrapped Christina's arm for a temporary sling wanted to know what relation the three of us were to one another. Christina, relieved that her forearm was only cracked in one spot and would heal cleanly, had located a box of latex gloves while we were alone in the doctor's office. She and Robin had blown two up into balloons for a turkey puppet show. It was the middle of the night, and we were all loopy and laughing, thankful that the injuries weren't worse.

"These are my sisters," Christina said proudly, swinging her legs against the metal bed.

"Oh, I can see that," the nurse said earnestly. "You look alike." This made us all laugh harder; in our practical, physical features, we have nothing in common. We're not the same race, we're not the same age, and Christina had just gotten the hell beaten out of her mere hours before—but somehow, in that moment, we all believed the nurse. We probably did look alike.

My biggest fear with Christina, of course, was that she'd been lucky in Pasadena—that next time could be worse. Every year transwomen and transmen are killed by enraged strangers who feel duped by their gender presentation. One of the most famous was Gwen Araujo—a transgender teenager killed in October 2002.

Gwen was so much like Christina and Ariel and all the kids I know that when her story broke, I followed it closely as a sort of warning, a talisman, against such tragedy happening again. I looked for a false step she could have made—all the kids did—but there wasn't anything she did that wasn't entirely familiar.

Gwen was seventeen when she went to a party in the working-class suburb of Newark, some thirty-five miles southeast of San Francisco. According to later reports, she drank a few beers, played dominos, sat on the laps of a few boys, and pecked them on the lips as she flirted. She liked two of them especially, had known them for a while, and had even had sex with them on prior occasions—though they didn't know she was transgender. It wasn't necessarily the sex that tipped the Newark boys off to Gwen's status. An acquaintance of the murderers said their suspicions came from Gwen's thick fingernails, unpainted toenails, and strong cheekbones. At the party the two men she had sex with, Michael Magidson and Jose Merel, were heard shouting, "Are you a man or a woman?!"

Later Magidson and Merel followed, or chased, Araujo from the party. A friend and eyewitness testified that the two stabbed her, beat her with a frying pan, and strangled her with rope. A third man— Jason Cazares, in his early twenties and a father of two—allegedly then hit her over the head with a shovel. The men then drove the body to Silver Fork Campground, 150 miles away, buried it in a shallow grave, and had breakfast at McDonald's.

This murder, according to the defendants' lawyer, was justified because of what's come to be known as the "gay panic defense." In essence, he told the jury, finding out that you're having a supposedly "gay" experience (when you thought you were having a straight one) is so horrible, you panic—and you lash out and maybe even commit a murder. The jury deadlocked and the trial was rescheduled. Cazares, the one with the shovel, was released on bail.

———

The difference between the Araujo case and Brandon Teena's, for instance—the transgender teenager who was murdered in 1993 to international attention—is the mainstream media and family response. Shortly after Teena's death, the *Village Voice* effectively called Teena a lesbian and his death a gay-bashing, with the story "Love Hurts: Brandon Teena Was a Woman Who Lived and Loved as a Man. She Was Killed for Carrying It Off." *Playboy* and even the gay newsmagazine the *Advocate* used the female pronoun for Teena, who clearly identified as male. Nearly a decade later, mainstream sympathizers were less afraid of the word "transsexual." There were immediate vigils held for Araujo, and hundreds of trans activists and supporters continued to gather on municipal steps in both San Francisco and Los Angeles as the murder trial dragged on. A few community funds were launched in Araujo's name, raising thousands of dollars for her family and to promote awareness about transgender people and issues in Newark public schools. And in an act of solidarity, the predominantly gay news agency PlanetOut named Gwen Araujo "Person of the Year" for 2002.

Also, Gwen's family was tremendously vocal. After Gwen's death, her mother, Sylvia Guerrero, publicly came forward about the child she had named Eddie. She said she had known Eddie was a girl for years, and she supported *her*—as did the child's aunt and uncle and other members of the extended family. It was time to speak up about transgender violence. (In 2002, the year Gwen died, twenty-seven other transgender people were murdered, ostensibly for being transgender. Many activists estimate that the numbers are much higher, but their deaths go unreported entirely because families can't be located, and names can't be listed, or obituaries paid for. Also, when bodies are too decomposed or found without clothing and coroners can't recognize them as trans, they're not tallied as such.)

There are few statistics on anti-transgender violence overall. The only national study, appropriately called the "First National Survey of Transgender Violence," was conducted by GenderPAC in 1997 with 402 transpeople, and it showed nearly 37 percent had been phys-ically attacked. Their sample was not, by and large, the street kids of L.A., however: the data is (as the organizers admit) overwhelmingly white, over thirty, and largely middle class—so it might be national in geography, but not demography. A different kind of statistic is the one from the 2000 "Washington, D.C., Transgender Needs Assess-ment Survey," where the respondents were 70 percent African American and 22 percent Latino/a. In this case 43 percent of the 263 transgender respondents had been victims of violence and/or crime.

One of my former students was murdered several years after I left the school. It was Bella, the one who wrote the story on hormones for *Out & About*. She was discovered shot to death in her Los An-geles apartment. There were no suspects. An organization called Remembering Our Dead, which collects data on reported trans mur-ders, lists Bella's murder as one of twenty-six that year. As they had for Gwen, the trans community in L.A. held a small vigil for Bella—but there were no splashy news stories, no major outcry from the city at large—mainly because Bella's family was not around to demand justice. Her murder, of course, frightened Christina and all the other girls, but they hadn't known her well at Eagles and nobody had known her as an adult. The case is still unsolved.

In 2005 a jury decided that Magidson and Merel were guilty of second-degree murder (instead of the "gay panic" manslaughter or felony assault) but without the hate-crime enhancement. The jury was hung on the case of Cazares, the one originally released on bail. In 2006 Magidson and Merel were sentenced to fifteen years to life. Cazares was given six years but was allowed to wait to start serving his sentence for a few months—until his wife delivered his third child.

After Fernando got out of jail, it didn't take long for him and Foxx to restart their relationship; a few days after his release, they were back together at Foxx's place, despite the court-mandated restraining order.

Fernando wanted Foxx to marry him; Foxx wasn't sure the fighting wouldn't start again so she said she couldn't answer right away.

Some weeks later Foxx's reservations proved right; Fernando beat her up so badly, Foxx feared for her life. This time she didn't call the police. As soon as Fernando left the apartment for a few minutes to get something from the bodega, she ran away, leaving everything—her music, her television, most of her clothes, and all of her furniture—for Fernando to destroy or abandon when he came home and found her gone. Because she had worried something like this might happen, Foxx had already brought her guinea pigs, Shelly and Fiona, back to the pet store where she bought them.

"I could have easily called the police on him and got him put away and then stayed in the apartment, but I chose to quit my job and stay in a shelter," Foxx said, explaining that she had to stop going anywhere that Fernando could find her—her workplace, her music haunts, friends' houses, anywhere.

Foxx actually called me right after the assault to help her find places to stay. I quickly researched battered women's shelters, but Foxx knew that most don't accept nonoperative transsexuals. This was a terrible and infuriating tragedy. Here was poor Foxx, looking like, as she said, "Quasimodo," stooped over with the bruises and the swelling; she needed as much "safe space" as anyone. And yet it wasn't the other victims' fault; it wasn't their burden to untwist a culture that hadn't yet opened a place for Foxx, hadn't yet created a societal understanding that said "woman" and not "man." Again, the problem was systemic and much bigger than Foxx or Fernando or me.

"Where else could you go?" I asked. Not my place or any other friends' apartments; Fernando knew where we all lived, or could easily find out.

"I guess the Gay and Lesbian Center," she said. "They accept people until they're twenty-four. And at least they have guards."

At the time, we were in such a hurry to get Foxx to safety, she couldn't really answer my questions about why she didn't want to just get Fernando arrested and be done with it. Now, though, she's spent time in domestic violence groups and therapy.

"Part of me didn't believe he deserved to go back to jail; I still loved him," she said to me one recent afternoon. "Maybe it was my low self-esteem; I thought I wasn't good enough in some type of way."

When Foxx moved into the gay and lesbian shelter after Fernando attacked her, she immediately reframed her reasons for being there. She didn't forget being beaten up, but she hated seeing herself as a victim. Without being able to play her music in places Fernando could find her, she needed a self-improvement project. She decided to make it about money.

"At this time I was heavily in debt. My car bill was something I couldn't deal with; I was struggling to pay rent; I was on the verge of bankruptcy—so I saw this as the easy way out," Foxx said, explaining that over the previous several months she had been tempted by over-priced cars and music equipment and clothes that had all added up on high-interest cards. Within a few weeks of settling at the shelter, she went to a county-sponsored session on filing personal bankruptcy and decided to do it. Within another few weeks, she had a new job and had started a savings plan. "When I did go back to a shelter, it felt so much better because I didn't have the burdens anymore."

Shortly after Foxx moved in, her drag daughter Ariel decided she wanted to live at the shelter too—not just because Foxx was there, though that was probably part of it. Ariel was twenty years old and she needed help moving out of her mother's house and into a place of her own. Ariel's mom didn't have the money to help her with a se-curity deposit on an apartment, especially with her older sister and two babies living at home. Also, Ariel was having a harder and harder time staying home and saving money. Her need to go out and dress up was escalating, and she found herself staying at friends' houses more and more, which meant her income dribbled away on night-clubs and takeout dinners. At the Gay and Lesbian Center, at least, she could dress up in her room.

Ariel didn't have a job at the time but was taking intermittent classes at the community college. Aside from Foxx, who used to enroll in Spanish classes at the community college in order to reach a bilingual audience for her music, Ariel was the only person in their immediate circle to go to college. Lenora, Foxx's other drag daughter, was still seventeen and not nearly through with high school, but she was attending. Christina wasn't going to high school, though she always said she wanted a diploma and not a GED. And Domineque was in juvenile hall. Other kids, like Lu, were too busy surviving to think about school.

I never got to see the inside of the gay and lesbian youth shelter, which everyone calls the KT, after its full name, the Kruks/Tilsner Transitional Living Program. Nonresidents aren't allowed, but I picture it as a cozy place. Foxx spoke of it fondly as she made friends with the staff and hung out at home to save money for a new apartment and car (a Trans Am, which she liked for its name)—both of which she'd have to pay for outright because of the bankruptcy declaration. Sure, there were negative influences at the shelter, Foxx admitted, but she just stayed away from them. She watched movies in the communal living room with Ariel, and she took advantage of all the groups and free therapy. She saw the early curfews as a welcome respite from the city's nightly temptation to spend money.

Christina was alternately intrigued, and then frustrated, by Foxx's Pollyanna attitude, which she teasingly called "blond." Sometimes she thought Foxx was just naive, but other times, when Christina noticed the way Foxx could use her stumbles as mere traction for her next life goal, she'd want to know her secret. Foxx told Christina, like I did, that it was about attitude and faith—that she had to believe in herself, 'cause nobody was going to do that for her.

After Christina's assault with the broomstick, she conceded that maybe the ride in the car had to do with her choices and not just dumb luck. So, just as the stint in jail made her decide to get a job, the attack, in a roundabout way, made Christina decide she could give a shelter one more try. This is how it happened that all three girls—Christina, Foxx, and Ariel—ended up living at the KT together.

At the KT Christina found out about a temp agency that places people in social service jobs. She had already quit her post at Ripley's; she was bored with the cash register, bored with the shrunken skulls, bored with what she called a "high school job." So together, Christina and I punched up her résumé, highlighting the many afternoons she spent at Bienestar and the Gay and Lesbian Center, receiving counseling but also volunteering: stuffing envelopes, answering phones, putting free condoms in outreach packs, and so on. We played up her skills as a bilingual and bicultural communicator and her "flexible, mature, and reliable nature," which was a line she lifted from *Cover Letters for Dummies.* We played down her lack of a high school diploma.

Almost immediately she got a job as a receptionist at a hospital's pediatric ward, which, for the most part, she loved. Her favorite part was the translation—helping the patients or the parents of patients, who were often nervous when they had to bring in sick children to doctors who didn't speak their language. A couple of times Christina called me from work, and I could overhear her interacting with the patients. She was always incredibly gentle, telling moms their babies were cute even if they were sweating and screaming with fever and then promising that the doctor would be able to help. The staff relied heavily on her as a translator because she could make families from all kinds of neighborhoods feel comfortable—she could be urban and street with the inner-city moms, and she could charm the tired grandmas, helping patients fill out paperwork and communicate with doctors. Christina felt useful at this job.

While living at the shelter, Foxx, too, had found new employment: customer service at 1-800-DENTIST and hawking drinks at a Jamba Juice across town. While Foxx had done her time as a community activist with GLASS, she no longer craved a day job that was emotionally taxing. She only wanted to elevate people through her music and found that, after all she'd been through, her style was bowing toward the harder, yet more visceral and direct, rap. She supported Christina in her efforts, though, and told her that working in a hospital would get her closer to her goal of becoming a social worker and counselor.

Foxx also tried to support Ariel, pep-talking her as she always had and giving her tips on dressing, urging her to go full-time. Ariel didn't have a job, and while she needed the help, she was outgrowing her role as a daughter figure. She was twenty years old. One night, as Ariel tells it, she, Foxx, Christina, and some other residents were watching television in the KT living room. Foxx was making fun of the people on the screen, and Ariel laughed so hard she got up and slapped Foxx. She doesn't really know why she did it, she said, but she meant it playfully.

Foxx, who hates getting slapped, hit her back. Ariel pulled pepper spray from her purse and sprayed it in her face. Fumes filled the living room, and all the residents ran out coughing and clutching their eyes. Ariel was expelled from the home.

The process of adolescent individuation from the parents, I've realized, often has to happen whether there are parents around or not. It's another reason for all the violence and misdirected rage in the places where family structures are fabricated and duplicated, like a bad strain of DNA—places like prisons, schools, the street. Foxx, being the proxy mom, got the pepper spray. At least this is how I saw it. Foxx did too, though she didn't forgive Ariel right away; hitting was now a deep violation for her, and she didn't have the patience of a real parent.

The expulsion, for Ariel, was horrible. She lived with a friend in a hotel room and had to prostitute for fast money for a month until she got her head together and could land a bed at the other shelter, Covenant House. She was immediately sorry for starting the fight and tried to reconcile, but Foxx wouldn't have it. A year later, when I asked Ariel about the incident, she viewed it as mutual and described it merely as "me and Foxx getting into it."

I thought it was probably more nuanced than that; trans-on-trans aggression, either verbal or physical, can be common in Hollywood.

For one thing, there's the claustrophobia and its subsidiary tension. For another, the transgender population in Hollywood is young, and adolescents everywhere are cruel.

"Look at sixteen-year-old girls in general," Alexis Rivera told me over lunch one day. We were eating Middle Eastern food across the street from the hospital where she worked and saw dozens of clients each week, listening to the rotating grievances between the fluctuating cliques. At any high school in America, Alexis said, young genetic girls are "best friends on the surface and then calling each other bitches and whores behind each others' backs."

Even Alexis, who is entirely well-adjusted and more self-aware than your average woman in her late twenties, wasn't able to have a transgender friend until she was twenty-five years old. "I'm not going to blame anyone else for my insecurity, but this is the first year that I invited a transsexual woman to my house. Ever. It was because of self-hatred," Alexis admitted. Alexis has dark brown eyes that fall to black the deeper you look into them, and she nodded carefully as she spoke. She said she had her transgender acquaintances at work and then she had her gay friends. Her boyfriend had an entirely other set of friends who were primarily straight and didn't know Alexis was transgender. The three groups never intermingled. "I look at it as transphobia. Even when I would invite over my gay friends, I would still not invite my transgender sisters. It's really sad."

It's an accelerated, intensified version of this that Alexis sees when the girls on the Boulevard beat each other up or call each other "man" or "faggot" in public. "What I see a lot of girls go through is this: They can accept that they're transgender, they can accept that they have a penis, but what they can't accept is seeing another transgender woman and reflecting on it because then they have to say, 'Oh, I'm that.'"

It's a sort of double consciousness. On the one hand, a person is acutely aware that she's trans; in every situation she's concerned she'll be clocked and exposed, aware that she's slightly different from the genetic women in the room. On the other hand, she's moving through the world precisely as a woman like anyone else, getting on the bus, ordering her dinner, pumping her gas—and when another transperson enters her sphere, she has to rearrange these two compartmentalized mind states somewhat, and question whether one part will have to manifest more and upset her normal balance. And Ariel always did have two separate universes—her male and her female; she was the mermaid trying to live in both. Perhaps Foxx was *too* transgender, too threatening, too woman, to live with, day in and out.

Of course, not all transpeople react like this. There are some who navigate gracefully. But most admit that the pervasive self-doubt or self-hate born of a dismissive larger culture will squeeze itself out from the soul's cracks somewhere.

## 10

## CHANGE

*F*ROM THE MOMENT Robin and I moved to Los Angeles, we knew we would leave. The plan was to stay only the five years Robin needed to finish graduate school, and then move back to New York. Los Angeles was never home for us, no matter how much Christina had become our family. She was nineteen the summer we left, and though we had all emotionally prepared for it for months, the actual departure was wrenching.

The promise was that we would see her at least three times per year: Robin or I or both of us would fly to Los Angeles a couple of times, and we'd fly Christina to New York City once a year. We would talk on the phone each Sunday, when Christina had free minutes, and whenever else she wanted, but Sundays were definite. All of this was to create for her a sense of continuity, a feeling of being held in, instead of free-falling in the open sky—abandoned like she'd been so many times before. In the past, the only way Christina could assure a connection was to hold people to her in actual, physical space—showing up in doorways defiant or laughing, with that "I know you don't want to see me" snarl curled onto her lips, a fear revealed in her blinking. Experience had proven to her that anyone who expressed care—case managers, group-home leaders, therapists—would vanish if Christina weren't there to stitch together the relationship. I hoped that if Christina was strong enough to tolerate the separation without severing herself from us, our leaving could teach her something entirely new about her own value. We would go the farthest away, but we would be the first to see her through.

Thankfully, Christina loves ceremonies as much as I do. She was always checking books on Wicca and witchcraft out from the library, mostly to do spells to make men or her mother love her, so she was open to having a good-bye ritual rather than some sort of teary last supper. Just before sunset on the eve of our flight to New York, Robin and Christina and I picked up some garlicky chicken from a Greek takeout place and drove deep into Griffith Park, which is the city's largest park, and, in parts, still feels sort of wild and untamed. We had brought paper and pens, candles, and a spade for digging.

Fingers greasy from the chicken, we wrote the things we loved most about one another on small pieces of paper and buried them in the center of a ring of trees, where, we said, the earth could hold our best selves, the three of us forever united in the Los Angeles tree roots. The sun was dappled, still golden, but the dusk was flattening the shapes of the forest. We lit the candles and made wishes for our futures. Christina was solemn, holding our hands, tears streaking the powder she had dusted on her cheeks into lines of clay.

"I wish that I make it," she said. "That I graduate from high school. That I have a job that helps people. That I stop caring if my mom hates me. That I don't die."

When we finished, we saw that a family of foxes—three of them—had crept down the hillside to watch us. The biggest one was the closest, his red-brown fur reflecting the dying sunlight, his eyes intelligent and quick. We sat there quietly and looked at each other, the three foxes and the three people, and at first there was a taut wariness, and then curiosity, and then a kind of happy acceptance, as if we were reluctantly assigned the same table for dinner and then discovered we enjoyed each other's company. It felt as though we offered our wishes to the wind, and the foxes appeared to show us they'd been heard and sealed. We left them the rest of our meal in gratitude.

Eight days before this ceremony, Domineque and a new boyfriend, David, had escaped from a residential drug detox facility in the city of Lancaster, where she'd been remanded for some prior parole violation. Domineque doesn't like to talk about that night now, but she did tell me later she was high out of her mind on crack. Somehow she and David made their way from Lancaster to Los Angeles, and somehow they got shotguns. According to court transcripts, they appeared on Soto and Sixth at 9:55 P.M. They spotted a white pickup with a woman and a baby inside and a man walking toward it carrying tacos. The family had stopped for dinner.

The corner of Soto and Sixth is in East L.A., in a poor and primarily Latino part of town. The family spoke Spanish but the transaction, at least from Domineque's side of the truck, took place in English. Domineque has always been frustrated that she doesn't speak better Spanish, as her mother never taught her and she was taken out of the home so young. She shouted at the woman to get out, opened the passenger side door, and poked her in the ribs with the barrel of the gun. The woman struggled to free her baby from the car seat next to her, but Domineque was in a hurry to get the car jacked and she tugged at the woman's belt loops, screaming at her to just get out. Finally the man, who was the baby's uncle and was fighting with David on the driver's side, was able to grab the baby and the pair relinquished the truck. David and Domineque sped away, leaving the family unharmed.

A few minutes later, at 10:10 P.M., the white truck pulled onto Cesar Chavez Avenue, several blocks away. A woman was leaving work carrying a handbag. David slowed and Domineque jumped out of the truck, wearing jeans, a gray sweatshirt, and a red bandanna tied around her head. Domineque still always wore bandannas.

"Give me your bag!" Domineque said, pointing the two-foot-long gun at the woman.

This victim didn't speak English either, and she told Domineque, in Spanish, that she didn't understand.

"Give me your bag!" Domineque said again, in English. Domineque cocked the gun. *Click-click* went the barrel.

This, the woman understood. She shoved her bag at Domineque, who jumped into the truck with David and raced away again.

It took more than an hour for the police to catch up with Domineque and David on the 10 freeway. The cops flashed their lights and sirens and chased them for thirty minutes, until David finally screeched off an exit ramp and went slamming to a stop at a 7-Eleven. David flew out of the truck carrying his shotgun, and Domineque followed, forgetting her gun for a second, then turning back around to grab it. They both ran through the front doors. The cop hit his brakes and shone his car lights into the store, to illuminate it. A second police car arrived, but no one barged in. When armed criminals enter an enclosed space, the authorities proceed very carefully.

Inside the 7-Eleven it was quiet. The clerk, whom I'll call Ernesto, was alone in the store when he heard the sirens from the freeway off-ramp squeal closer and closer to his parking lot. He wasn't sure, when he was asked to retell the story in a courtroom six months later, whether it was the man or the woman who told him to turn around and face the wall behind his cash register, so he wouldn't see his attackers. He was only staring at the shotgun.

David ordered Ernesto to kneel on the floor facing the wall.

"Do you know what this is?" David demanded, shoving the shotgun alongside Ernesto's face, the barrel between his shoulder and his ear. Ernesto remained kneeling, eyes to the wall, while Domineque pulled beers from the refrigerator. She and David drank.

Serviceably drunk, David motioned Ernesto up with the gun and forced him to a back room of the store, where David demanded money from the safe. Ernesto pulled out the few rolls of bills that were stashed there, and David tossed them to Domineque, who counted them. They marched Ernesto back to his original spot near the cash register and allowed him to sit when he asked. Then, while David watched their hostage, Domineque wandered back to the 7-Eleven's small kitchen area, used for washing up and for rinsing out the coffee pots. She found a knife.

"We should cut his hand—show the cops we're serious," Domineque said when she came back. At this, Ernesto told the court, he became even more afraid, and David saw it. For fifteen minutes, he tortured the clerk, threatening to cut off a pinkie, holding the cool blade pinned against the skin, moving it back and forth. He never drew blood.

When Domineque and David tired of this game, they went back to drinking. David told Ernesto he should drink too—that he should die drunk, that it would hurt less that way. At gunpoint, Ernesto drank. Ernesto believed he would die. This went on for four hours.

Finally, as their high wore down and they realized the cops weren't going to go anywhere, Domineque knew they'd have to surrender. The temporary power she wielded over a 7-Eleven clerk had lost its allure. David fired a shot into the ceiling. At the pop of gunfire, the SWAT team—which had been poised outside the 7-Eleven's doors for hours—rushed inside. In a flurry of boots and helmets and guns, the SWAT officers swarmed Domineque and David.

Domineque was sentenced to twenty-four years and four months in a state penitentiary for three counts of carjacking (because there were three people in the car), two counts of second-degree robbery, false imprisonment of a hostage, criminal threats, and being armed with a loaded weapon. Court documents stated that the "defendant is a man who impersonates a woman." She was sent to an all-male prison.

Robin and I came to visit Christina about six weeks after we'd left, as we had promised. She hadn't known about Domineque's crime when we said our good-byes, because she had cut all ties to Domineque after they crashed the car, and she still hadn't heard when we returned. I was happy that Christina had stayed at the KT house, and when her temp job at the hospital had timed out, she had landed herself a new job at a GNC, selling supplements at the mall.

Since Robin and I had moved, we talked to Christina nearly every day, often twice—Christina reporting to us her daily food intake, her sleep habits, her boy-crush choices, how she almost got into a stranger's car but didn't, so she could be rewarded from afar for all of her infinite good decisions and chided into alignment for her poor ones. We were too far away to chase her down if she truly misbehaved and also too far to rescue her, and I don't know if this was the reason for Christina's continued growth and improvement or if it was simply timing, but in any case, she had made a surprisingly easy transition into the new distance.

The best news was that since we had left, Christina had signed herself up for high school. She had found a self-paced alternative school where students completed as many worksheets and readings as they could each week on their own. Every Friday they dropped the papers off to a teacher, who corrected them and sent students home with more. Christina couldn't wait to show me the school.

"It feels like we're going to the country," I said to Christina, as we sat at the back of the city bus, which was careening around golden-brown hillsides dotted with poppies. We were on Interstate 5, so the blue sky view was open and unbroken by buildings or even billboards. The windows were open, and we hung our heads back, letting the wind rush across our faces.

"I know, I love that," she said. A few minutes before, the same bus had driven through downtown Los Angeles and passed Twin Towers, the main jail for female inmates and for all prisoners with mental health problems. In front of the whole bus, Christina had lifted my skirt to my upper thigh, saying, "Show some leg, girl! There's the jail!" But now, in the relative tranquillity of the countryside—which in reality was just Elysian Park, right near Dodger Stadium—Christina was calm.

As we rode into the neighborhood of Elysian Heights—a community of auto-repair shops, industrial plants, and families—Christina got a call from her case manager at the KT house. It seemed she was returning too late at night from her job. Christina immediately started plucking her eyebrows, staring into a compact, cradling the phone between her ear and her shoulder. I noticed she didn't have any hairs to pluck on the left side at all, just an arched line, drawn on with pencil. On the right, she had five. She fiercely pinched around these hairs, looking for tips that may have just budded through.

"My job gets out at 9:45; you know about the buses," Christina said into the phone, her voice acidic. I gave her a look that said "Stay cool," but she avoided me and stared at her compact.

"No, I can't get proof from my boss!" Christina yelled. She was so quick to ignite. "What? Tell them I'm homeless and live in a shelter? No." She hung up on her case manager and dodged my eyes. She plucked three of her remaining five eyebrow hairs.

"That bitch is only a few years older than me. Don't say nothing," she said to me. I didn't, but I knew the KT wouldn't last now, not for much longer.

By the time we got to the school, Christina was all smiles. The place looked like a former auto garage—of which there were two, across the street and next door—with a metal pull-up door that opened onto a long tube of a room with cement floors and no windows. Various workstations were demarcated by colorful circular rugs or children's bright plastic school chairs neatly clustered around wood veneer tables. At the back was a small computer lab and a few rotating library book stands, filled with tattered young adult romances.

The two women who ran the place seemed tired but kind, and they clearly adored Christina. They chided her in Spanish for her good attendance, saying that if she wasn't careful, she'd graduate from high school next year. Christina beamed; she was nineteen but still technically only a freshman. The teachers gave her a book, *Farewell to Manzanar,* to read.

When Christina left the school for the afternoon, she said she usually sat by the Los Angeles River, which was at the end of the block, for a while, just to think about her life. That day she wanted to think about her sister.

A few weeks prior, Christina's mom had shipped Vicki off to Guatemala to live with Vicki's grandfather—a studious, serious man that Gloria hoped could control Vicki better than she herself could. Vicki was now fifteen and, by virtue of the neighborhood she lived in, was running around with the gangster boys. The Guatemalan family was more strict, more Catholic, and far more poor than the Los Angeles one, so presumably Vicki would be surrounded by virtuous elements and fewer resources with which to harm herself. Gloria knew Vicki wouldn't willingly board the aircraft alone so, according to Christina, she somehow enlisted the help of the police to drag Vicki onto the plane and then make sure the flight took off with her on it.

We sat at the top of a steep cement ravine, which housed the stinky trickle of the river. Scrub grass poked up through cracks, and plastic grocery bags clung to twigs and rocks. Christina laid her head in my lap. She asked me if this meant her mother loved Vicki more.

"I don't know," I said. I didn't.

"I mean, she doesn't even call to find out where I'm living—if I'm living—and she's so worried about Vicki, she sends her to Guatemala?"

I stroked Christina's head. Her hair was breaking. She had dyed it platinum so many times that her normally wild curls were brittle and thin. Here and there, plastered down with hair spray, were three- or five-inch sticks of hair that had simply snapped from too much processing.

"Then again, this could just show that your mom couldn't deal with either of you," I said. "In a way, this could prove that your mom's rejection doesn't have to do with you personally, or with you being trans. She was afraid of Vicki growing up too."

"Let's go to Guatemala!" Christina said. "I could show you everything."

The last time Christina had been to visit, she was four, though her mother had taken Vicki to the country more than once. "We could stay with my family and see my sister," Christina continued, her eyes getting dreamy and far away. I didn't know what Christina's extended family thought about her being transgender, but I was pretty sure they knew. Her grandparents, who lived there, had been to Los Angeles and had seen Christina a few times. Her grandmother dealt with her transformation by not talking about it; she didn't use gender pronouns in Christina's presence, and while she didn't use her girl name, she also didn't call Christina Eduardo. She invented a gender-neutral pet name, something like Puppet. Christina loved her grandmother. "Just imagine, you could have your own room, with a nice big bed."

I let Christina lie there with her head in my lap, alone with her fantasy. Was Christina tossing out a daydream the way that I was fantasizing about Vicki and Christina being equal in their mother's eyes? Christina often issued fibs to match my own; it was her nice way of showing me I was being Pollyanna. There was no big bed in Guatemala, no private room. This was the family, Vicki had told me, in which the kids had no shoes.

Christina showed me the other things she had been doing since we had left, the haunts she'd been haunting. We went to the candle shop on Olvera Street, the touristy little boulevard downtown, designed to look like an old Mexican shopping district. Christina couldn't have candles in her room at the shelter, but she loved to smell them and imagine which ones she'd buy when she had a place of her own— deep red, "for the drama." She took me to La Placita, Our Lady Queen of Angels Church, where well over a thousand baptisms are performed each month, where people leave flowers and small dolls on an outdoor altar to the Virgin Mary. Christina still liked the idea of being Wiccan, but she loved the romance of the Catholic Church and came to this place to pray.

Here we talked about drugs, and how she hadn't used any, aside from pot, in months. She said, simply, that she didn't feel like she needed them so much anymore, that she was feeling better in her life and didn't need to distract herself as often. She also knew that Robin and I weren't right there to pick her up from jail or the emergency room anymore, so she had to take responsibility for herself, which I was amazed she could admit. Also, I thought Foxx and her "hugs not drugs" ways were a good influence on Christina, along with the curfews and regularity of a group home; for all her rankling against the rules and restrictions, urban village living was familiar and comfortable.

When Andrea heard what Domineque had done, her first reaction was "Not my child!" She got a call from the rehab where Domineque had been locked up, and an intake worker there asked Andrea if she'd been watching the news.

"It was on the news as a crime spree," Andrea told me. "Richard went on the Internet, and we found a couple of news clippings about these two men. They said they stole a car and there was a baby in the car, and I was like, 'Oh my god.' And then they barricaded themselves in a 7-Eleven. It sounded so unreal to me."

Throughout Andrea's years of trouble with Domineque, through all the fights and court dates, through the drugs and nights gone missing, Andrea never skipped a day of work. It was the way she coped, to just get up and keep going. "It sounds so silly now, but I remember the next day I called in sick. Emotionally I was flat. I was just empty. It was almost a dead feeling."

At that time, Andrea was pregnant with her first biological child. For the first few months, before Domineque's formal trial, Andrea went to visit Domineque at Men's Central Jail, where she was being held, on over a million dollars bail. Andrea knew, however, that after the sentencing, it would be time to cut Domineque loose. She had warned Domineque about this consequence, and she meant to stick by her word.

"I told her, 'I will be with you through the juvenile court process, but if you commit any adult crimes after the age of eighteen and you go into the adult system, I will not be there—I cannot handle it,'" Andrea said. After Domineque's conviction, however, her lawyer asked Andrea to appear at an 8:30 arraignment hearing to speak on Domineque's behalf. When Andrea arrived at the courthouse, she learned that the hearing had been bumped back to 7:00 A.M. It was already over, so Andrea couldn't speak at all.

"In retrospect, it was probably better that I wasn't there," said Andrea, who had recently given birth and had the baby with her. "What could I have said? This is a damaged kid."

When we talked about it later, I suggested Andrea could have started with Domineque's biological family, using some of the neglect and trauma to explain Domineque's behavior. Or she could start with Domineque's family's family, because abuse always cycles back. Or she could start with society's class-based punishments for drug addiction, or with poverty, or the prison industrial complex, or with any of the other injustices that tip people sideways inside themselves so they try to right the balance by hurting others.

"Exactly," Andrea agreed. "But then it's almost like you're blaming everything else for the decision Domineque made—and she really did do it. This is the decision she made, and these are the consequences of that decision."

Domineque, too, took full responsibility for the crimes she committed, though she said her reason was her drug addiction. She said she planned it—not the exact nature of the crimes, but she did intend to break the law somehow.

"I knew as soon as I turned eighteen I needed to commit a crime to go to prison. It's because I'm stubborn," Domineque said. "Before, there was always another way out. With Andrea, if I was grounded,

I could still walk out. If I was in rehab, I could escape. So I knew I would have to commit a crime to really detox. That was my plan."

Andrea said that she and Richard had warned Domineque that if she continued down the destructive path she was heading, she'd end up doing adult time, but Domineque never seemed to listen. "I think she thought that because of her time in the halls and her time on the streets that she was prepared for prison. In many ways—and this is my perspective—I don't think she knew what she was getting into."

Though Domineque and Andrea weren't communicating with one another at that time, Domineque parroted Andrea's words almost exactly when I talked to her. While she did want to go to prison, Domineque said, she wasn't expecting it to be so horrible. "I needed a slap in the face," Domineque said, something like a notch up from juvenile hall. "What I got was a kick in the gut and a slam in the head."

Then why, I asked, didn't she just do a smaller crime? Something that wouldn't land her twenty-four years, something that wouldn't psychologically harm four people?

"Because once I started, it was like a rush, you know? It's like the cars I've stolen. It's a rush. Like drugs," she said. "So then once I started doing the crimes, I felt like for once *I* was in control. I could do anything. So we just kept going."

When I came back to L.A. to visit Christina about a month later, we got to celebrate: she had landed a job at Bienestar, the Latino AIDS organization where I saw her perform that Britney Spears song so many years ago. She was given a position doing interviews with the transgender sex workers on Santa Monica Boulevard, establishing their HIV risk and teaching them about safer sex. She returned to the place she had run from—but as a counselor and educator—and she was proud. It was her first real social outreach kind of job.

In the weeks since I'd seen her, Christina had also left the KT house and secured a boyfriend. His name was Horatio, and he was twelve years older than she was and nearly inarticulate. The one time Christina put him on the phone with me and I asked him about where he worked, the closest he could get to a description was "I mix things in buckets." They fought all the time—mostly because of Christina's impatience with Horatio's stupidity—and to prove his loyalty to her after one particularly nasty argument, Horatio decided to carve Christina's name across his chest with a razor blade. He did this by watching himself in the mirror, so the end product was a chest scar that read "AИITX." Still, Christina let Horatio spend the night at the residential hotel where she was living, and he helped defray the $250 weekly cost.

The lobby of the Stillwell Hotel boasts a bar called Hank's and an "international" restaurant that serves only Mexican and Central American food. There are clutches of old sofas, sagging and brown, clustered around faux Oriental rugs, and the only windows are at the front, so the back of the lobby is dark and cavelike. I was relieved to find there were no crack addicts lurking about; instead, old men with tufty white hair and stained pants stood around the sofas coughing milky phlegm and staring into space. I climbed to room 307 and knocked on the door. Nobody answered.

"Where are you?" Christina shouted into my cell phone when I called her. She was waiting in front of the building. The hallway outside her door smelled of sour smoke, and the noise from four televisions clamored for dominance.

"I'm at your room—I want to see your space," I said.

"Girl, no. Let's go!" Christina whined. She hadn't wanted me to come in. She was embarrassed by the hotel. "My room's too messy."

Christina was wearing a pink skirt with Indian deities dancing across it, a white Diesel tank top, and black knee-high boots. She had cut her hair short because of all the damage from the hair dye, and it was now in a loose, curly, faux-hawk on top of her head, back in her natural brown. She looked adorable. As soon as we drove away in my rental car, she opened the door, leaned out, and threw up.

"What's that about?" I asked, my hand on her knee.

"It's Horatio," she said. "This time we broke up for real, and last night I drank because of it."

"I thought you already did break up," I said.

"We did, but we broke up again," Christina answered. At a stoplight she ran out of the car and into a gas station. She came back with a Coke. "I'm hungry."

"What do you think you could eat?" I asked, shaking my head at her rebound, knowing this skill had, and would continue to, rescue her from more than hangovers.

"*Mmm*, Japanese food? I think that raw egg they put over them noodles would be good for my stomach."

Over lunch, I asked Christina how much of her interest in Horatio was in simply having a warm body in her bed.

"A lot, girl, a lot," she admitted, stirring her noodles. "Because, you know, I've been trying to get my mother's love. Even if she doesn't give it, I want it. And that's what Horatio is like. I'm looking for my mother in him."

"Oh sweetie, I know about that," I said, impressed by her evolving insight. "The trick is to find people with something worthwhile to give."

This last breakup, Christina said, happened because Horatio was ashamed of her. He first wouldn't introduce her to his family, and then he told her she wasn't normal. "'I don't know what to call you,'" Christina said he told her. "'You're not a woman and you're not a man.'"

I told Christina how I was proud of her for demanding respect. And then she took it further.

"Horatio doesn't have any goals beyond just staying sober. He thinks that's enough. But I want someone that doesn't just stop. I want someone with a mission," Christina said. "And when they get that mission, I want them to have another one."

At this, we toasted Christina's job and the way, even in her roughest times, she'd always held fast to her own mission of wanting to do outreach and social activism. And now she was getting paid to do it.

As she had during the last visit, Christina wanted to take me to more of her secret places. Today it was the downtown library. I was shocked to learn she'd recently obtained a library card.

"Girl, yes," she said. "To get magazines."

Christina liked the historic look of the library, designed as it was to evoke old Egypt, with a central pyramid tower mosaicked with a golden sun. The day outside was beautiful, so there weren't many people loitering, or reading at the heavy tables. Christina and I milled about, browsing through the literature section, which, I lamented, wasn't very well stocked. Suddenly a young guy, in his early twenties maybe, passed by the stacks and eyed Christina up and down, lingering a little too long at her hips and breasts. He smiled at her and turned toward the elevator.

Christina chased after him.

"Excuse me," she said, a couple of paces behind. The man turned. "Do you have a mission? Do you have a goal? What is your reason for being on the planet?"

The guy's eyes bugged out like Christina was crazy, and she smiled congenially and waved him on. He shook his head quickly as though he had water in his ear, and then he grinned vaguely back, pretending to be in on the game. He walked away.

When the man was out of earshot, Christina said to me, "I just think if they's going to look at me like they want to get with me, they better have a mission, is all."

Later that afternoon Christina did let me come see her hotel room, and she was right; it was a mess. The walls were blue, and the carpet was stained and buckling. Christina's clothes lay in twisted heaps all across the floor, and her makeup sat in its own spilled and cakey dust on the bureau. I had to go to dinner without her that night, so she let me take a shower, handing me her raspberry body wash, and then she carefully ironed the extra pair of pants I had brought along. Christina is a meticulous ironer.

At the hotel I found out that she used the library for more than just magazines. She had checked out a Sandra Cisneros book because a year before I had given her *The House on Mango Street,* and she loved it. She was also reading a cheap romance and finishing *Farewell to Manzanar* for school. *Farewell* is about the Japanese internment camps during World War II, about being trapped in your own country. Christina lit a candle on top of the television—a red one, like she had wanted when she got her own place. Nodding toward the *Manzanar* book, Christina said, "I can relate."

Pleasant Valley State Prison takes up 640 acres of hot, dusty land in central California off of the main Interstate 5, 180 miles south of San Francisco and 180 miles north of Los Angeles. You can smell the region—sun-baked cow dung—long before you see it, because the prison is nestled near an enormous cattle ranch and slaughterhouse. Folks who regularly drive the 5 refer to the area as "Cowschwitz."

In the early weekend mornings around 6:00 A.M., visitors queue up their cars in the road shoulder outside the main entrance gates so they can be the first to be processed for the 10:30 visits. The prison is often covered in a thick fog, which is spookily lit from within by the enormous floodlights. Each building is two stories high and clearly marked with the letters *A, B,* or *C,* and tall, electrically charged metal fences surround everything, forming corridors between the buildings. Nearly five thousand inmates live here. Guard towers dot the landscape like windowed trees, and the floodlights help officers see through the fog—though by 10:00 A.M. or so, it all burns off and the air is shimmery hot again.

The first sign a new inmate or visitor sees when driving onto prison grounds is a standard warning against bringing in weapons and firearms. The next sign is cuter; it looks hand-painted, and it's hung on a wooden post. It reads, "DON'T REST UNTIL YOU'VE DONE YOUR BEST," and it's followed by an identical post with curlicue decorations on its horizontal arm. "SMILE, YOU MAKE A DIFFERENCE," this one says.

A prison visitor-processing area is probably the only place in

North America, outside of a synagogue, where you'll find hundreds of people gathered together on a Saturday morning, and not one of them will be in jeans. The dress code is strict: no denim or blue chambray of any sort (because the inmates all wear state-issued blues), no skirts or shorts that rise more than two inches above the knee, no tight or transparent clothing, no gloves or hats, and no bras with metal underwires. Visitors are allowed to bring two keys on one ring, one ID, one small, unopened package of Kleenex, up to $30 in quarters for the vending machines, and ten non-obscene, non-gang-affiliated photographs, all in a transparent change purse no larger than six by eight inches. Prison handbags have a fashion all their own; I saw see-through purses with pink piping and clear vinyl purses that were cinched at the top with a glittery string, purses that zipped and purses that snapped. A Ziploc full of quarters like mine indicated a onetime visitor; the fancy bags signaled a regular.

When I went to see Domineque, she had already been at Pleasant Valley for more than a year, and I was her first visitor. She had to initiate the process to get me approved for a visit months before, as inmates request background-check forms for the people they'd like to see. When an officer finally called my number, I walked toward a high counter with six men in uniform behind it and handed him my approval form. He asked me questions and sent me through a metal detector that promptly beeped. I took off my belt and my watch and went back through. It beeped again. This got the attention of a few more officers.

"Maybe it's the zipper on your sweater," the officer suggested. "Try taking that off."

I was wearing a black zip-up cardigan with a white tank top underneath. I am naturally flat chested and, because of the "no bras with underwire" rule, I had simply not worn a bra. The sweater was somewhat thick and covered me entirely. "Um, I'm only wearing a little tank top underneath," I said, and added, very quietly, "and I'm not wearing a bra."

The officer smirked a little and shot a quick look to his coworker.

"Well, just cover yourself with your arms and go through fast. Then put the sweater back on."

So I did. I dropped my sweater into one of the plastic baskets people use for their coins and stepped forward toward the detector, my arms folded across my chest.

"Ma'am, you have to wear a bra in here!" a voice boomed. Another officer, broad shouldered and thick jawed, had stepped forward. "You can't have a visit without a bra on."

I reached for my sweater, one arm still protectively covering my chest. By now the entire room of a hundred visitors was openly staring. "But you have the rule about no underwires," I said.

"That's right, but you have to wear a bra," the man said loudly. Three of the guards behind him had started to crack up, one of them folded over in laughter. "You can't visit these men without no bra."

"But wait, you wouldn't have even known I didn't have a bra on if I didn't have to take my sweater off," I protested. Knowing they were just trying to humiliate me, I stood a little taller and said, "A bra doesn't do anything for me, and you can't see anything with that sweater."

"Ma'am, I saw you weren't wearing a bra," the officer continued, keeping a stern face while the men laughed behind him. "And we got a rule. Now you can go to Kmart down the road and get yourself a bra and come back."

I looked at the clock on the wall. It was almost 11:00. I had been waiting since 6:30. Visiting hours were over at 3:00. If I went to Kmart, bought a bra, and reentered the line, I would miss seeing Domineque altogether. I told the officer this, and, to my surprise, the original officer I had been working with interrupted.

"Sir," he said to his superior with the booming voice. "This lady's going to visit one of the he-shes. So I don't think there'll be that much of a problem."

The officer screwed up his face and waved me through. As I passed alone through metal gates that clanked shut and creaked open in front of me, I wondered how Domineque could be faring in this world; ten minutes in and my civilian breasts were the subject of derision and control. Her prisoner breasts were three times the size of mine. The ironic thing was, she wasn't allowed to have a bra in jail.

The visitation room looks and smells like a public school cafeteria, with the exception that all the food comes out of vending machines and there's a small children's play area off to one side where a few blocks and children's books and toys lie scattered about. At the front of this room, three guards sit at an elevated desk area, where they communicate with central command and make announcements over loudspeakers. The center guard has a photocopied map of all the tables and, like a host at a restaurant, writes down which inmate is sitting at which table to keep tabs and ensure that no fights break out. Next to the guard station is a wallpaper picture of tropical mountains and a green lake where inmates and their families can pay for a Polaroid photograph of themselves standing in front of the scene, as though they were all on vacation together. Another wall, inexplicably, proffers a small laminated jigsaw puzzle of two parakeets while the side walls show posters of blond children looking at water with the word "PRIORITIES" in bold letters above their heads. The posters read, " A hundred years from now it will not matter what my bank account was, the sort of house I lived in, or the kind of car I drove . . . But the world may be different because I was important in the life of a child." Given that the inmates in this room had neither cars nor houses and likely felt guilty over their lack of influence in their children's lives, I thought this an odd decorative choice. Later, when Domineque saw me glancing at the posters, she shrugged and said, "They just like to come up with ways to be cruel."

I had been in the visitation room for about ten minutes when a guard opened up the special inmate door at the back and Domineque walked in. She actually looked beautiful. Her hair was dyed blond and pulled back in a bun at the nape of her neck. The skin on her face was soft and radiant, and she had drawn black eyeliner into the inside of her lower lids. She smiled and her teeth were a pure white;

the small gap between the front two looked disarmingly vulnerable. She wore her state jeans low and slouchy; her blue chambray shirt was tucked in and ironed smooth with perfect creases in each arm, the buttons down the front drawing a line between breasts that hung loose. In this room of men, Domineque was undeniably a woman.

"Do I look fat?" Domineque asked as she hugged me.

She did not look fat. In fact, she looked healthier than I had seen her in all the years since she was a student in my classroom years ago. This surprised me; from Domineque's letters, I knew prison life was hard.

"It's because I'm off the drugs," Domineque said. Not that drugs weren't available to her. Domineque pointed out an inmate who was holding hands with a woman with red hair and a flower-print dress. His eyes were dilated, and the couple was staring at a wall. "See, they're high right now."

Domineque guessed that about 10 percent of the men in the visiting room had had dope slipped to them in a baggy during the one mouth kiss inmates are allowed when they first encounter their visitor. She had been offered crack in this prison, she said, but she didn't take it; she didn't even smoke weed. When I asked her why not, she looked at me, incredulous.

"Because I know drugs are what got me here in the first place. I have a lot of regrets. Whenever I'm tempted, I think about what got me here," she said, looking me square in the eye. She seemed so firm and so bare, with so little to lose, that I believed her. "The only thing I'll do very rarely is drink wine, which is disgusting because it tastes like feet."

The inmates make liquor in their cells, Domineque said, by sneaking fruit from "chow," where they eat their meals, and leaving it to rot in their rooms. They fashion a grater out of the top of a sardine can and grate the fruit, which preferably is some kind of citrus, into small bits in a plastic bag. They then add a high-sugar item like ketchup, barbecue sauce or, the holy grail, Skittles (which Domineque knew contained forty-five grams of sugar per bag), and some water. Over three to four days, the fruit rot will cook the sugar, and a rough form of hooch will emerge.

As we were talking, a little boy in a black T-shirt and red jeans came running up to us. He was maybe four years old.

"You're a lady!" he shouted, dancing back on his heels and smiling. "Why're you in jail?"

Domineque laughed and covered her mouth with her hand, embarrassed. She looked at me and back at the boy. He laughed, too, and ran away. I smiled at Domineque and held her hand, on top of the table—the only place where visitors and inmates were allowed to touch. Her eyes welled, and she bit her lip to stop them.

"I honestly don't know why people let their children in this place; this is the block for all the child molesters," Domineque said, her mouth sneering in disgust, one eyebrow raising. In an instant, this was the Domineque I remembered from the streets, the one who fought dirty and mean, the one who could silence a gangster with a glance. I looked around. Unlike other visitation rooms where the inmates were segregated by race just as they were in their blocks, the men were mixed in here. They were predominantly black and Latino, and about 15 percent were white. I saw one Asian man. Many had tattoos, big Olde English letters that wrapped around their tree trunk necks, and many had shaved heads. Many were smiling and laughing as they bounced young children on their laps or held hands with their wives or girlfriends; some sat somberly with their parents; some played cards; some prayed.

Domineque had been placed in the Sensitive Needs Yard, or SNY, which is the unit for any inmate who needs special protection, who could get hurt or killed in the regular prison, or mainline. The mainline is segregated by race, supposedly to circumvent gang wars, though many inmates and outsiders alike think that this fuels, rather than impedes, racism. Prison personnel refer to the blocks by their gang or racial names; for instance, a sign in the visitor-processing room that morning said that Southern Hispanics and Bulldogs were on lockdown that day and were not permitted visitors.

Domineque was placed in the SNY because she's transsexual; most of the gay inmates are in there too. Used to be, she said, the "queens" would go into the mainline, but then there was trouble when some of the men with life sentences, or lifers, fell in love. The lifers' deepest loyalty would fall to his lover, not to the prison gang, and the gang leaders didn't like that, so the gangs started ordering the queens to be killed. To protect them, the authorities sent the gay men and transsexuals into the SNY. The other people in the SNY were the criminals the mainline prisoners hated most: the rapists and the child molesters and, sometimes, the more "sick" serial murderers.

Whenever someone new enters the mainline, he has to show the gang leaders his papers—the court reports he's legally allowed to keep with him that detail the nature of his crime. In this way, the gangs keep tabs on their members and clean their rosters of, or kill, any undesirables. In the SNY there aren't any gangs, so nobody knows for sure what crimes anyone else has committed, and Domineque is tense with round-the-clock vigilance.

Domineque didn't want to go into the SNY; she was terrified of being raped again and said that if anyone touched her, she might black out or attack madly without any awareness of what she was doing. But she wasn't given a choice; outside the protective custody of the SNY, Domineque could be murdered. So Domineque made friends with the D.O.'s, or "dropouts"—the gang members who had tired of life in the mainline and wanted to ease up with the "weirdos" in Sensitive Needs. To be accepted into the SNY, Domineque explained, the dropouts were forced to supply the prison authorities with a significant amount of information about gang operatives; they had to rat out their former friends, which put them at great risk if they were ever released. If he didn't tattle, the reasoning went, the D.O. could be a "sleeper," or someone who penetrated the SNY to kill someone who was "in the hat"—meaning with a contract on his life, often for snitching—and then transfer back into the mainline.

"Ugh," I said. I was eating mini donuts and sliced peaches in syrup from the vending machine, trying to soften the bleak surroundings with sugar. Domineque was tapping at a piece of chocolate cake with a plastic spoon. She said she didn't want to let the other inmates see her eat; she never let them see her eat. "It's all pretty ugly. How are you handling it?" I asked her.

"I feel like a fifty-year-old person in a twenty-year-old body, for real," Domineque answered. She looked sad. Her eyes, which were always sunken, now seemed deep and more penetrating. "I have to be so hard in here—people think of me like that—hard. Only my cellie knows I goof around."

I told Domineque that she was strong for getting off the drugs, that other addicts take decades to do it, that some never succeed. And here she was in prison, finally off crack.

Domineque's eyes brightened. "I *am* strong," she said. "That, I know I am. Especially in here."

I remembered Domineque when she was younger, when her face was usually distant and vaguely wanting something, like she was re-membering a meal she ate three weeks ago and trying to mentally find the taste. Sometimes I felt like I could put my hand right through her, as though her flesh were a mirage, she was so vacant in-side herself. But now when I looked at Domineque, the image of a tree came to mind. It was strange, I knew, but I just said it.

"You're more like a tree now," I said. "I know you really fucked up, but you're also better, more solid. You always seemed sort of spaced out to me before, and now, you feel more like a tree."

Domineque smiled, and in that moment she did look fifty and not twenty. I could tell we understood each other. "Exactly," she said. "I am more like a tree."

The next day the number of visitors had thinned out considerably throughout the whole prison. There was more of a bleakness to the visitation room, maybe because there were fewer children squealing and running about, and maybe because the weekend visits were end-ing and the inmates knew their loved ones would be leaving today for another week or month or year. Domineque's mood got sadder too. She told me what she hadn't told me in her letters—that she only left her cell for, at max, an hour or two a day. While the other inmates went to jobs or the dayroom or religious services or the yard or to chow—to be with other people—Domineque never knew when she was going to be harassed, by either the prison staff or other inmates. She hadn't taken a real shower in over a year.

"Birdbaths in my cell sink," Domineque said when I asked her how she kept clean. The open showers at Pleasant Valley are apparently set up in what's called a "270," meaning a 270-degree angle to all of the cell doors, so that any inmate can look out his door and watch the other inmates showering. This, for Domineque, is not an option. "With me looking the way I do, knowing there are people in here for rape and child molestation . . . that's just evil. That's why I don't really leave my cell."

A couple of correctional officers, or C.O.'s, have asked Domineque to change her appearance. One gave her a write-up for 180 days more time and took away dayroom privileges for a stint when he caught her with paint, made to look like fingernail polish, on her nails. Another threatened to make her cut her hair, but she refused. Domineque said he called her a "faggot." Incidents like these make her extremely depressed.

It's the depression, though, that gains Domineque access to her doctors, whom she likes. Domineque told her doctors that they'd "have to take me out on a gurney"—meaning dead—if they didn't prescribe her her hormones in prison, and she now gets them, along with antidepressants, every day. She also keeps herself up with peroxide, which is handed out in the nurses' office for gargling. She dyes her hair with this and keeps it straighter and light by washing with the state-issued body soap, which has a lot of lye in it. For makeup she uses a ballpoint pen to draw in her eyebrows and a grease pencil on her eyes.

"Inmates who work as clerks get these and sell them to the queens," Domineque explained. I told Domineque I was surprised to hear her call herself that. A curtain of grief pulled across her face, but briefly.

"I changed my vocabulary to meet theirs," she said. "In here we're called queens. Me, I know I'm a girl, and with the inmates, I say 'if you don't call me "she," don't talk to me.' With the C.O.'s, since they have the authority to write me up or send me to the hole, I let a lot pass. And no matter what, they're not gonna say 'she.'"

Domineque said that when she first got locked up, being called "gentleman" and "sir" at every turn made her angry and suicidal. She had transitioned at fifteen and grown accustomed to people accepting her as a woman. After a while hopelessness trumped fury, and blinding headaches framed her days. "Tylenol became my best friend, " she said. Now what's hardest is the loneliness and isolation. "I would say, if I could be in a women's prison, that would take maybe 90 percent of my problems away. If you feel comfortable somewhere, you can go to groups, participate in things, get involved. In a women's prison, I would go to school and a job, but I can't so easily here because everyone looks at me."

Domineque won't talk about the crimes she committed. Her process of alleviating her conscience is a private one, though she will say, in broad sweeps, that she has regrets and takes responsibility for what she's done. She knows part of this responsibility is prison time, but she doesn't think she should have to endure what other inmates don't: the daily trauma of being a woman in a men's prison.

In one of the most comprehensive legal articles on the topic, lawyer Darren Rosenblum writes that transgender prisoners all over the country have tried to get reassigned to the opposite prison. Most only succeed if they have had genital surgery, though some not even then. One postoperative female in a federal prison in Kentucky was housed with men because she was "anatomically male." Another transwoman in Colorado tried to self-castrate and, after the prison completed the surgery, forced her onto testosterone supplements against her will, presumably because she was still in a men's prison. A court later ordered the prison to provide her with estrogen. In all the cases he studied for his article, Rosenblum found only one instance of a preoperative transsexual being housed with the gender that matched her psychological status—and in this case, her cell-mate sued because she felt uncomfortable using the toilet or shower-ing with her so near.

Domineque thought surgery might be her best, if far-flung, hope for getting rehoused. Given that medical insurance won't cover the cost of SRS for unincarcerated citizens, I told Domineque it was un-likely that she could get the state to pay for hers while she was locked up. Many prisons won't even pay for hormones, and no state has ever covered the full genital surgery. In fact, when a transwoman in Wis-consin launched a recent federal lawsuit—claiming that denying her access to the operation (and thus keeping her in a men's prison) vio-lated her Eighth Amendment constitutional protection from "cruel and unusual punishment"—state legislators one-upped her. They introduced a bill that would prohibit the state from ever using state money for inmate SRS, now or in the future.

The way transgender people are treated in prison often violates the Eighth Amendment, said Alex Lee, a lawyer for the Transgen-der, Gender Variant and Intersex Justice Project, an advocacy group based in San Francisco. They're more easily victimized—verbally, physically, and sexually—and less often protected by gangs. Also, the guards and prison staff, because of their own transphobia, can turn a blind eye to inmate assaults, or even participate in the harass-ment and assaults themselves. Still, when Domineque first got to prison, her only solution to what she called "this hell" was to find a way to complete her transition process. She shrugged off the notion that it would be nearly impossible to do.

"I don't care," she said. "Hit me over the head with a bat and do the surgery with a broken bottle; just get me out of here."

Christina and I were originally supposed to visit Domineque to-gether. After Domineque had been locked up for several months, Christina finally found out what had happened. I was gone, so I didn't see her reaction, but I know it upset her enough that she didn't want to talk to me about it. When I found Domineque's address and gave it to Christina over the phone, she kicked a tree so hard that she was limping and had to hang up. Still, Christina wrote to Domineque, referred to her as "sister," and said she missed her. Domineque sent her the visiting papers, but at first Christina lost them, and then she didn't fill them out in time to be processed for our trip. She didn't really want to go.

When I drove back into Los Angeles after seeing Domineque, I picked Christina up first thing. I asked if she wanted to go get coffee, and she shook her head. "Just drive," she said. Like the old days, she turned the radio up loud.

After fifteen minutes Christina shut the music off. "Talk," she said quietly. "I'm ready."

I told her everything, and she listened, her jaw set and her eyes distant. Then she sobbed. I pulled over and held her, but she was somewhere else—with Domineque, letting go. She cried for a half an hour solid, and then she asked me to start up the car, and to "never talk about that place again."

I thought for a long time about why Domineque was in a men's prison and why Christina was in a good job and how most everyone I know ends up where they are because they're looking to answer some core question seeded in childhood, the question that shapes them and sets their bones for walking forward. If it's a hopeful question, like "How can I live out my family's dreams?" their lives will be hopeful ones, if riddled with difficult expectations. But if it's a bad question, their life will be hard. For Domineque, her question was one she posed to me long ago: "I wanted to know what could be so good about a drug that could make my mom give up her kids for it." This question nearly killed her.

Christina's question, I think, was "How can I find love?" which is what's kept her always looking, always surviving. She, like Domineque, didn't get the love she needed as a little girl, but something made her ask a different kind of question. Maybe the difference was drugs, or character, or maybe she had those extra ounces of stability early on, I don't know. I do know that Foxx was well-loved enough as a child for her question to be "How can I be a star?"

My question, I realized, was similar to Domineque's, only turned in on itself. My mother had let me go at fourteen and never thought of me again. My question, still sounding for all the world like it came from a child's wounded soul, was this: What kind of kid could be so bad that a mother would give her up?

Domineque had gone to prison for her question, and Christina had ping-ponged her way from acting the druggie thug to accomplished activist for her question, and what had I done for mine? I had found one of the most outwardly difficult kids, and I had mothered her. I said to Christina, "You—you, who will challenge me, and run away and test my limits—I will love you, and I will not let you go." Because I had to find out there was no "bad" kid worth discarding. Even Christina. Even me.

## II

## COMMENCEMENT

*W*HEN ROBIN AND I got to Los Angeles for Christina's high school graduation, the first thing she did was make us homemade wontons.

"If y'all are going to fly three thousand miles for this day, y'all are going to get a home-cooked meal," Christina said, dicing imitation crab and cucumbers and carrots. She was living back at her mother's house, in the room she and her sister used to share, since Vicki had gone to Guatemala. At $250 a week, the hotel was more expensive than an apartment, and Christina still didn't feel ready to get one of those on her own: it was too permanent, too stable, too detached, or too independent, depending on the day. Christina didn't join us in the feast, however, as she still didn't feel comfortable eating in her mother's house (even if Christina had done the shopping, she was afraid her mother would accuse her of stealing her expensive food).

It was 10:00 A.M. and both her mother and stepfather were out. It turned out Gloria was buying tapes for the video camera and was planning on attending the graduation. Christina was cautiously thrilled. The graduation was a big deal, Christina said, because she was the first person in the American part of the Guatemalan family to graduate from high school. An aunt dropped off a few cousins to join us—one fourteen, one twelve, and the youngest, Neely, six. All the kid cousins now called Christina by her girl name and treated her with respect; she was older, she had street credibility for having left the home and family so much younger, and they loved her. Plus, when they were out of line, she threatened to hit them. We goofed around, taking pictures of Neely in Christina's graduation cap, waiting for Gloria.

When we were just about to stuff all the kids in our little rental car, Gloria showed. Christina's smile was so big you could tuck it behind her ears, but she didn't say anything—just scooped up Neely and tumbled with her into our backseat.

Gloria followed us to the ceremony, which was held in a football field near Temescal Canyon State Park, a beautiful area of brown, sun-dried mountains and wildflowers. All the alternative schools were graduating together that day—about nine hundred students from adult schools, schools for pregnant moms, schools for probation kids, and schools, like Christina's, for independent learning.

Christina waved to us as she ran up to get her diploma, her high-heeled boots and baby pink cords blurring in a happy skip beneath her blue graduation gown. Robin and I and the cousins and Christina's mom leaped up to cheer, just like all the other families who sat bored and listless during the litany of names until they heard the announcer call out their special one, but for us there seemed to be an extra surge of relief and joy. Neely pointed and jumped up and down, and Robin picked her up so she could see better. Christina's triumph was electric.

"It was like my whole life was there," she said afterward. "For my mom to see nine hundred people not saying *anything* about me, not seeing anything wrong with me—that helps so much. There were all these people that thought I was bad and disgusting, and in a way I believed them—and then I go and do something like this; it just fucks with the frequency."

Still, she told us afterward, things had not been all sunshine and Technicolor on the field. As she was lining up, she said, she ran into a teacher from a continuation school that she attended after she left a mainstream junior high. Seven years prior, this teacher stopped the class to announce, "I don't think you should be wearing a bra to school, *Mr.* Ramirez." When Christina saw this teacher again, she wanted to settle the score.

"I told her, 'We had an *experience* together,'" Christina said. "'You disrespected me.'"

Christina said the teacher walked toward her, concerned, asking, "How?"

"For me to tell you that, we'd have to go somewhere private," Christina said she told her, smirking nastily. "But that bitch didn't look like she wanted to go nowhere private with me. I looked at her like I could throw down—even with all my makeup on. She just walked away with this tight-ass smile on her face."

After the graduation, after the last car had left the parking lot with a giant foam finger in the shape of an "I'm #1" wagging from the window, after we had taken pictures of every family member holding Christina's diploma, it was clear without discussion that Christina would be leaving with us. We were the parents who took a child out after a graduation; Gloria would do no more than attend the ceremony.

At the restaurant Christina was too tired to even flirt with the waiters. "I'm feeling every kind of emotion at once," she said, and started to cry. She couldn't eat her carne asada, which was her favorite. She said she missed Domineque, whom she knew would never share milestones with her again.

On the drive home, Christina's spirits lifted. She asked if we could open all the windows, and if I would sit in the back with her so she could lay her head in my lap while Robin drove. We laughed at Christina's Janet Jackson CD, which we all agreed sounded like a sexy gerbil, if small rodents could sing, and Christina watched the billboards passing from her vantage on my lap.

"Girl, what would you do if you won thirty-seven million dollars?" she asked me when she spotted the California Lotto sign.

"Oh, I don't know. Probably start a school. Pay for your college. Buy a lot of shoes," I said. "What would you do with thirty-seven million dollars?"

"Buy thirty-seven million vaginas."

"Really?" I said. Christina had continually maintained that she didn't want sex reassignment surgery. She was protective of her body as it was. She liked the way the hormones changed her outward appearance, but she always said she would keep her penis, because removing it would be about pleasing a man instead of herself. "Have you been thinking about surgery?"

"I always am," she said.

"*Hmm,*" I answered. "Are you getting tired of having to struggle with the dating thing?"

"This isn't about men," Christina said, looking up at me. Her eyes were perfectly clear and serious. "I'm not comfortable with my body naked. I want to do it for me, to be comfortable with my body naked."

In a way, this broke my heart. It was such a simple statement, but it was so complicated. On the one hand, Christina wasn't comfortable with her body, because other people weren't comfortable with her body. And it was the other people I wanted to fix. On the other hand, she could be changing; she could simply want to look more like the genetic women that she knew. In any case, this was the first time that Christina had talked about the surgery in relation to herself instead of men, which was tremendous progress, and I was proud of her for that. It was no coincidence, I thought, that this shift came on her graduation day. I took her hand.

Christina lightened the mood. "Besides, it'll be cuter."

I laughed. "Pussies aren't always cute," I said.

"Well, I'll just make mine look like my lips"—and she narrowed her eyes and pursed her lips Marilyn Monroe style.

"Well, it'll certainly make it easier for us all to go to the Korean baths together," I said. Christina laughed and sat up and hugged me.

The next day, when the three of us were hanging out with Foxx, surgery came up again. We were drinking fancy, frothy coffee drinks at an outdoor café on Melrose. Foxx, because she still hated coffee, was drinking a smoothie. Christina told this story:

"The other day, I woke up and decided to go to the grocery store and get some cheese for nachos. It was like eight in the morning. And these guys were at the gas station, and they said, 'Come over.'"

"Why'd you go up to their car?" I asked, knowing she did.

Both Foxx and Christina looked at me, incredulous, their long spoons held in midair.

"Because they'll clock you if you don't," Christina said.

"They smell your fear," Foxx said.

"Later that night the guy called," Christina went on. "He was watching a movie and he said, *'Ewww!* There's a guy having sex with a transvestite!' And I was like, *'Ewwwww!'*"

Foxx cracked up.

"And then the guy said, 'What's up, Pretty?'" Christina said. "And I said, 'I'm some pretty-ass transsexual.'"

"What'd he do?" Foxx asked, stirring her smoothie and smiling.

"He said, 'What?!' And I said, 'You heard me. I'm a pretty transsexual, honey,' in my sweetest voice. And then I hung up the phone."

Foxx laughed and said, "No matter what, men aren't going to understand." She felt this way since Fernando, that real love wasn't possible. She'd had boyfriends, but none of them were great, and she chalked it up to a lack of options.

"In the transgender world, you're either going to get a man that'll abuse you, try to get money out of you, a man that just wants sex, or a man that's not mentally all there to figure things out," she said to me once when I asked her about her romantic prospects. I told her I thought she was being uncharacteristically negative; she made love sound impossible.

"It's not impossible; out of twenty t-girls, there are maybe two in healthy, equal relationships," she said. "The thing is, when you do get a man who comes along, and he has some flaws, you think, '*Hmmmm,* I can work with that.'"

Unlike in the past, when Foxx used to disclose her status right away, she now often waits. She told Christina and Robin and me the story of meeting some guy in a Quik Stop who asked for her number because he'd never kissed a black girl before. After they'd made out for a while, Foxx asked the guy if he knew she was transsexual.

"He just said, 'Yeah?'" Foxx said. "A lot of times guys will say that because they don't want to admit they don't know something."

Christina nodded; she'd experienced this too. "So what happened?" she prodded.

"I said, 'It means I was born a male, but now I'm female,' and he said, 'Ohhh,'" and here Foxx made her voice sound both disgusted and disappointed. "The guy said, 'That changes my feelings about you.'"

I had to interrupt. "You picked up these two losers at a gas station and a Quik Stop!" I said. "What if you only handed out your number to guys who looked like they had brains in their heads?" As soon as I asked the question, I knew it wasn't just intelligence that made genetic men comfortable with transwomen's bodies; still, I was frustrated with smart girls stooping for dumb men.

"It wouldn't matter," Christina answered. "No matter who they are, you've got to tell men something so personal so fast before anything can happen—and then they get to reject you. And then even if you want to reject them, you can't because you've already told them this thing: it's like, yeah right, you're rejecting them."

It was then that I understood why Christina didn't go out with the men she met in the library where she sometimes hung out; she had lower hopes for the guys on the street and therefore less to lose.

"I'm tired of being a freak to everybody. With men, I'm disgusting, and with women, they want to check and see how passable I am. With everyone, I'm an 'it,' and it's like I'm not fully human," Christina said. "It's like Michael Jackson—he can say he's white, but people can go back to his baby pictures and be like, 'Ummm, no, you're not.' With me, they see me down there, and no matter what I say, they're like 'Ummm, no, you're not.' That's why I want the surgery."

Even Foxx, who for years had led many of the kids in their proud thinking that women could have penises, now conceded that life would be easier without one. She wasn't planning for surgery, but, she said, if someone came along and proposed to pay for it, she'd probably take the offer.

"It's something I might like to do, but nothing I'm in a rush to get," she said to me later. "I guess the main reasons I would do it would be to not have to tuck anymore and to not have the big burden to disclose that I have a penis. But other than that, you still have the same problems in life after the surgery that you do before."

In her musical persona, Foxx had stopped disclosing her transsexuality too. She had recently joined, and then left, a hip-hop group with Tito and two brothers from New York. Tito, with his honeyish baby voice, did a lot of the singing, and the boys, who were straight, rapped. Foxx provided the sex appeal and did backup dancing and some rapping. Foxx wrote the band member bios.

Hers read, "I'm a simple girl and I know I'm not the best rapper or even the finest rapper, but I'm real," hinting at the knocks she'd weathered since she'd moved to Los Angeles, bright eyed with confidence. Foxx then went on to lie about her age and birth gender. "On February 15, 1984, Serena and Derek were blessed with a beautiful caramel girl. She grew up in Birmingham, Alabama. At an early age, she began to emulate Janet Jackson, Chaka Khan, and even Prince."

When she had just joined the group, Foxx said to me, "The world's not ready for a transsexual pop star yet. I've tried that route, and it hasn't been that successful." We were lying on her bed in Long Beach. Her bedspread was green with pink roses, and her three cats climbed over us as we talked. The room had three mirrors, along with a television and a computer, and a T-shirt memorializing Gwen Araujo pinned to the wall. "I'm not saying it can't be done, but I'm more realistic than I was four years ago. Back then I was much more like, 'I'm gonna go in and change the world. In four years I'll be a big star.' That's just not so easy; I need to get my foot in the door before I can do that, so right now I'm going through the hip-hop community."

Here, Foxx paused. She meant she was going to be giving up her pop music, and her politics. No more singing about coming out, or about being proud of being transgender. From here on out, she would rap about hip-hop's sanctioned subjects: money, sex, and being better than anyone else. She petted one of her cats and looked out her window. Atop it, two black Barbies stood sentinel. "The hip-hop community is already homophobic and very male driven—they barely let a female artist come through," she said. "So if you're a transgender woman trying to come through, it's a challenge."

Foxx ended up playing mother to the boys; she said she had to foot the bills for most of the demo recording sessions, and she copied all the flyers and carted the band around in her car. After several months, she grew tired of what she perceived as the others' irresponsibility, and infighting naturally gave way to the group's dissolution. For the first time in years, she decided to take a short break from music.

Because she had originally come to Los Angeles for acting, Foxx thought perhaps she should go back to her roots. Maybe that original vision was the channel through which she could prove herself—and from some success there, she could morph herself back into a musician. She thought she'd go on a few auditions, maybe put her head shots together.

Almost as soon as Foxx resolved to shift her focus, she landed a speaking role in a Wayans brothers movie. The brothers were looking specifically for a transsexual, and when Foxx walked into the auditions at the Laugh Factory on Sunset Boulevard, she said, "Damon Wayans's eyes were fixated right on me. I knew I had the role."

Damon Wayans was making his directorial debut on a movie about a comedian (Marlon Wayans) down on his luck. One of the jokes is that Marlon makes out with a transsexual whom he thinks is a genetic woman, takes her to a motel, and the next day runs into her again at the nightclub where he's performing. It's then that he, as Foxx said, "clocks her T." The audience, who's in on the "joke," gets to laugh at the duped fool, who runs away in horror.

"Damon asked me if I could make my voice go deeper," Foxx said of the audition. "He said I was too convincing as a woman, and in order to get a reaction from the audience, I'd need to have a deeper voice."

Foxx had called to tell me her exhilarating news—that finally she had gotten a break. I didn't want to temper her excitement, always the one handy with a bucket of cold water. Still. Where were her lyrics, her anthems to transgender pride?

"It's a portrayal of life—it's exactly as men act," Foxx said, defensive. Then she paused. "Yeah, I wasn't happy with it at first. Like you, I thought, 'Is this gonna send the wrong message?' But then I thought to myself, a lot of transgender women are not blessed to have a feminine voice, and that was the woman I was playing."

Foxx's big break was such a complex gift. She had been working for five years for artistic recognition, and she wanted to use the recognition to raise awareness and acceptance for transsexuals. When some fame finally arrived, it had a sting for the trans community she was originally looking to uplift. "When I was watching them rehearse, there were parts that hurt deep inside because the character says things like 'I'm a black man. The only thing lower than a black man is a black woman. The only thing lower than a black woman is a black faggot.' Still, as a character, it all comes back on him," Foxx said. And for her, the potential end justified the means.

"I'm gonna just try to be a J.Lo—use acting as a way into music," Foxx said. "I really want to show people I have talent, and you can see I have talent in this movie."

Foxx is remarkable that way: her resilience, optimism, and tenacity are unflagging, and so is her faith, since she goes to a queer-friendly church nearly every Sunday. She believes in a divine order and, after the movie, was praying that both creative avenues would allow her to express her message.

"I'm hoping that somebody would like to put me in a queer show that's based on transgender women," Foxx said. She imagined a serialized program where transgender characters weren't reduced to their stereotypes of call girls or awkward "bricks" just learning how to waddle around in a dress, but rather be fully drawn people with love lives and jobs and families—more like the community Foxx had cultivated and grown into.

Foxx also wanted to produce more dimensional music, that had strands of both pop and hip-hop, a sound that represented Foxx's varied interests and attracted multiple audiences. She said she was too independent to be joining any bands again anytime soon; she was back to writing her own music. Her songs weren't solely promoting transgender pride but were more about, as she said, "women empowerment," with transsexuality as one more way to be a woman.

A little over a year later, though, Foxx would struggle again with her own dreams versus outsiders' expectations. Her music wasn't picking up, and she hadn't booked any acting gigs, and none of her dates had developed into boyfriends. She decided she needed to do something drastic: she decided she needed the sex reassignment surgery.

It came to her in a kind of flash; she was talking to friends one day, and it hit her—the one thing that was holding her back from stardom and from love was what was between her legs. She looked around her church and saw that the gay men had lovers, the lesbians had wives, but the transsexuals sat alone. She listened to rap music and heard the way women were discriminated against; how would she ever be accepted? For years she had been trumpeting a woman's right to live her own life in her own body—and suddenly she worried that the life she planned was slipping away.

So Foxx started saving money. She made an appointment with a good surgeon in Thailand, where the prices are low, and she bought an airline ticket. She was frantic with the saving, the planning, the vision. She called with weekly updates about her finances and her fears. She started obsessing about her looks; she got a nose job and a tracheal shave, so she'd look even more feminine before the surgery—and after, she'd be close to perfection. And then, exactly one week before her scheduled departure, she changed her mind. Once again, Foxx's center held.

"I think I had to get this close to the surgery to remind myself that I like being a transsexual," Foxx said right after she canceled the trip. She was happy again, sounding like her old confident self. "If I got it, I would feel like I was just a regular woman—nothing special."

Foxx would go on to use the surgery money to record three new songs in the studio, and put together a top-quality media package. This time, she came out as transgender in her bio.

"There was a time when black people couldn't get starring roles in the movies; they could only be servants or nannies. And they couldn't be major singers. It's like that with transsexuals too—they can only be seen as prostitutes," Foxx said to me later, her kind, teacherly voice coming through. Even though we were on the phone, I half expected her to hand me some fruit punch, make a spot for me on the couch. "I'm not saying I'm going to be the person to break down the door, but it'll happen—and it might be me. A lot of the reason I'm doing this in the first place is for a fourteen-year-old to see me and say, 'I did not know it was possible for a transsexual to do this. And she's beautiful. And she can rap.' It's to give him hope."

At the end of the summer of the Wayans brothers filming, Christina had applied for a new research job. It was a job with the county, investigating and compiling data on HIV risk for gay men in the Latino community. It was a desk job; Christina would get her own business cards and computer and be trained to counsel her clients and have a caseload, like the social work she wanted to do but didn't yet have the degree for. She would learn computer skills and how to design studies. She wanted this job more than anything—it surprised her to say it, but more than a boyfriend. Christina was twenty-one, and she was finally growing up.

When Christina called to tell us she got it, she was crying and laughing at the same time. "Girl!" she just kept saying. "Girl!" as though she had to scold some sense into herself; all this hysteria just would not do. "I kicked some *ass* in those interviews," she said. "Down!"

Later she would tell me what this job meant to her: that she was finally hired, and valued, as Christina. Not Christina, named after Christina Aguilera or Geri Halliwell, but plain old Los Angeles Christina with the skills and compassion she had learned from living her specific life. She was hired because she spoke two languages and was fluent in two cultures, because she'd done outreach with sex workers and knew about HIV and had also worked in clinical hospital settings. She'd also had a hard life and could muster empathy for clients who made shockingly poor choices. Suddenly, Christina was an expert. She said, "Girl, what if I'm not only looking up to Pink no more; what if I look up to Christina? In ten years, I don't even know who she'll *be*."

That fall, there were also two major breakthroughs, from Christina's perspective, with her mother. The first was that Gloria asked one of her work clients to reach her through her "daughter," "Christina"—verbalizing both the feminine noun and the proper name, which Christina had never seen her mother do, and certainly not with people from her job. Even more sweet, for Christina, was when Gloria was sorting through old photos and pulled out one to show Christina. It was a picture of Christina's father with her when she was a baby. Gloria said, "Look—that's the only toy your dad ever bought you, and it's pink. He must have known you were going to be a girl."

Christina called to tell me this story, utterly shocked. "My mom didn't even say, 'He must have known you were going to be *this way*,' like she usually would have. She said '*a girl*'!" she gushed. "And my dad had bought me a pink rattle."

These incidents came on the heels of Gloria's fiftieth birthday party, which Christina semi-crashed. She knew about the party because she was living in her mother's house and it was going to be held in the backyard, but she also said she wasn't expressly invited. Christina debated for weeks whether or not she'd go, and finally she decided there was a toast she'd like to make.

Christina wore a relatively understated outfit—cords, a white tank top, and a black-and-white checkered necktie with, as she said, some Victoria "Posh Spice" Adams–inspired heels. There were seventy people at the party, many of whom had known Christina since she was a child, along with all of the extended family who had not reached out to help her when she was homeless and struggling. Many, she said, still called her by her boy name, and many gossiped behind her back. After everyone had been dancing for a while, Christina walked up to the DJ and asked him for the mic.

"I thanked God for getting my mother to fifty," Christina said, when she called me at 1:00 A.M. after the party. Her voice was still shaky with relief. "And then I thanked my mother for being my mother, and for the person she's become to me recently. And then I said I appreciated my aunts and what they do for her, and I named all of them. And then I said, 'For the ones that judge me or point fingers, don't—'cause I know y'all got shit in your closets!' That felt so fucking good!"

The trajectory with her mother wasn't always upward, of course, and Christina's mother still called her by her boy name, or ignored her, Christina said, or still made jokes about AIDS with her stepfather that made Christina uncomfortable. For Christmas that year, Christina said, her mother didn't give her a present, though the house had been full of wrapped gifts to be bundled off to Guatemala for weeks. Christina decided it was time—she was ready—to move out on her own. I flew to Los Angeles to help her.

She was squirrelly when I first showed up. I was waiting in a rental car outside her office, as we had arranged, to go look at some listings, and she jumped in another car with a coworker, headed toward South Central, to get her hair done. She wanted me to follow her there. We got in a huge argument.

"I fly all the way from New York to take you apartment hunting, and now you want me to chase you all over town?! Christina, no!" I snapped into the phone when she called from the road. "Who do you think I am?"

Christina skipped the hair appointment and made her way back to my car, but her back was still up. After an hour of protesting that she really just wanted to have some fun and all I do is try and stop her from that, the truth tumbled out: she was terrified.

It wasn't about the money or the responsibility; Christina had already moved herself back into a hotel for a few weeks (this time closer to her job) as a transition to mentally psych herself up for the bigger move. It was that people in her old neighborhood were gossiping about her. Some said Christina had been arrested; others claimed she had been killed. These were the reasons people left her street in East L.A.; nobody got a good job and moved into a studio apartment in a better part of town. There just wasn't precedent for it, or the kids she knew hadn't heard of it. Also, Christina admitted, she was afraid she'd feel confident and supported enough to find an apartment and maybe even sign a lease while I was in town, but that assurance could disintegrate once I left.

"I get more nurturing from you in one minute than I do from other people in my whole life," Christina said. "There. I said it."

"Thank you, but, Sparrow, you're already doing it, doing your life, on your own. You think it's me holding the bicycle, but you're riding it by yourself already," I said. "You've got the great job, and had other jobs now, for a while. You've been paying rent—to hotels or to your mom—for well over a year. You're actually *good* at living on your own."

It was 9:30 at night before we actually got out of the car to look at apartments. I said it was too late, but Christina said, "Girl! The managers are up!" and just marched toward their doors, a forced smile on her face. She had made one of her power-surge turnarounds. Once she released some of the bottled anxieties, Christina could choose to do well on a dime.

And she was right. At each apartment complex, a manager opened his door halfway, the television blaring in the background. And each one shook down his enormous ring of keys from the wall to show us an apartment.

Christina fell for the fourth place we saw. The manager was a woman named Beatrice, who immediately connected to Christina and told her there were a lot of single women in the building, and it was perfectly safe.

"We don't have any parties here—it's really quiet," Beatrice said. "You'll like it."

The unit was a studio with an enormous walk-in closet and a separate kitchen. There was a tree outside the kitchen window, and Beatrice said that in the day the place got good light. Christina asked for an application.

Two weeks later Christina moved in. I was back in New York by then but had been a part of the intimate blow-by-blow via telephone. Christina e-mailed photographs of the lease, before signing and after. She called to say her friend Joseph would help her move her stuff from the hotel to the apartment; did we think that was a good idea? It could probably all fit in one or two trunkloads. She called to say she bought some sage to burn around the corners of the room to smoke away the energies of the last tenants; they hadn't been able to pay their rent and had been forced to move. Robin and I were ordering Christina a futon couch online, and we endlessly pored over Web sites with her, trying to find the perfect one.

She moved in on a Sunday. Beatrice the manager said the earliest she could be there was 7:30 in the morning, so that's exactly when Christina showed up. By nine or so she was settled; she only had her clothes to unpack, some blankets and sheets, some pans and a lamp my dad and stepmother had given her, and the vacuum cleaner she had presented to her mother for Christmas a few years back, when she said her mother gave her a handful of pennies and dimes, scooped from the edge of the coffee table, in return.

Christina went out and bought coffee and some tacos and then sat around her apartment and didn't know what to do. She didn't have a television, and her boom box had broken while she was staying at the hotel. She lay on the floor. She walked around from corner to corner. She wanted to call someone, but she didn't know who. She lit a candle; she blew it out. She went to sleep at noon, tangled in a sheet on the brown carpet because the futon hadn't come yet, and woke a few hours later to drink more coffee. By nightfall, she was a wreck.

"Girls, the refrigerator makes a terrible sound!" Christina said when she called us around 9:00 P.M. "This place is scary at night!"

"What kind of sound is it making?" I asked.

"Like a motor—it's so quiet in here, you can hear everything!"

"Well, how close are you to the refrigerator? Move farther away if it's bothering you," I said.

"I can't," she said. "It's right next to me. I'm in the sink."

"*In* the sink? The kitchen sink?"

"Girl, shut up!" Christina said. She was chewing something furiously that was making a loud crunching sound. "This place is big!"

She meant the apartment felt too spacious, too quiet, too consuming. The sink was somewhere that could contain her. I pictured her perched there like a bird, with her legs crumpled beneath her, and I stifled a laugh. "Are you eating Doritos?" I asked. She loved Doritos.

"*Mmm-hmmm,*" she answered, and stuffed more in her mouth.

"Do you have all the lights on?"

"I have the kitchen one on and the lamp, but not the bathroom," Christina said, her mouth still full of chips. "But I'm too scared to go in there. I can't leave the sink. Do you think I made a mistake?"

"What?" I asked. "Made a mistake with what?"

"Moving in here. Maybe I'm not ready. I can't live in a sink."

"True," I said. "And you can't live on Doritos either. But you're only doing both of those things right now. Tomorrow'll be different."

And it was. After talking for three hours—about Brad Pitt and Jennifer Aniston, about Christina's hair, about horoscopes and money management and how to make curtain rods—Christina decided she was probably tired enough to fall asleep. By then she had climbed out of the sink and onto the floor and had cuddled herself into her softest blanket. The next day she went to work, and there she was, a woman with a career and a high school diploma and an apartment of her own. No one could look at her and say she wasn't.

"We've all made it. Me, Foxx, Ariel, everybody. It's kind of amazing, but we all made it," Lenora said, when I went to visit her shortly after Christina had gotten her apartment. Lenora was Foxx's drag daughter—the one who filled her bra with water balloons—and was still the youngest of the bunch. Lenora and Foxx were close, and so were Lenora and Ariel, but Foxx and Ariel never regained their friendship after the pepper spray incident. Christina and Foxx were friends, but not the way Christina and Domineque had been, so there was no real cohesive community between all the girls—it was more like independent relationships, and they were all, more and more, going their own ways.

Lenora was the only kid I knew who had actually graduated from one of the young adult shelters into an independent living program. She had earned her own one-bedroom apartment, which, as long as she maintained a job, was nearly entirely subsidized by the shelter. Still, Lenora wanted to move. Her apartment was in a part of South Central so bad that there weren't even the fast-food restaurants ubiquitous in other poor neighborhoods; here there were only hand-painted signs on plywood boards. Furniture and appliance stores didn't bother putting up signs; they just spilled their mostly second-hand wares onto the sidewalks for people to see. The churches were storefronts covered in gang tags with folding chairs and plastic flowers. Both Lenora and a friend who lived nearby said they heard gunshots every day.

At Lenora's apartment, which was clean and spare—save for a single coffee table piled high with celebrity magazines in both English and Spanish—she said she would still like to transition to full-time womanhood. "Men when they get into their late forties are looking ugly and, you know, women—they stay pretty," she said. "A young man will still try to hit on a grown lady, but ain't nobody gonna want me as an old man."

Lenora has conceived of herself entirely as a female since she was five years old, but she's kept her external male appearance to protect her family. She dresses now maybe once a month when she goes to the clubs with Ariel or when she calls the party lines at Foxx's house, but she projects her full-time transition into a vague and undefined future—when she starts looking "ugly" or "old" to potential dates.

"I don't want to break my grandma's heart because she's already done a lot for me. I love her, and it would hurt her so much," Lenora said. Once when Lenora was in her early teens, she sent a photograph of herself—as a boy—but with her eyebrows plucked into thin lines. Her grandmother sent the pictures back. "She said, 'Don't send me pictures like that!' and that just hurt my heart," Lenora said, adding that her grandmother cares deeply about what other people think of her and her family, and she doesn't want Lenora changing her appearance.

Still, when Lenora turned twenty, Foxx gave her some little blue pills for her birthday. They weren't estrogen, so they wouldn't encourage breast growth, but they were testosterone blockers—the drug that's too expensive and hard to prescribe in the States. Said Lenora happily, "I take one every morning and every night—Foxx said they'd make my skin softer!"

Ariel, too, was doing fine: She was working at a coffee shop and earning enough to support herself in a one-bedroom apartment downtown. She had a car, and was volunteering a few times a month at the Boys & Girls Club. She was dressing two or three times a week, even during the day—even sometimes at the Boys & Girls

Club, where, at twenty-two, she could show the teenagers that a boy was sometimes really a girl. She couldn't have done this when she was a teenager herself. She thought it was the mere accumulation of years that had provided her with courage for such acts. I asked if self-love had anything to do with it, and, just like the old days, she held up her hand and looked away, her eyes welling with tears.

Ariel's major wrestling in life was still to be had with God. God was the reason she couldn't go full-time, like she wanted. I met her at the coffee shop where she'd been working for more than a year, as Luis. She wore the uniform—a polo shirt with the shop's logo—about eight sizes too big, so it looked like a dress over her equally oversize khakis. She had grown her hair out long, which she could have never done living at home, and her fingernails were long too, though unpainted.

When we sat outside on a bench to talk, Ariel was still short enough to swing her legs, her platform sneakers barely scraping the ground. She told me she had eight wigs and two closets—one for her boy things and one for her girl things.

"I feel that now I look at being transgender as more normal," Ariel said, in her same old quiet way. Her head was tipped to the side, and her whole countenance was curled inward and down, though her eyes peeked up, in quick butterfly glances, to look at me. I told her that was good news, given that four years ago, she was struggling with the idea of sin. At this, her face clouded, and she looked at her shoes. I asked her, gently, what she thought about God and transsexuality these days, and she didn't answer me for a few minutes. Finally, she looked away, out into the busy downtown street, where cars were pumping hip-hop music and honking at traffic. "Personal," she said softly. "It's personal."

Still, the fear is stopping her less and less, perhaps because, as Ariel said, "I'm getting used to it." She still doesn't know if she'll ever take hormones or even transition to full-time, but for now, she's content just to have her own place and to not have to cart her girl clothes around the city in a wheelie suitcase. After so many years of hiding herself in pieces—in Foxx's apartment, in her backpack, in the shelter's closet—she keeps her wigs out on display stands, and even hangs dresses on the walls as decoration. She's determined to always have her own apartment, and, at the time we met, was paying off a Ford Focus. Ariel was usually the designated driver for Lenora and the other girls when they went to the clubs.

"We all made it, even after all we been through," Lenora repeated, somehow both impressed and vaguely skeptical, when I saw her. Then she paused. "We all made it, except Domineque."

When I went to visit her, Domineque had already written to Andrea several times and received no reply. This, she said, was difficult, but not unexpected. "I put the family through hell," she said. "I understand why Andrea doesn't write to me."

It wasn't out of bitterness or anger or resentment that Andrea hadn't written or gone to see Domineque; it was because she didn't believe Domineque would change. "The problem with Domineque is I feel that there's going to be such limited movement—emotionally, economically, physically—I hope and wish she'll get her GED while she's in there, that she takes advantage of the college program that's offered there, but a large part of me knows that's not going to happen," Andrea said to me, and in fact Domineque hadn't been to school in the nearly two years she'd been locked up. Classrooms, like the cafeteria and dayroom and everywhere else in prison, are sites for potential harassment, which is why Domineque said she doesn't go. Then again, I sent Domineque two GED books to read on her own time, and she hadn't cracked those either. Said Andrea, her voice thickening with grief as she spoke, "Do I want to be in my midfifties parenting a child at thirty-five who's acting like she's seventeen or eighteen? It's not going to happen for me."

Shortly after Domineque's sentencing, Andrea and Richard got a call from a social services agency asking them if they'd consider fostering another transgender child. Her name was Jessica; she was fifteen years old and had already been in twenty-one foster and group homes, running from most of them. A few months after their baby turned one, they brought Jessica home. Late that year Richard got a job offer in northern California, and they moved the whole family, including Jessica, to a suburb of San Francisco. Andrea said that she learned from Domineque not to ride the emotional waves of adolescent rage, and she's able to be more even-tempered with Jessica, who also struggles with drugs, though nowhere as badly as Domineque. And while Andrea said she will always love Domineque as her first child, she still hasn't figured out how to interact with her in a way that takes care of her current priorities: a two-year-old and a sixteen-year-old.

"There are multiple players here, and it comes down to the need to protect whoever is in the home at the time—and hopefully there'll be other kids, whether they're foster, adopted, or biological," Andrea said. The absolute earliest Domineque could be released, if she can get out on good behavior, would be 2015. Andrea's toddler would be twelve. "Contacting her is something I know I need to do one day, and I don't know what my decision will be. I know it can't be, 'Come on back when you're out,' and yet part of me emotionally knows she has nobody else out there for her. It's such a hard thing.

"For me to have contact with a child," Andrea continued, "I need to be able to know that I'm going to continue to be there for them. And with Domineque, I can't make that statement."

So Andrea will wait, until she reaches an inner clarity that allows her to set a boundary and promise she can keep. In the meantime, Domineque continues to grow up, in her own way, in prison. When I saw her, she had inked over the tattoo she had gotten as a young teenager—Juliana's name scripted on her right arm—in homage to her drag mother who had bought her her first hormones, told her she'd look good as a girl.

"Juliana didn't stand up for what she believed in," Domineque said, referring to the fact that she went home to her own biological mom in Texas and returned to living as a boy. "I mean, I'd still be her friend. If she wrote, I'd write back. But I stand up for what I believe in—even in here, I'm female. And for Juliana's family, she became male."

In prison, Domineque said, they make tattoo guns with the batteries and motors from small appliances, like Walkmans. They attach these to the springs from pens, so the needles—made from guitar strings—can go up and down. They concoct the ink by making soot: they pour baby oil into a sardine can and fashion a wick out of a strip of cloth; then they light the "candle" and throw a bag over the top to collect the soot, which they then mix with a little water, toothpaste, and shampoo to form a permanent purply-black ink. There are guys in prison known for their tattoo skills, and Domineque had one of them turn Juliana's name into a heart with the words "Fire and Desire" scrolled in above, after the Teena Marie and Rick James song. Domineque wrote me a letter saying these words have special significance because "my soul is filled with so much fire and especially desire."

Ironically, it's prison that's giving Domineque a principle to fight for, but it's costing her. When she was caught with paint on her fingernails and given a "115"—which, in her case, added 180 days to her release date—Domineque recognized this as discrimination. She wrote to me, "Nowhere in the Title 15 does it state that males can't paint their fingernails. I'm transgendered. I'm not a man. I'm a woman, and they're making me extremely depressed."

Title 15 is the California Department of Corrections' list of minimum standards for the state's detention facilities. According to lawyer Alex Lee, there are rules against inmates in male facilities exhibiting female appearance—and vice versa. "Women are not allowed to have facial hair. Some genetic women have facial hair naturally, so they're getting written up—it's exposing the sexism behind the grooming standards," Lee said.

The sexism is turning Domineque into somewhat of a feminist. "I'd burn my bra if they'd give me one," Domineque wrote in a subsequent letter when she was feeling a bit better. "I'm all for human rights."

Domineque's decided she wants to work for improved transgender conditions for all incarcerated transsexuals in California, as best she can from behind bars. When a sergeant tried to make her cut her long hair, which she wears in a bun at the nape of her neck, she refused. She had researched the Title 15 grooming standards for women, and wrote to me about them.

"If hair is long, it shall be worn in a neat, plain style, which does not draw undue attention to the inmate," she wrote, citing the regulation. "I comply with the female grooming standards! I'm a female who just happens to be in a men's prison."

Unfortunately, as long as she still is genitally male, the state will likely see her as such and make her comply with the men's grooming standards—which require hair to be cut short. Prison law won't allow the authorities to physically restrain an inmate and cut her hair, so as long as Domineque refuses the scissors, she can keep her hair long. The authorities, however, can punish her in other ways.

Domineque was told several times to cut her hair, and she refused every time. Her punishments have included time in solitary "administrative segregation" (or "the hole"), temporary suspensions of all of her day privileges, and yet another 180 extra days added to her sentence. I connected her with the lawyer Alex Lee, who said he would write letters on her behalf and, if she wanted to, help her connect with a legal team, who would likely help her initiate a lawsuit against the state. Domineque said she wants to; Lee told me that he gets letters from people in exactly Domineque's position at the rate of about two or three a week.

A non-profit legal team had already recently fought to overturn the grooming standards on hair length for Rastafarian and other inmates on the basis of religious practice, Lee said, and he thought that Domineque could get someone to take on her case pro bono. In the end, however, this religious hair-length law would end up serving Domineque as well. More than a year after all of Domineque's run-ins with her correction officers, the state of California issued "emergency regulations" simply stating that "an inmate's hair may be any length but shall not extend over the eyebrows, cover the face, or pose a health and safety risk." Not being a religious institution, or in the business of determining which religions necessitated which hair dimensions, the Department of Corrections and Rehabilitation decided to simply allow everyone the same rights, carte blanche.

This would be an obvious victory for Domineque, but the law wasn't designed for what the state considered "men" to look like women. Domineque's hair color would still be illegal, along with her long or painted fingernails, her eye makeup and, if she could ever score or concoct one, her bra. If Domineque wants to fight for these rights or any others that allow her to live as a woman in a men's prison, it'll take patience and perseverance—traits that Domineque hasn't exhibited in the past with her temper and depression and short fuse. She'll first have to write formal protests to any 115s (with the hair length hurdle removed, she could be written up for other violations) requesting that she be allowed to maintain her female expression. Lee says prisoner protests are often ignored and have to be resubmitted repeatedly, and they will likely be denied. Then she'll have to protest again, and these will be reviewed by her guards' supervisors, then by prison administrators, and so on, all the way up to state correctional authorities in Sacramento. When her plea finally gets to Sacramento and she is once again denied, a legal team such as, for instance, the Prison Law Office could step in and file a habeas corpus on her behalf. If she won, she'd get to keep her look, and there would be a legal precedent for other transsexuals in her situation. Also, any extra time that had been added to her sentence would be lifted.

Whether Domineque will take it that far and whether she will succeed remains to be seen. Many days she feels like she can't do much besides wait for her favorite shows, *Will and Grace* and *The King of Queens*, to come on the TV in her cell. Still, when Domineque was first in jail and frustrated with the isolation and discrimination, she wrote me a letter that said, "I wish my purpose in life would just walk up and slap me in the face." After these years in prison, now drug-free, she feels like it has.

When Christina first got her job, she said, she was a little confused. She'd been hired to find and interview Latino men who had sex with men to assess HIV risk and behavior in the Latino community as a whole. She would be trained as a counselor of sorts, instructed to comfort people if their confessions got serious or sad, or to direct them toward other resources. Down the line, she'd be administering the HIV test, and delivering the results. She had to be ready for tears and fear and anger, and she had to learn how to listen to other people's problems. "I felt like I lacked these skills," she said. "I did not know that I knew how to talk to people—I did not know that I could be nonjudgmental."

But Christina learned. She started calling us after she interviewed clients to say that she got someone to smile a little, with some hope, after he felt depressed and afraid upon admitting to sleeping with men without condoms. She herself had been judged so many times and by so many kinds of people, she knew what judgments meant by now—that they came from ignorance and fear. She was good at her job. She wasn't judgmental, she was thoughtful, and she noticed every small thing.

"This guy I did intake on tonight, girl—he said he had sex with, like, five men and then five women, all unsafe, and he didn't tell the women about the guys," Christina said to me in a recent phone call.

"What do you think about that?" I asked.

"I think he's telling the truth," Christina said. "Because I noticed that he smelled like a house. No, like a room—that nobody pays attention to. He needs somebody to pay attention to him."

When Christina came to visit us on her most recent trip to New York, she decided she wanted to get a tattoo. It was wintertime, and we had been sledding in Riverside Park, near our apartment. We'd also eaten pizza that burned the tops of our mouths, and crunched down the glitter-bright snowy streets arm in arm—the three of us taking up whole sidewalks together. Despite the temperature, Christina insisted on wearing flimsy blouses under her open suede coat with faux-fur trim. She said she was looking to get a "chest cold," but she was catching the eyes of several men hungry for skin in the drought of winter.

"I used to think sparrows were baby pigeons, because they're always hanging out together," Christina said as we passed a group of birds pecking at a frozen puddle in a patch of sun. "But I'm so glad I found out they're not, because I don't like pigeons at all."

Christina had decided she wanted a sparrow tattoo—to commemorate Robin's and my special name for her, and to mark the flight she'd been making into her adult life. She'd already had a friend cover over her A.T.C. gang tattoo with an image of some crabs, for her astrological sign, Cancer. She asked my brother, Andrew, who's an illustrator, to design the sparrow tattoo.

"I want it to be flying, definitely, and looking up toward the sky," Christina said to Andrew. He gave it a brown head and small probing eyes, and brown and black wings, spread wide.

Before we left for the tattoo parlor, we went online to research sparrows and their symbolic significance. In some cultures, sparrows can mean nobility, and in others, humility. In Sappho's poetry, the sparrows brought love, as Aphrodite's chariot was "yoked with swift, lovely sparrows." Because sparrows don't fly south for the winter, always living in one place in groups, they're seen as "community birds" or "markers of human attachment." Christina saw this as a sign she didn't have to be alone.

Of course, the sparrow is also one of the most regular birds—the least eccentric or strange. In human terms, a sparrow might be a woman like any other. In Christian symbolism, many experts cite the sparrow as a symbol for God's love for even the smallest, most overlooked creatures.

The tattoo parlor was classic—a small storefront on the Lower

East Side with three stations, each crammed with pinned-up examples of the artist's work. Christina had an appointment with a man named Skull, who, appropriately, designed all manners of colorful skulls, from the droopy and harrowing to the grateful and dancing, along with several Tibetan "om" symbols. Skull was British and bald, wearing black jeans and scuffed boots. He smiled at Christina as he photocopied Andrew's drawing onto a special inked paper, which he would press onto Christina's skin to serve as an outline.

"Where do you want this, love?" Skull asked.

Christina lifted the back of her blouse and twisted around to look at herself in a full-length mirror. "On my back," she said. "But can you make it bigger? I want it as big as my hand."

"I can make it as big as you want," Skull said. "But where on your back do you want it?"

"Right here on the side," Christina said. She gestured to the part of her back that had the least flesh. "I want it right here, going from my back to my side, right along my ribs."

Skull's smile dropped from his face, and he sat down on a metal folding chair directly across from all of us. He clasped his hands. "That is, I'm afraid, *the* single most painful part of the body," he said. "People always think it's the feet. The feet hurt—anywhere you don't have fat will hurt. But along the ribs, on your side and back—that hurts more than anything else. And this tattoo is big. It'll take hours."

Christina looked from Skull to Robin to me. She took the xeroxed copy of her sparrow tattoo and held it up along the back part of her ribs. She stared into the mirror and then she smiled. "That's okay," she said. "I want to put my wings in my most painful place."

# AUTHOR'S NOTE

All of the stories in this book are true. It spans seven years—from 1998 through the summer of 2005—and nearly all interviews were taped, except when I had to reconstruct scenes from memory, such as those in the classroom or the more personal moments with Christina. I've captured these scenes as faithfully as I could, and they are as accurate as memory will allow. Except for a very few cases, I've verified my accounts with the primary sources before publication.

The characters here, as is the way with books, found me. Or we found each other. In any case, this is merely the story of four transgender young women and their friends living in a particular place at a particular time: they do not represent the trans community at large, nor are they meant to. There are few transboys in this book simply because my main sources didn't run with them much; this is more memoir than social science, and there is clearly more room on the shelf.

The main characters in this book all go by their real first names (though I've changed most boy names), and outside "experts" providing inside commentary are correctly identified as well. Family members' names and identifying details as well as those of many secondary characters have been altered to protect their privacy. There are no composite characters.

# ENDNOTES

## CHAPTER TWO

"SCIENTISTS HAVEN'T BEEN ASKING THAT QUESTION": See, for instance, the recent overview article by Larry Cahill, "His Brain, Her Brain," *Scientific American*, May 2005, 40–47. Ultimately, the structural differences between men's and women's brains are pretty small. Some evidence shows that the slightly smaller female brain has a higher percentage of gray matter—the substance that processes information—and a male's brain has more white matter, which sends information between gray matter regions and other parts of the body. The female cortex may have somewhere between 12 and 20 percent more neurons in the language-related temporal lobe, and the female brain expresses roughly 15 percent more blood flow than a male brain at any one time.

"IN A FAMOUS NETHERLANDS STUDY": J. N. Zhou et al., "A Sex Difference in the Human Brain and Its Relation to Transsexuality," *Nature* 378 (1995): 68–70. In this initial study, all of the transsexuals had undergone hormone treatment, so the concern was that the extra hormones could have changed the brain structure long after birth. To control for this, the same scientists conducted a follow-up study several years later. Frank P. M. Kruijver et al., "Male-to-Female Transsexuals Have Female Neuron Numbers in a Limbic Nucleus," *Journal of Clinical Endocrinology and Metabolism* 85, no. 5 (May 2000): 2034. They looked at a postmortem transman and transwoman who had never taken hormones. They found the same results. The transman's BNST was in line with the genetic men, and the transwoman had the same number of neurons as a genetic woman.

"THE BNST IS OFTEN CONSIDERED": E. A. Phelps and J. E. LeDoux, "Contributions of the Amygdala to Emotion Processing: From Animal Models to Human Behavior," *Neuron* 48, no. 2 (October 20, 2005): 175–87; and A. J. Calder, A. D. Lawrence, and A. W. Young, "Neuropsychology of Fear and Loathing," *Nature Reviews Neuroscience* 2, no. 5 (May 2001): 352–63.

"THE BNST ITSELF IS BELIEVED TO MEDIATE": M. I. Forray and K. Gysling, "Role of Noradrenergic Projections to the Bed Nucleus of the Stria Terminalis in the Regulation of the Hypothalamic-Pituitary-Adrenal Axis," *Brain Research Reviews* 47, nos. 1–3 (December 2004): 145–60; and J. P. Herman et al., "Limbic System Mechanisms of Stress Regulation: Hypothalamo-Pituitary-Adrenocortical Axis," *Progress in Neuropsychopharmacology and Biological Psychiatry* 29, no. 8 (December 2005): 1201–13.

"TESTOSTERONE, WHICH ENTERS HIS BRAIN": This comes from a paper called "Atypical Gender Development: A Review," prepared by the Gender Identity Research and Education Society (GIRES), assisted by Trans Group, and was slated to be published in the *International Journal of Transgenderism* 1, no. 9. At press time this was in prepublication. This paper was retrieved from http://72.14.207.104/search?q=cache:8SXumCVdn4kJ:www.gires.org.uk/ Text_Assets/ATypical_Gender_Development.pdf+stress+%2B+utero+%2B+ transsexuality&hl=en&gl=us&ct=clnk&cd=33&client=safari, and the information came from p. 9.

"BABIES GOT TOO MUCH OF ONE HORMONE": ibid., 9–11.

"RESEARCHERS OFTEN BLAME STRESS": ibid., 11. Also, people (researchers and laypeople alike) can (often mistakenly) link cross-gender behavior in gay adults to transgender conduct. There's a large body of research that shows prenatal stress can produce gay and lesbian offspring, who behave in gender-atypical ways. See, for instance, L. Ellis and S. Cole-Harding, "The Effects of Prenatal Stress, and of Prenatal Alcohol and Nicotine Exposure, on Human Sexual Orientation," *Physiological Behavior* 74, nos. 1–2 (September 1–15, 2001): 213.

"TOO MUCH TESTOSTERONE AND A GIRL BABY": D. F. Swaab, "Sexual Differentiation of the Human Brain: Relevance for Gender Identity, Transsexualism and Sexual Orientation," *Gynecological Endocrinology* 19 (2004): 302, 304–5. Also see the "Atypical Gender Development: A Review," 9–11.

"MAMMALS LIKE RATS": Melissa Hines et al., "Testosterone During Pregnancy and Gender Role Behavior of Preschool Children: A Longitudinal, Population Study," *Child Development* 73, no. 6 (November/December 2002): 1678–79.

"AND GUINEA PIGS": Carina Dennis, "The Most Important Sexual Organ," *Nature* 427 (January 29, 2004): 390.

"CONVERSELY, CASTRATED RABBIT FETUSES": ibid., 390.

"A MEDICAL GROUP IN LONDON SAMPLED": Hines et al., "Testosterone During Pregnancy and Gender Role Behavior of Preschool Children," 1680–85.

"SOME OF THE NEWEST RESEARCH GOES BEYOND THE HORMONE WASH THEORY": Arthur P. Arnold et al., "Minireview: Sex Chromosomes and Brain Sexual Differentiation," *Endocrinology* 145, no. 3 (2004): 1057.

"BIRDS, FOR INSTANCE": Dennis, "The Most Important Sexual Organ," 391.

"GENDER IN THIS PREHORMONAL BRAIN": ibid., 391.

"SO FAR VILAIN HAS FOCUSED": phone interview with Eric Vilain, October 2005.

"CLINICAL ESTIMATES SAY": In "The Harry Benjamin International Gender Dysphoria Association's Standards of Care for Gender Identity Disorder, Sixth Version," part II (Epidemiological Considerations), 2. Retrieved from http://www.hbigda.org/soc.htm.

"DOMINEQUE'S MOM WAS ALSO": The child abuse is self-reported. Because the victims were minors, all DCFS and court reports are sealed.

"THE LOS ANGELES ALMANAC CLAIMS": Los Angeles Almanac, Given Place Publishing, Los Angeles, California. Retrieved from http://www.laalmanac.com/crime/cro3v.htm.

CHAPTER THREE

"LESLIE FEINBERG'S *TRANSGENDER WARRIORS*": Leslie Feinberg, *Transgender Warriors: Making History from Joan of Arc to Dennis Rodman* (Boston: Beacon Press, 1996).

"ANCIENT PAINTINGS": ibid., 56.

"MARBLE SCULPTURES OF HERACLES": ibid., 58.

"GREEK GOD DIONYSUS": ibid., 56.

"AS SHOWN IN MESOPOTAMIAN": ibid., 40.

"THE GREEK HISTORIAN PLUTARCH": ibid., 40.

"STATUES OF ARTEMIS": ibid., 40.

"A WOMAN MUST NOT WEAR": Deuteronomy 22:5.

"HE THAT IS WOUNDED": Deuteronomy 23:1.

"THESE BIBLICAL LAWS": Feinberg, *Transgender Warriors*, 50.

"SYRIANS WORSHIPPED": ibid., 50.

"KNOWN COLLOQUIALLY AS 'POPE JOAN'": There are several books about Pope Joan. One good one is Peter Stanford's *The Legend of Pope Joan* (Boston: Beacon Press, 1996).

"A SPECIAL PAPAL CHAIR": ibid., p. 4 of photo insert after 116.


## CHAPTER FOUR

"DANA INTERNATIONAL ACTUALLY": All information about Dana International comes from her official Web site (http://www.danainternational.co.il/). The Eurovision win and Israeli controversy is also reported in Ilene Prusher, "Of Visions and Eurovisions," *Jerusalem Report*, April 26, 1999. Her performance at the Gay Games was mentioned, among other places, in Joshua Gamson, "The Officer and the Diva," *Nation*, June 28, 1999.

"SOME CLAIM AROUND FIFTEEN THOUSAND": The San Francisco Human Rights Commission, a branch of the city government, estimates that a full 2 percent of San Francisco is transgender. See "Economic Empowerment for the Lesbian Gay Bisexual Transgender Communities: A Report by the Human Rights Commission City and County of San Francisco Final Report," November 30, 2000, 33. The city's population is roughly 750,000—which means 15,000 transpeople. An article by Torri Minton, "Not Ready for Prime Time: Kitty Kastro Hosts Nation's First TV Talk Show for Transsexuals," *San Francisco Chronicle*, March 30, 2001, cited a Human Rights Commission figure at 16,000, and an Oakland-based transgender activist I interviewed doubled this figure to 30,000 for the much larger Bay Area.

These numbers are far higher than the widely accepted Harry Benjamin figures, which claim 1 in 11,900 people are female to male and 1 in 30,400 are male-to-female. Following these guidelines, San Francisco would be home to only 43 transpeople. While this figure is obviously low given San Francisco's status as a magnet city, it does shed some perspective on the 2 percent estimate.

Other cities, like Los Angeles, are reluctant to offer up figures of their own—largely because it's impossible to count. "Estimating the number of transpeople in L.A. county is as difficult as determining the number of undocumented workers. We've got a hidden population," said Masen Davis, founder of L.A.'s FTM Alliance. Davis, who has lived in both Los Angeles and San Francisco, thinks the 30,000 Bay Area number is grossly overstated and believes that the population in Los Angeles is larger than that of San Francisco.

"ACTIVISM AND POLITICAL ORGANIZING": from an interview with Simon Aronoff, August 2004. Also see Rona Marech, "Throw Out Your Pronouns— 'He' and 'She' Are Meaningless Terms in the Bay Area's Flourishing Transgender Performance Scene," *San Francisco Chronicle,* December 29, 2003.

"GENDER OUTLAWZ, TRANNYFAGS, AND QUEERBOIS": See, for instance, Rona Marech, "Nuances of Gay Identities Reflected in New Language," *San Francisco Chronicle,* February 8, 2004; and Marech, "Throw Out Your Pronouns."

"HAVE BEEN THROWING": The history of the ballroom scene is vibrant but scattered and often oral, and academic scholarship is scant. Gerard Gaskin (identified in the subsequent paragraph) claims the roots started in the forties; a new documentary called *How Do I Look* (see www.howdoilooknyc.org) pegs the contemporary Harlem scene specifically to around 1980. Guy Trebay, in his January 12–18, 2000, *Village Voice* article "Paris is Still Burning," says that the tradition dates back to the nineteenth century (retrieved from http://www .villagevoice.com/news/0002,trebay,11690,5.html), and Aaron Pierre Brown, on the official House of Enigma Web site, claims that there was an earlier semblance of the balls in Harlem in the 1920s (see http://www.balls.houseofenigma .com/what_world.html). *Ebony* magazine ran an authorless feature with photos, in its March 1953 issue, called "Female Impersonators" (page 64) that depicts what we'd now call transgirls competing for trophies and cash prizes. Because people have been transgender, doing drag, throwing parties and performatively critiquing gender roles in various ways for a long time, it's difficult to discern a precise timeline.

"THE 'BALLROOM SCENE' ": Information about the houses and balls in this and the next three paragraphs comes from 2005 interviews with Gerard Gaskin.

"INSTEAD OF GETTING SLAPPED OR MOCKED": The rest of the information in this paragraph about the *alyha* comes from Walter L. Williams, *The Spirit and the Flesh: Sexual Diversity in American Indian Culture* (Boston: Beacon Press, 1986): 23–24.

"*ALYHAS* WERE . . . GENETICALLY MALE": ibid., 24.

"DID WOMEN'S WORK": ibid., 58.

"THERE WERE FOUR DISTINCT SEXES": ibid., 242.

"*ALYHA* AND *HWAME* DIDN'T TRANSITION": ibid., 239.

"THESE SONGS FOR THE *ALYHA* CEREMONIES": The rest of the information in this paragraph comes from Randy P. Connor et al., *Cassell's Encyclopedia of Queer Myth, Symbol and Spirit* (New York: Cassell, 1997), 52.

"MEN WHO MARRIED *ALYHA*": Williams, *The Spirit and the Flesh*, 119.

"SAME CHORES AS A TRADITIONAL WIFE": ibid., 115.

"WOMEN WHO WERE CONSIDERED SEXUALLY LICENTIOUS": ibid., 114.

"GENETIC MALES WHO EXHIBITED": ibid., 3–4.

"*BERDACHE* IS A PEJORATIVE": Midnight Sun, "Sex/Gender Systems in Native North America," *Living the Spirit: A Gay American Indian Anthology,* ed. Will Roscoe (New York: St. Martin's Press, 1998), 34.

"THESE GENDER NONCONFORMISTS HAD EVERYTHING": Williams, *The Spirit and the Flesh*, 92, 115.

"*NADLE* (SOMEBODY WHO EXHIBITS": ibid., 77–78.

"THEY BOTH DRESSED": ibid., 111.

"A *NADLE* PERFORMED": ibid., 60–61, 63.

"IN POLYGAMOUS TRIBES": Maurice Kenny, "Tinselled Bucks: A Historical Study in Indian Homosexuality," in *Living the Spirit: A Gay American Indian Anthology,* ed. Will Roscoe (New York, St. Martin's Press, 1998), 30.

"HE HAD A *WINKTE* SPOUSE": This comes from an interview with an informant cited in Williams, *The Spirit and the Flesh*, 112.

"THREE-QUARTERS OF HIGH SCHOOL–AGED": "The 2001 National School Climate Survey: Lesbian, Gay, Bisexual and Transgender Students and Their Experiences in Schools," under Key Findings. A publication from the Office for Public Policy of the Gay, Lesbian and Straight Education Network, New York. Retrieved from http://www.glsen.org/cgi-bin/iowa/all/library/record/827.html.

"THE MOST COMPREHENSIVE STUDY": The study was known as AESOP, which stood for AIDS Evaluation of Street Outreach Projects, and was part of a larger five-year study designed by the Centers for Disease Control and Prevention (CDC) in collaboration with researchers representing agencies at eight sites. Its purpose was to "support studies to describe outreach services to injection drug users (IDUs) and youth in high-risk situations, calculate the costs of such services, and develop and evaluate enhanced on-the-street services for these populations." (From the "What We Have Learned from the AIDS Evaluation of Street Outreach Projects," Centers for Disease Control, Atlanta, 1998.) In Los Angeles the participating agencies were Angel's Flight, Covenant House California, Hollywood YMCA, Los Angeles Gay and Lesbian Community Services Center, Los Angeles Free Clinic, Los Angeles Youth Network, My Friend's Place, PROTOTYPES, Teen Canteen, and The Way In. These statistics come from the more detailed "AESOP AIDS Evaluation 93–95 Homeless Youth Fact Sheet," which reported findings from one of the AESOP studies. It shows data from 1,103 youth aged 12–23 who had been living on the street for two or more consecutive months and were part of the "street economy" (prostitution, drug dealing, stealing, etc.).

"ACTIVISTS AND OUTREACH WORKERS HAVE CROSS-REFERENCED": The three to four hundred figure comes from Marvin Belzer, who has worked with multiple service agencies to cross-reference data.

## CHAPTER FIVE

"HARRY BENJAMIN, THE MAN": The information in the paragraph about Harry Benjamin and Magnus Hirschfeld is widely documented. It can be found in Friedmann Pfaefflin, MD, "Sex Reassignment, Harry Benjamin, and Some

European Roots," *International Journal of Transgenderism* 1, no. 2 (October–December 1997).

Harry Benjamin was forced to leave Germany during WWI because he was traveling on an ocean liner that had been intercepted by the Royal Navy and diverted to a British port. When Benjamin returned home, he was dubbed an "enemy alien" and the condition of his release was that he move away from Berlin and to the United States. Retrieved from "Magnus Hirschfeld Archive for Sexology" at the Humboldt-Universitat zu Berlin, http://www2.hu-berlin.de/sexology/GESUND/ARCHIV/COLLBEN.HTM.

"THE TRANSSEXUAL PHENOMENON": *The Transsexual Phenomenon* is indexed and available online on the Web site of the *International Journal of Transgenderism.* A recent address is http://www2.hu-berlin.de/sexology/GESUND/ARCHIV/COLLBEN.HTM.

"ASSOCIATION WAS STARTED IN 1979": The Harry Benjamin International Gender Dysphoria Association was launched as a renamed assemblage of the International Symposia on Gender Identity, which was started by a rich and eccentric transman named Reed Erickson in the late sixties. Erickson was born Rita Mae in El Paso in 1917 and attended all-girls schools and Louisiana State University before she inherited her father's lead smelting business in 1962. By 1963 Rita Mae had become Reed under the care of Dr. Harry Benjamin, and six years later Reed had sold the family business for $5 million. He grew this money to $40 million and started a philanthropic organization in Baton Rouge that funded doctors and advocates for gay and transsexual people as well as new age spiritual projects—pushing transgender medical, social, and psychological research ahead perhaps more than any other single individual in history. (He also married four times and lived with a pet leopard in a house in Mexico that he called the "Love Joy Palace.") A good article on Erickson is Aaron H. Devor and Nicholas Matte, "ONE Inc. and Reed Erickson: The Uneasy Collaboration of Gay and Trans Activism," *GLQ* 10, no. 2 (2004): 179–209.

"A TWENTY-TWO-PAGE DOCUMENT": The Harry Benjamin International Gender Dysphoria Association maintains an extensive and updated Web site where readers can download the complete "Standards of Care" (along with earlier versions), read more about the organization, and so on. Their Web address is http://www.hbigda.org/.

"TO START HORMONES": In the "Standards of Care," 10–11. Retrieved from http://www.hbigda.org/soc.htm.

"WOMEN'S HEALTH INITIATIVE STUDY": In the summer of 1992, the National Heart, Lung, and Blood Institute of the National Institutes of Health stopped a major clinical trial of combined estrogen and progestin in healthy menopausal women due to an increased incidence of invasive breast cancer. See article in the *Journal of the American Medical Association* 288, no. 3 (July 17, 2002): 321–33.

"CHICAGO HAS A MULTIFACETED": The information about adolescent services in Boston comes from a January 2006 telephone interview with Rob Garofalo, MD, director of youth services at the Howard Brown Health Center, which focuses on serving Chicago's GLBT community. Garofalo also launched the first program serving transgender adolescents in Boston, where he said the laws about providing hormones to kids under eighteen tend to be similar to those in Illinois. For information about San Francisco, I spoke with Lori Kohler, MD, director of the Medical Consultation Network and associate clinical professor at the Department of Family Medicine at the University of California, San Francisco. Dr. Kohler is a family physician in a free clinic and provides hormones to kids under eighteen, provided they are emancipated or have parental consent. She has about ten adolescent patients at any given time.

"DEPENDING UPON WHERE IT'S INJECTED": Y. Gaber, "Secondary Lymphoedema of the Lower Leg as an Unusual Side-Effect of a Liquid Silicone Injection in the Hips and Buttocks," *Dermatology* 208, no. 4 (2004): 342–4; and L. A. Farina et al., "Scrotal Granuloma Caused by Oil Migrating from the Hip in 2 Transsexual Males (Scrotal Sclerosing Lipogranuloma)," *Archivos Españoles de Urologia* 50, no. 1 (January–February 1997): 51–53; F. Vilde et al., "Fatal Pneumopathy Linked to Subcutaneous Injections of Liquid Silicone into Soft Tissue," *Annales de Pathologie* 3, no. 4 (December 1983): 307–12; and T. Duong et al., "Acute Pneumopathy in a Nonsurgical Transsexual," *Chest* 113, no. 4 (April 1998): 1127–29.

"TRANSWOMEN HAVE HAD LONG LATENCY PERIODS": J. J. Hage et al., "The Devastating Outcome of Massive Subcutaneous Injection of Highly Viscous Fluids in Male-to-Female Transsexuals," *Plastic Reconstructive Surgery* 107, no. 3 (March 2001): 734–41.

"IN THE LUNGS SILICONE HAS LED": F. Vilde et al., "Fatal Pneumopathy Linked to Subcutaneous Injections," 307–12; and T. Duong et al., "Acute Pneumopathy in a Nonsurgical Transsexual," 1127–29.

"A FEW PUMPING DEATHS": C. G. Wallace, "Death Shows Danger of Silicone Injections," Associated Press, April 1, 2004; and Elliott Minor, "Transvestite Who Gave Silicone Injections Pleads Guilty to Manslaughter in Man's Death," Associated Press, February 4, 2005.

"IN AUTOPSIES": F. Vilde et al., "Fatal Pneumopathy Linked to Subcutaneous Injections," 307.

"ONE WAS SO FULL": Wallace, "Death Shows Danger of Silicone Injections."

"SILICONE CAME INTO VOGUE": Judy Foreman and the *Globe* staff, "Women and Silicone: A History of Risk," *Boston Globe,* January 19, 1992; M. Sharon Webb, MD, Ph.D., "Cleopatra's Needle: The History and Legacy of Silicone Injections" (1997), in *Food and Drug Law: An Electronic Book of Student Papers,* ed. Peter Barton Hutt, retrieved from http://leda.law.harvard.edu/leda/data/197/mwebb.html.

"BY THE MIDSIXTIES": Sander Gilman, "The Amazing History of Silicone Implants," in *Aesthetic Surgery,* ed. Angelika Taschen (Los Angeles: Taschen America, 2005), 1010–2, and Foreman and the *Globe* staff, "Women and Silicone."

"SILICONE IMPLANTS ARE BANNED": The FDA banned silicone gel implants except in cases of post-mastectomy breast reconstruction in approved clinical breast cancer studies in 1992. See Lori S. Brown's article "Epidemiology of Silicone-Gel Breast Implants," *Epidemiology* 13, no. 3, supplement: S34–S39 (May 2002).

"OTHER SITES ARE MORE MODERATE": Nonmedical Web sites about pumping tend to be casual, bloglike sites. Even when the advice is more moderate, it should not be followed, as pumping is dangerous and illegal.

"GENDER IDENTITY DISORDER IS A MENTAL ILLNESS": American Psychiatric Association (APA), *Diagnostic and Statistical Manual of Mental Disorders* (American Psychiatric Association, 1994), 4th ed. (*DSM-IV*), Washington, D.C.: 534–38.

"THE FIRST AMERICAN TO UNDERGO": All information about Christine Jorgensen comes from Joanne Meyerowitz, *How Sex Changed: A History of Transsexuality in the United States* (Cambridge, MA: Harvard University Press, 2004).

"MOBBED BY REPORTERS": ibid., 64.

"Ex-GI Becomes Blonde Bombshell": *Daily News,* December 1, 1952; reported in an obituary by Michele Ingrassia, *Newsday,* May 5, 1989.

"Christine stories ranked": Meyerowitz, *How Sex Changed,* 66.

"letters addressed to": ibid., 92.

"part of the reason Jorgensen enflamed": ibid., 52, 67–68.

"Her case literally": ibid., 51.

"Jorgensen ultimately used her fame": ibid., 74–76.

"Her beauty": ibid., 79.

"Christine wasn't 'American' ": ibid., 76.

"she was denied a license": ibid., 51.

"She lived off and on": ibid., 74.

"died of bladder cancer": ibid., 282.

"the other option is penile reconstruction": A good article on the sexual outcomes of SRS for FTMs is Harold I. Lief, MD, and Lynn Hubschman, MSW, "Orgasm in the Postoperative Transsexual," *Archives of Sexual Behavior* 22, no. 2 (April 1993): 145.

"In the States": All costs are loose estimates and change all the time. Good links to doctors and surgical information, including pricing, can be found at www.gender.org, www.thetransitionalmale.com, and www.tsroadmap.com.

## CHAPTER SEVEN

"A famous case is": All information in this paragraph and the one following comes from *Littleton v. Prange,* 288th Judicial District Court, Bexar County, Texas, Trial Court No. 98-CI-15220.

"one in five hundred people": Julie A. Greenberg, "Defining Male and Female: Intersexuality and the Collision Between Law and Biology," *Arizona Law Review* 41, no. 2 (Summer 1999): 283.

"Turner Syndrome": ibid., 284.

"Swyer Syndrome": ibid.

"IN KANSAS A SIMILAR MARRIAGE CASE": "Kansas Supreme Court Says Transsexual Marriage Invalid; Rejects Claim for $2.5 million," Associated Press, March 15, 2002.

"THE JUDGE RULED IN FAVOR": See "Syllabus by the Court," in the Supreme Court of the State of Kansas, No. 85030 in the Matter of the Estate of Marshall G. Gardiner, Deceased. Retrieved from http://www.kscourts.org/kscases/supct/2002/20020315/85030.htm.

"ABOUT 1 PERCENT OF ALL LIVE BIRTHS": This figure comes from the Intersex Society of North America (ISNA). Greenberg, "Defining Male and Female," 267–68, claims the percentage could go as high as 4 percent. The ISNA admits the numbers are tricky because it's hard to define intersex. "How small does a penis have to be before it counts as intersex?" they ask in their online materials. Still, they claim, "if you ask experts at medical centers how often a child is born so noticeably atypical in terms of genitalia that a specialist in sex differentiation is called in, the number comes out to about 1 in 1500 to 1 in 2000 births." But that's only what's visible, externally, at birth.

Here are their numeric estimates for the frequency of sex variations: Not XX and not XY, 1 in 1,666 births; Klinefelter's (XXY), 1 in 1,000 births; androgen insensitivity syndrome, 1 in 13,000 births; partial androgen insensitivity syndrome, 1 in 130,000 births; classical congenital adrenal hyperplasia, 1 in 13,000 births; late onset adrenal hyperplasia, 1 in 66 individuals; vaginal agenesis, 1 in 6,000 births; ovotestes, 1 in 83,000 births; idiopathic (no discernible medical cause), 1 in 110,000 births; iatrogenic (caused by medical treatment, for instance, progestin administered to pregnant mother), no estimate; 5 alpha reductase deficiency, no estimate; mixed gonadal dysgenesis, no estimate; complete gonadal dysgenesis, 1 in 150,000 births; hypospadias (urethral opening in perineum or along penile shaft), 1 in 2,000 births; hypospadias (urethral opening between corona and tip of glans penis), 1 in 770 births.

"BROWN'S HOUSING QUESTIONNAIRE": Fred A. Bernstein, "On Campus, Rethinking Biology 101," *New York Times*, March 7, 2004.

"THE WOMEN'S COLLEGE SMITH": ibid.

"AT WESLEYAN": ibid.

"OHIO UNIVERSITY": Sam Whiting, "Ohio University Designates Unisex Bathrooms," Associated Press, June 9, 2001.

"AT THE NEW COLLEGE": Patricia Leigh Brown, "A Quest for a Restroom That's Neither Men's Room nor Women's Room," *New York Times,* March 4, 2005.

"THE SAN FRANCISCO HUMAN RIGHTS COMMISSION": San Francisco Human Rights Commission, "Gender Neutral Bathroom Survey," summer 2001, retrieved from http://www.pissr.org/research.html.

"CHANGE THE GENDER ON YOUR PASSPORT": Information in this paragraph as well as the next comes from an interview with Chris Daley, Esq., a lawyer with the Transgender Law Project in San Francisco, January 2006. Information from the Transgender Law Center can be found at www .transgenderlawcenter.org.

"OTHER STATES ARE MORE EXPLICIT": Current state statutes for changing birth certificates are compiled and maintained by Lambda Legal Defense in a document called "Sources of Authority to Amend Sex Designation on Birth Certificates Following Corrective Surgery." It's available online at http://www .lambdalegal.org/cgi-bin/iowa/news/resources.html?record=1627.

"IT'S LISTED IN THE AMERICAN PSYCHIATRIC ASSOCIATION'S": APA, *DSM-IV,* retrieved from http://www.behavenet.com/capsules/disorders/ genderiddis.htm.

"INTERESTINGLY, GID RARELY MANIFESTS": Domenico DiCeglie et al., "Children and Adolescents Referred to a Specialist Identity Development Service: Clinical Features and Demographic Characteristics," *International Journal of Transgenderism* 6, no. 1 (January–March 2002): 1–3.

"IN THE LATE 1800S": Nancy H. Bartlett, Paul L. Vasey, and William M. Bukowski, "Is Gender Identity Disorder in Children a Mental Disorder?" *Sex Roles: A Journal of Research* 43, nos. 11–12 (December 2000): 756.

"THERE'S BEEN SOME MOVEMENT": ibid., 753–56. The American Psychiatric Association held a debate about whether or not to include GID in the next edition of the *DSM* at a recent annual meeting symposium. See Ken Hausman, "Controversy Continues to Grow Over *DSM*'s GID Diagnosis," *Psychiatric News* 38, no. 14 (July 18, 2003): 25.

"A COMMON THERAPEUTIC RESPONSE": The kinds of treatments children receive can be found in Kenneth J. Zucker, "Gender Identity Development and Issues," *Child Adolescent Psychiatric Clinic North America* 13 (2004): 564–65.

Zucker runs a Child and Adolescent Gender Identity Clinic in Ontario and has written several seminal papers on the topic, though this type of treatment is also described in memoirs. See, for instance, Daphne Scholinski, *The Last Time I Wore a Dress* (New York: Riverhead, 1994).

"AMERICAN PSYCHOLOGICAL ASSOCIATION RELEASED A STATEMENT": The information about the APA denouncing reparative or "conversion therapies" can be found on the APA Web site, along with their position on homosexuality in general, at http://www.apa.org/pubinfo/answers.html#conversiontherapies.

"MANY GENDER-VARIANT CHILDREN": Zucker, "Gender Identity Development and Issues," 556.

"SOME PARENTS ARE LOOKING TO CURE": Zucker, "Gender Identity Development and Issues," 563, and Nancy H. Bartlett, "Is Gender Identity in Children a Mental Disorder?" 754. A good article on the controversy about treating young children diagnosed with GID is Duncan Osborne, "An Attack on Our Most Vulnerable: The Use and Abuse of Gender Identity Disorder," *Lesbian and Gay New York*, October 28, 1997.

"A MORE FAMOUS CASE": The rest of the information in this paragraph comes from John Cloud, "His Name Is Aurora," *Time*, September 25, 2000.

"PARENTS HAD VARIOUS MENTAL HEALTH": Kevin Mayhood, "Parents in Gender-Identity Custody Dispute Now at Odds," *Columbus Dispatch*, September 19, 2000.

"NOW THERE'S A GAG ORDER": Noa Ben-Asher, "Paradoxes of Health and Equality: When a Boy Becomes a Girl," *Yale Journal of Law and Feminism* 16 (2004): 280.

"THE PARENTS DIVORCED": Kevin Mayhood, "Boy Forced to Act as Girl Thriving in Foster Family," *Columbus Dispatch*, September 23, 2001.

"THE GAG ORDER ITSELF IS INTERESTING": Ben-Asher, "Paradoxes of Health and Equality."

## CHAPTER EIGHT

"THE FBI TALLIED": Federal Bureau of Investigation, "Hate Crime Statistics, 2004," U.S. Department of Justice, Washington, D.C., retrieved from http://www.fbi.gov/ucr/hc2004/section1.htm.

"SAN FRANCISCO DEPARTMENT OF PUBLIC HEALTH": San Francisco Department of Public Health, "The Transgender Community Health Project," Descriptive Results, published February 18, 1999, retrieved from http://hivinsite.ucsf.edu/InSite?page=cftg-02-02#S4.4X.

## CHAPTER NINE

"THE GAY MEN'S DOMESTIC VIOLENCE PROJECT": From the Gay Men's Domestic Violence Project Web page "Similarities and Differences," retrieved from http://www.gmdvp.org/pages/differences.html.

"IN A STUDY JOINTLY CONDUCTED": "Extent, Nature, and Consequences of Intimate Partner Violence: Research Report, Findings from the National Violence Against Women Survey," National Institute of Justice, Centers for Disease Control, July 2000, NJC 181867, Exhibit 20, p. 53.

" 'INTIMATE PARTNER VIOLENCE IS PERPETRATED' ": ibid., p. v of the Executive Summary.

"TYRA HUNTER": Derrill Holly, "DC Settles Transvestite Death Suit," Associated Press, August 10, 2000. For a rebuttal to the language in this article, see "Note to AP Regarding Errors in Reporting Death of Tyra Hunter," on the National Transgender Advocacy Coalition Web site, http://www.ntac.org/pr/000813tyra.html.

"GWEN WAS SEVENTEEN": Information in this paragraph, save for the bit about the sexual encounters, comes from Daily Headlines, "Araujo Testimony Brings Up Earlier Suspicions," *Advocate*, February 20, 2003. Reports of the sexual encounters come from several sources, including Michelle Locke, "Legacy of Gwen Araujo: Death of Gay, Trans Panic Defense," Associated Press, September 16, 2005.

"LATER MAGIDSON AND MEREL FOLLOWED": Yomi S. Wronge, "After Burying Araujo, Men Ate Breakfast at McDonald's," *San Jose Mercury News*, online edition, posted February 25, 2003.

"THIS MURDER": Vicki Haddock, "'Gay Panic' Defense in Araujo Case,'" *San Francisco Chronicle*, May 16, 2004; and Locke, "Legacy of Gwen Araujo: Death of Gay, Trans Panic Defense," Associated Press, September 16, 2005.

"THE *VILLAGE VOICE*": Donna Minkowitz, "Love Hurts: Brandon Teena Was a Woman Who Lived and Loved as a Man. She Was Killed for Carrying It Off," *Village Voice*, April 19, 1994.

"*PLAYBOY*": Eric Konigsberg, "Death of a Deceiver: The True Story of Teena Brandon," *Playboy*, January 1995.

"EVEN THE GAY NEWSMAGAZINE": Ingrid Ricks, "Heartland Homicide," *Advocate*, March 8, 1994.

"A FEW COMMUNITY FUNDS": Kelly St. John, "Gwen Araujo Fund Has Almost $10,000," *San Francisco Chronicle*, May 4, 2004.

"IN AN ACT OF SOLIDARITY": News & Politics, "Gwen Araujo: Person of the Year," PlanetOut.com, January 14, 2003, retrieved from http://www .planetout.com/news/roundups/package.html?sernum=446.

"AFTER GWEN'S DEATH": ibid.; and Daily Headlines, "Araujo's Family Seeks Posthumous Name Change," *Advocate*, May 27, 2004, retrieved from www .advocate.com/new_news.asp?id=12566&sd=05/27/04.

"IN 2002, THE YEAR GWEN DIED": The transgender death statistics come from Remembering Our Dead, compiled by the Transgender Day of Remembrance, and can be found at http://www.gender.org/remember/day/how.html.

"THE ONLY NATIONAL STUDY": Riki Anne Wilchins, executive director, GenderPAC, "GenderPAC: First National Survey of Transgender Violence," *GenderPAC*, New York, April 13, 1997.

"A DIFFERENT KIND OF STATISTIC": Jessica M. Xavier, principal investigator, "The Washington Transgender Needs Assessment Survey," funded by the Administration for HIV and AIDS of the District of Columbia Government (conducted from September 1998 to May 2000). Executive summary retrieved from http://www.glaa.org/archive/2000/tgneedsassessment1112.shtml.

"IN 2005 A JURY DECIDED": Locke, "Legacy of Gwen Araujo."

"IN 2006": The rest of this paragraph comes from Yomi S. Wronge, "3 Men Sentenced in Slaying of Transgender Teen," *San Jose Mercury News*, January 28, 2006.

## CHAPTER TEN

"THE 'QUEENS' WOULD GO": The history of transpeople in the SNY comes entirely from Domineque. A spokeswoman for Pleasant Valley State Prison would only say that gay and transgender people, along with child molesters and other inmates at risk from other prisoners, are indeed housed in the SNY.

"IN ONE OF THE MOST COMPREHENSIVE": Darren Rosenblum, "'Trapped' in Sing Sing: Transgender Prisoners Caught in the Gender Binarism," *Michigan Journal of Gender and Law* 6, no. 1 (1999): 499–571. The other good article on the topic is Christine Peek, "Breaking Out of the Prison Hierarchy: Transgender Prisoners, Rape and the Eighth Amendment," *Santa Clara Law Journal* 44 (October 2004): 1211–48.

"ONE POSTOPERATIVE FEMALE": Rosenblum, "'Trapped' in Sing Sing," 522, n. 108; also see *Michelle Murray, Plaintiff-Appellant, v. United States Bureau of Prisons,* United States Bureau of Appeals for the Sixth Circuit, filed January 28, 1997.

"ANOTHER TRANSWOMAN IN COLORADO": Rosenblum, "'Trapped' in Sing Sing," 547, n. 238.

"ROSENBLUM FOUND ONLY ONE INSTANCE": ibid., 520, n. 108.

"WHEN A TRANSWOMAN IN WISCONSIN": Gina Barton, "Bill Would Halt Use of State Funds for Sex Change," online *Milwaukee Journal Sentinel,* posted February 9, 2005. Also see editorial, "Taxpayers Shouldn't Foot the Bill for Inmate's Hormone Therapy," online *Milwaukee Journal Sentinel,* posted February 17, 2006, retrieved from www.jsonline.com.

"STATE OF CALIFORNIA ISSUED": From "Text of Proposed Emergency Regulations," p. 2. Retrieved from http://www.cdcr.ca.gov/BudgetRegs/pendingrulespage.html#IGRP. The emergency regulations were adopted December 29, 2005, and, after a public comment period, were filed with the Office of Administrative Law (OAL) on June 22, 2006. The OAL has thirty business days to make changes to any emergency regulations, and then they become law; at press time the OAL was still deliberating. A government analyst and coauthor of the new regulation said she expected the law to go through; in her nine years of employment, the OAL had never overturned a regulation she had submitted.

"NOT BEING A RELIGIOUS INSTITUTION": The state published an "Initial Statement of Reasons" behind their alterations to the grooming standards (retrieved from http://www.cdcr.ca.gov/BudgetRegs/pendingrulespage .html#IGRP). Because the hair length change was made to accommodate religious practice, they offer this explanation: "The Department would be unable to meet the staffing demands required to adequately review requests from inmates to determine if a specific inmate produces prima facie evidence to support a claim alleging a violation of the inmate's exercise of religion specific to grooming standards. Additionally, the Department is not a religious expert and would be unable to determine specific requirements of a particular religion."

"APHRODITE'S CHARIOT": This comes from a poem traditionally called "Hymn to Aphrodite," written by Sappho, but in this particular translation by Diane Rayor, it's left untitled. Diane Rayor, *Sappho's Lyre: Archaic Lyric and Women Poets of Ancient Greece*. (Berkeley and Los Angeles: University of California Press, 1991), 51.

# SELECTED BIBLIOGRAPHY

Boenke, Mary, ed. *Trans Forming Families: Real Stories about Transgendered Loved Ones.* Imperial Beach, CA: Walter Trook, 1999.

Bornstein, Kate. *Gender Outlaw: On Men, Women, and the Rest of Us.* New York: Routledge, 1994.

———. *My Gender Notebook.* New York: Routledge, 1998.

Bowles, Norma, ed. *Friendly Fire: An Anthology of 3 Plays by Queer Street Youth.* Los Angeles: A.S.K. Theater Projects, 1997.

Boylan, Jennifer Finney. *She's Not There: A Novel in Two Genders.* New York: Broadway Books, 2003.

Califia, Pat. *Sex Changes: The Politics of Transgenderism.* San Francisco: Cleis Press, 1997.

Evelyn, Just. *Mom, I Need to Be a Girl.* Imperial Beach, CA: Walter Trook, 1998.

Israel, Gianna, and Donald Tarver II, MD, *Transgender Care: Recommended Guidelines, Practical Information and Personal Accounts.* Philadelphia: Temple University Press, 1997.

Istar-Lev, Alene. *Transgender Emergence: Therapeutic Guidelines for Working with Gender-Variant People and Their Families.* Binghamton, NY: Haworth Clinical Practice Press, 2004.

More, Kate, and Stephen Whittle, eds. *Reclaiming Genders: Transsexual Grammars at the Fin de Siècle.* London: Cassell, 1999.

O'Keefe, Tracie, and Katrina Fox. *Transsexual: The Naked Difference.* London: Extraordinary People Press, 1996.

Pettiway, Leon E. *Honey, Honey, Miss Thang: Being Black, Gay, and on the Streets.* Philadelphia: Temple University Press, 1996.

Prosser, Jay. *Second Skins: The Body Narratives of Transsexuality.* New York: Columbia University Press, 1998.

Sims, Michael. *Adam's Navel: A Natural and Cultural History of the Human Form.* New York: Penguin, 2004.

Walworth, Janis. *Transsexual Workers: An Employers Guide.* Westchester, CA: Center for Gender Sanity, 1998.

Wilchins, Riki Anne. *Read My Lips: Sexual Subversion and the End of Gender.* Milford, CT: Firebrand, 1997.

# ACKNOWLEDGMENTS

My deepest thanks go to the people in this book who shared their lives and generous spirits with me. First and foremost to Christina, who had the courage to tell her story and then want a new one; you are now on a strong, beautiful path and I am deeply honored to be your family. You are my daughter, my heart. And to Foxx, who taught me what it means to be a woman, about authenticity and innocence and kindness; your friendship is a rare gift that I hold among the closest of my treasures. Domineque: thank you for your raw honesty, even though I know it hurt sometimes to go there; you are a bright spark of intelligence and goodness and I cherish our letters. Ariel, thank you for your quiet opening and for trusting me every time I kept coming back, and Lenora: you are one powerful woman who's only becoming more so; I'm glad to have you in my life. To the rest: Tito, Lu, Miguel, and all the others who gave of your time and creativity, your complex thinking, and your patient translations from your experiences to mine—thank you. I hope you feel as honored on the page as I have been in knowing you.

Thank you to the Point Foundation, without whose generous financial support I couldn't have written this book.

Thank you to a host of experts who contributed their knowledge and expertise. Doctors Eric Vilain and Susan Bookheimer at UCLA were the brains behind the brain section. Alexander Lee, Jen Aarons, Jared Goldman, and Daniel Slifkin all shared legal advice. Nancy Bonvilain read over the Native American writings, and Tarynn Witten, MD, contributed her medical knowledge as well as information about violence in the transgender communities.

Masen Davis gave me much-needed perspective on transgender population figures and activism in L.A., and Simon Aronoff generously talked with me about the San Francisco scene. Patrick Knowles did a little research on a lot of everything. Gerard Gaskin, in addition to providing much of the background research on the ballroom scene, took photographs of all the kids in L.A. back in 1999, providing them with a different way to see themselves, and shot an image for the jacket as well. He's been a welcome sounding board and dear friend through this journey.

In Los Angeles, thank you to the Jeff Griffith Youth Center, Wendell Glenn at GLASS, and especially Chris Haiss at Eagles. Also, thank you to Andrea Biffle, who helped me understand about parenting as Robin and I scribbled our messy way along. Thank you to Felix Pfeifle, Saije Bashaw, Batyah Shtrum, Paul Park, and Dean Larkin for providing beds, cars, food, and friendship during the countless trips to L.A. once we'd moved away. Alexis Rivera read a full draft and spent many hours over many days with me affirming and correcting my perceptions about changes in transgender communities. Pat Viera translated beautifully, Adam Davidson provided key connections and vital humor—I'm grateful to you all for your commitment and your friendship. Thank you also to Marvin Belzer for your charity of spirit and for continuously answering my questions.

Thank you to *This American Life* for airing an early version of some of these stories.

This book would be a mess without the cadre of readers who helped me see it, shape it, and start it all over again. To my writing group, Jennie Yabroff, Carol Paik, and Kelly McMasters: thank you from the most core part of me— you've read more chapter drafts than any living human should have to endure and you unerringly gave vital, discerning, and enlightened responses, along with real sisterhood. Betony Toht, Rebecca DiLiberto, Melissa Heltzel, and John Cochran also read several chapters. Merrill Feitell and Lisa Davis read early versions and provided critical feedback; Lisa also inducted me into the world of book publishing and for this I will always be grateful. Andrew Solomon graciously read an entire manuscript, as did Sharon Krum: thank you both for your feedback and your faith.

I worked on much of this manuscript while completing an MFA at Columbia, and the faculty there was unfailingly supportive and thorough. I'd like to especially thank Lis Harris for her abundant impressions and for keeping me real, Honor Moore for her encouragement and intelligent notes, and Alan Ziegler for his reflections on teaching, which helped me frame my own. Richard Locke and Leslie Sharpe read a shorter version of this book and both provided wonderful feedback on shape and structure. And then there's Patty O'Toole, who showed up whenever I needed her: Patty, your wise counsel on everything from line edits to career moves means the world to me, and I'll cherish your friendship always.

Teresa Dinaburg understood parts of this book before I did; across continents, your wisdom into our shared childhood kept my heart open. Trista Sordillo and Lacy Austin also believed in this project and in me for years; thank you for the sustenance and the wings, respectively. Raina Moore always gave me new ideas; Felicia Sullivan gave me new places to read; and Alison Froling gave me a ceremony when the writing was done. Lisa Hanauer and Gemma Baumer fed me, both gastronomically and creatively. Jane Lerner, Lucia Matioli, Karen Gilliam, and Kathy Szilagyi also all provided invaluable support and are dear friends. Thank you also to Heather Myers, Laurie Sutton, Barbara Freedgood, and Marie-Hélène Charlap for helping to heal the broken parts.

Thank you to my family—my brother, Andrew, and my parents, who were so excited about this book coming out and, in difficult spots, loved me anyway. I also thank my extended family, too numerous to mention, but you all know who you are and how I adore you.

My agent, Amy Williams, is a dream. Assured, thoughtful, responsive, and honest, she was a giver and a fighter for me, always in the best possible combination. And then there's my editor, Andrea Schulz, to whom I owe the biggest debt of gratitude. Andrea was able to see *Transparent*'s deeper intentions even when I could not; her intuition and intellect worked in a kind of whip-speed tandem that always left me dazed and delighted. She made this a tighter, cleaner, and more graceful book.

Finally, I thank the incredible Robin, with whom everything was, and is, possible.